FOR ACTION

The Autobiography of
a Canadian Industrialist

JAMES E. HAHN
D.S.O., O.B.E., M.C.

FOR ACTION

The Autobiography of

a Canadian Industrialist

JAMES E. HAHN

D.S.O., O.B.E., M.C.

Toronto

CLARKE, IRWIN & COMPANY LIMITED

1954

FOR MY WIFE

DOROTHY McLAGAN HAHN

CONTENTS

PART ONE
EARLY YEARS

vii

Part Five
SOME INTERESTS

Part Six
RECONVERSION

Part Seven
CANADA AGAIN

ILLUSTRATIONS

PREFACE

MOST THINGS ARE PLANNED; others happen. This autobiography belongs in the latter category.

From the days of my youth I have enjoyed the forests and streams. Later, in the course of an active life, two periods of which were occupied by the duties imposed by war, I spent a good deal of such time as was available with rod, gun, camera, and sail. After my retirement from active industry three years ago, travel, which has taken me twice around the world, enabled me to occupy myself more fully with the pastimes I had always enjoyed.

In the winter of 1953, friends who had seen movies of our travel and hunting experiences urged me to record them. At the insistence of my wife, who has accompanied me on most of my journeys, I completed some of these anecdotes not for publication but for the edification of our grandchildren. The publishers of this book, who saw this manuscript, believed that the record of hunting and fishing experiences in various parts of the world might be of general interest, but from the outset kept insisting that I should complete a full record of the story of my life to date. I was most reluctant to do this, and the complete record would not have been compiled had I not been subject to the warnings of several heart seizures which made it apparent that from now on I must steam at reduced speed.

Recording the events that follow has afforded me recreation during this long period of restricted activity to which I am completely unaccustomed. Fortunately, my parents had preserved many records of my youthful activities, and all my correspondence during the first World War. I myself had accumulated many records of the following years.

I make no pretensions to being an author. I have simply related incidents in my life as concisely and accurately as I could, and I trust that the reader may find them of interest.

As I have reviewed the story of my life, I have become more convinced than ever I was that few, if any, other countries in the world afford youth as great opportunities as this country of ours. We enjoy here one of the highest standards of living in an atmosphere of vigour, freedom, and solidarity, and our citizens may well be proud of their heritage.

I strongly believe that the young men of today who are prepared constructively and with intelligence to "fill the unforgiving minute with sixty seconds' worth of distance run" will agree with me in the future, when they look back, that Canadians can find a full life in their own country.

All the chapters with the exception of those dealing with hunting in India have been written during a long period of illness either in my home or in hospital. I wish to express my grateful thanks to my many friends who were good enough during this period to provide me with such data or information as I required.

I am most appreciative of the assistance of Mrs. Peter Cameron, one of the secretaries of The Toronto General Trusts Corporation with which I have had many years of pleasant association as one of its Directors. Mrs. Cameron transcribed all my notes and the original manuscript sometimes under rather trying conditions. Miss Liella Finlayson and Miss Jessie McBroom were also helpful during my various stays in hospital.

Peter Lash, Q.C., son of my old friend, was good enough to read the manuscript and the help of my wife and two sons, as well as the other members of my family, was invaluable as the work progressed.

I am also greatly indebted to the extremely patient publishers, old friends of ours, their Editor, Mr. R. W. W. Robertson, and the members of their organization, whose continued cooperation enabled me to complete this book.

JAMES E. HAHN

Toronto,
October, 1954.

PART ONE

EARLY YEARS

CHAPTER I

A BOYHOOD IN WATERLOO COUNTY

MY FATHER, Alfred Hahn, arrived in New York in 1890 at the age of twenty-nine and was shortly afterwards joined by my mother, to whom he had been engaged prior to his arrival on this continent. The marriage of my parents to whom I owe so much, in 1890, might quite properly be taken as the beginning of this story.

Father was a well-educated man. When he arrived in America, he had served his one year voluntary in the German Army, and wore a decoration bestowed on him by the Government of Roumania. He was an ardent lover of music and an accomplished violinist. In Bavaria he had been in business with his father, who was a grain merchant. My father was devoted to his mother, and when, after her death, my grandfather married a woman not much older than his son, this circumstance caused my father to leave home for America, where he arrived with a silk hat, but possessing very little money.

My mother, a Viennese, was the daughter of a publisher. I recall to my memory her love, guidance and counsel: I recall, too, her courage. It was never more clearly demonstrated than when she stood on the station platform in Stratford in 1917, smiling and waving goodbye to me as I returned to the Front after having been severely wounded.

I was born in New York on the thirtieth of July, 1892. I have no recollection of my early years in that city, since by the time I was six my family had reversed the trend of the times and had moved from the United States to Canada. In the States my father had obtained employment as a salesman with a company which specialized in the manufacture of builders' hardware. His travels took him up into Canada where he saw opportunities which

3

encouraged him to come to this country at the close of the last century. He settled in New Hamburg, Ontario. There, he and the late Louis Hahn, the local furniture manufacturer of the same name but no relation, founded the Hahn Brass Company, which is still operating, and has expanded over the past fifty years.

We arrived one bright crisp winter day in the village of New Hamburg, some fourteen miles from Berlin, the capital of the County of Waterloo. Berlin is now called Kitchener; its name was changed in an access of patriotism during the first World War. Many of the settlers of Waterloo County were of German descent, and the County was already noted for its progressiveness, enterprise and thrift. There was still a great deal of German spoken there and the services in some of the churches were conducted in that language. The attractive crest of the Berlin Technical and Collegiate Institute, which I attended in later years, included in it the words "Höher Hinauf", Strive Higher.

It was in this environment that I spent the days of my boyhood. I attended public school, and then continued through to Junior Matriculation in the village of New Hamburg.

In my earliest days I enjoyed fishing and boating on the River Nith and hunting in the woods in the surrounding countryside. Hunting, fishing and boats, and the equipment associated with all three, have remained among my main hobbies throughout my entire life. It is no accident that at one time or another in later years, companies that I directed produced fishing tackle, guns, and the complete propulsion equipment for ships at sea.

My first gun, an air rifle, was given to me as a Christmas present by my parents. It was a type of gun, popular at the time, that furnished a considerable amount of amusement for boys of my age. My next acquisition in the way of guns was a single-shot target pistol, which broke like a shotgun for loading, was safe at half-cock, and had an extremely light trigger pull.

I had had this pistol for a few days only when I went swimming with a friend in a pool of the Nith. As we sat by the swimming pool dressing, I fired a few shots from my pistol into the river. It was my friend's turn to shoot. I was horrified to see him close the barrel of the pistol, with the little finger of his left hand over the muzzle, and a finger of his right hand on the trigger. There was a report, the weapon fell to the ground, and the boy cried out that he had been shot. The bullet had passed right through the centre bone of the little finger. We rushed him to the local doctor. I still do not quite understand how his finger was saved, but it was. I immediately told my father of the incident and as quickly lost possession of the target pistol. The episode was a lesson to me in gun handling for the rest of my life.

This preoccupation with guns was probably very disconcerting to my parents. I had other activities more to their liking. I attended Sunday School regularly and still have a number of pewter medals given for regular attendance at the Evangelical Lutheran Church, where I also sang in the choir. I like to recall my trips with the veterinary surgeon, Tom Stirling, as he took me with him into the country to attend calls from the various farms.

During this period I dutifully attended my piano, violin, and mandolin lessons and enjoyed every one of them. It must not be thought, however, that enjoyment and proficiency were synonymous terms. Though I inherited my father's ear for music, I never attained to his proficiency and technique. He was an artist on the violin and as a boy had appeared on occasion as soloist with a symphony orchestra. Poor Father! He never could bear to hear me practise. Without ever losing my fondness for music, I turned more to competitive sports and played and pitched for the school baseball team.

During the school holidays I occasionally worked at odd jobs. Once I ran a disc on a farm with not too great success. On another occasion I worked for a delightful old character called Fred McCallum, who owned the local drug store. He was also the village telegraph operator. His store was the main source of supply in that district for wallpaper, his stock of which was always in the most indescribable confusion. The summer that I worked for him the wallpaper, together with its matching borders, was in such a state that he could not find anything. His stock was kept in a warehouse room above the drug store, and I was given the job, at 25 cents a day, to inventory and organize it. I found it lying about on the floor and on chairs all over the room. After making a study of this confusion, I suggested to him that racks should be built all round the room and that if he would have them built, I would index them, put each type of wallpaper in a separate compartment, and provide him with an inventory from which he could go immediately to any rack and procure from it whatever type of wallpaper he required.

He agreed to my plan. Carpenters were brought in, the racks put up according to my specifications, and inside a couple of weeks I had the chaos converted into an orderly layout. I worked out an inventory, with key letters and numbers that corresponded with a plan of the racks, which permitted an immediate selection to be made. When all this had been completed, I asked Mr. McCallum to come upstairs and test the new system. I laid before him the inventory and asked him to select any particular type that he wanted to find. He placed his finger at random on a certain number; then he found it on the key plan of the racks. Together we went over to the rack indicated. He pulled out the roll of wallpaper, looked at it, and saw that it corresponded with the inventory number. Then with the greatest smile of approval he pushed it into a cubbyhole about four racks from where it should have been.

My father always gave me the greatest encouragement in anything that could be considered useful or constructive. He helped me provide in our home a dark-room where I developed and printed my own pictures. I also became interested in wireless telegraphy and built the first spark-transmitter and coherer type receiver in the village, which I operated with another local enthusiast. The dark-room, again with my father's co-operation, finally expanded into an electrical, chemical, and mineralogical laboratory in which I spent many happy hours with Rhumkorf coils, bunsen burner and florence flask, and blowpipe. I found these interests and activities most absorbing when I was ten years of age, and the knowledge acquired then proved very useful in my later days at collegiate, at university, and throughout my life.

In view of my own experience as a child and its usefulness throughout my life, I encouraged my children in similar activities from their very early years. I was astounded to find out how much they could absorb.

In 1907 I was confirmed in the Evangelical Lutheran Church, where the service was conducted in German. The entire Confirmation class at that time agreed to take a pledge that its members would remain total abstainers until the age of twenty-one. This undertaking I kept through my years at high school and university. I had my first drink when a toast in champagne was proposed on Armistice Day in 1918 by my Commanding General, Sir David Watson. On the night of November 10th I was Staff Officer on duty at H.Q. near Valenciennes. About daybreak on the following day, the message came through that we had all been hoping for. There was to be an armistice at eleven o'clock, the morning of November 11th. This news was accompanied by some necessary instructions. I went over to the chateau, woke the General and informed him of the message. The General, overjoyed at the news, said, "Hahnsie, you are going to take the first drink of your life this morning." By this time all the Staff had been aroused. Glasses were passed around, filled with champagne. I shall never forget the toast proposed by the General's A.D.C., McLeod Moore. Moore was a prominent English newspaper man who had survived the War although twice wounded. Ironically, he was killed in an accident a few weeks later.

I cannot begin to quote his words, nor convey the brilliant command of English which was his, but I can paraphrase his closing words. After a moving tribute to the fallen he said, "At this moment there are men who are fortunate to be on the Honours Lists, there are men who are fortunate to be on Lists of Decorations; but at this moment how fortunate are we, who are on the list of the survivors."

IN THE YEAR 1909, at the age of seventeen, I was appointed Lieutenant in the 29th Waterloo Regiment of the Canadian Militia. The Warrant, which I have before me as I write, was from His Majesty King George V. It was signed on his behalf by Earl Grey, then Governor-General of Canada, and R. W. Borden, the Minister of Militia, and later Prime Minister of Canada. It is with some emotion that I look back to this step in my boyhood which marked the beginning of a course that has charted itself through so many years of my life.

An extract from this Warrant which reads, "James Emanuel Hahn, Gentleman, Greetings . . ." makes me pause and compare the military requirements of today with those of nearly fifty years ago. At that time officers for the Canadian Militia were selected from a so-called "cadre of gentlemen" chosen from the community from which the local regiment was recruited—an interesting reminder of the "purchase system" which prevailed in the British Army till the middle of the nineteenth century. It was then necessary for the candidate to qualify for the rank of Lieutenant in the first instance, and later for senior ranks, by attending courses of military instruction held at the Headquarters of the Military District. These courses were conducted by officers of the Permanent Force. If the candidate were successful, certificates were issued which qualified him for his rank. I remember the courses I took in 1913 for the certificates of military instruction qualifying me for the ranks of Captain and Field Officer when promotion might occur. With today's system, training, competence and merit, and not social standing, are the main requirements for an appointment as an officer in Canada's Army.

The "gentlemen" of fifty years ago in the main officered the First Canadian Contingent, which before the end of the first World War expanded into a Canadian Corps of four Divisions. It reflects the greatest credit on these officers, and the men under their command, that they adapted themselves to field conditions so rapidly and successfully that the Canadian Corps became recognized as one of the most effective fighting units in the field.

Militia training fifty years ago consisted of weekly or biweekly parades and a week or so of annual training at one of the military camps within the district in which the militia regiment was located. It was very difficult for rural regiments to get their units to turn out anywhere near full strength for this type of training. I look back with great pleasure at the instruction, training and pleasant days from 1909 to 1914, when I attended militia camps at London and Goderich. The Permanent Staff which trained us at these camps was limited in number but efficient.

With Canada apparently so far removed from the possibility

of being involved in any conflict, the training that was received at these courses was not taken too seriously by some. There were twenty of us in the class when I took my course to qualify as a Lieutenant. The instructors made every effort to teach us the rudiments of military tactics. Among other things, we had to know the commands necessary to move a battalion of men in any formation the examiner might require of us. In the last stage of the examination the General Officer commanding the Military District called out each member of the class who had taken the course and instructed him to put the battalion through a few movements. Then the provisional Lieutenant would take his place before the battalion. He was expected to issue the proper words of command in the sequence that would bring about the required formation. In the class we had with us an officer from Northern Ontario who took his course of instruction rather lightly and his drinking seriously.

We all dreaded this day. The General Officer Commanding Military District No. 1 at that time was the likable and explosive Colonel Peters. When the name of our northern friend was called out, he walked to the appointed place in front of Colonel Peters, who was mounted, and saluted very smartly. He was then instructed to take his position and move the battalion into a formation which required three consecutive orders.

The first order was properly given, but after this, the same formation continued for seconds, and finally for nearly a minute. It was obvious that our applicant had forgotten the proper words of command. The Colonel became restive. The candidate, however, was not at a complete loss: he finally gave the command, "Buck up, boys; buck up." Fear of censorship will not permit me to record what followed.

In 1910 I completed my matriculation examinations in New Hamburg. As an Honour Matriculation course was not available there at that time, I attended the Berlin Technical and Collegiate Institute, an institution which will celebrate its 100th anniversary in 1955. I travelled from New Hamburg by train every morning and returned in the early evening.

My memories of school life at Kitchener are among my happiest. Apart from my studies, I spent many hours on the tennis courts after school, pitched for the Collegiate baseball team, and enjoyed the games with collegiates from the nearby towns and cities. There were other activities that, if one is to be charitable, could best be put under the classification of "mischief". There were three of us in the Fourth Form who, I am afraid, contributed to the difficulties of a teacher's life as we were constantly up to one prank or another.

Most of these took place in the chemistry laboratory or during chemistry lectures. A standard trick was to release a flow of hydrogen sulphide either in the chemistry lab. or into one of the other classrooms of the school. We devised another method of exasperating our instructor. Shortly before a chemistry lecture we would put a few innocent-looking drops of carbon bi-sulphide into the bottom of an open-mouth jar. We would then place over the top of the apparently empty bell jar a piece of moist filter paper upon which we had put finely divided pure phosphorus. During the progress of the lecture, the filter paper would dry up, the finely divided phosphorus would become spontaneously combustible, and would ignite the highly volatile and explosive mixture of air and carbon bi-sulphide. The accompanying boom would seem to originate from nowhere at all. I am sure, however, our chemistry master had his suspicions both as to the cause of the explosion and its authors.

It happened that all three of us in the Fourth Form were particularly fond of shooting. One noon we amused ourselves in the chemistry lab. by setting florence flasks on their necks and using them as targets for a .22 calibre pistol.

Another stupidity in which we indulged, and which did not add any lustre to our behaviour, was to break off the tip of an electric light bulb (it will be remembered that bulbs at that time in the process of manufacture were sealed by a tip drawn out at the end and were not completely rounded as they are today), filling the bulb with water and screwing it back into the socket, with disconcerting results.

Nothing is more true than that the wheels of justice grind inexorably and slowly, and in due course retribution overtook my youthful exuberance. This occurred after a friendly tussle in the school library, in the course of which I pushed one of the lads into a bookcase so that the panes of glass on both sides were broken. When this was reported by the janitor, I was called up on the carpet by the Principal of the school. On admitting this misbehaviour, and in view of my previous misdemeanours, I was expelled from school. The Principal told me that I was not a "bad boy", but mischievous, and that I could return after I wrote a letter of apology and gave a promise of future good behaviour. This I promised to do. In the meantime, the Principal announced to the other classes that I had been expelled and that my two companions would be shortly accorded similar treatment. I remember handing in the letter of apology after lunch, getting a very kindly lecture from the Principal, and being re-instated in my class.

The behaviour of the three of us was somewhat more subdued after that. The other two did not follow me in my shame, as the Principal had predicted.

While at the Collegiate I became interested in the activities of the Literary and Musical Society, whose motto was "Dum vivimus vivamus" (While we live, let us live). I remember participating in many debates and playing a mandolin in the Society's string orchestra.

In the first year I was elected to the Committee of the Society. The Honourable W. L. Mackenzie King, then Minister of Labour in the Federal Government, had been one of the first presidents of this Literary Society and during his regime the Society had bought a piano, which by my time was in a very dilapidated state. I had heard that each president set the purchase of a new piano for the Society as the main objective for the year. In 1910 I was elected President of the Society. The day following my election I went to one of the local music dealers in Berlin and told him that I would buy a piano on behalf of the Literary Society, if he would take the risk involved concerning payment within the year to come. This he agreed to do and the piano was shipped to the school. At our first meeting I displayed the instrument and told the students that it was our mutual job to pay for it during the school term. I am glad to say that we accomplished this by holding extra concerts and appealing to the generosity of the parents of the students.

In the same year I entered the oratorical contest for the medal donated by the Honourable W. L. Mackenzie King, who still maintained an interest in the school of his boyhood. I was successful in winning the medal. His letter to me at that time brings back a warm memory of my boyhood days.

Ottawa, January 31, 1910

My dear Mr. Hahn,

I was very pleased to see by the Berlin papers of Saturday that you had won the medal which I have had the privilege of donating in connection with the second Annual Oratorical contest at the Collegiate. I am doubly pleased in that the subject of your oration was "Canada".

I am writing this little note to congratulate you heartily, and to say that I look forward with much pleasure to presenting you with the medal and I shall always have a personal interest in your future and career. You have made a splendid beginning, and I wish you every success.

With kind regards,

Believe me,
Yours sincerely,
W. L. Mackenzie King

James Hahn Esq.,
Fourth Form,
Berlin Technical and Collegiate Institute,
Berlin, Ont.

For some reason that I do not now recall, Mr. King did not himself present me with the medal, and I did not make his acquaintance until 1937, when after the Dominion Conference which followed the Coronation of King George VI I met Mr. King aboard a Canadian destroyer at the naval review at Spithead. My second and last meeting with him took place in 1942 when he came to visit the John Inglis Company in Toronto, which was engaged at that time in producing weapons for the Allied troops in World War II.

Among other things in my speech in Kitchener in 1910 I said that many peoples of the world, and even our great neighbour to the south, believed Canada to be "a land of nine months of winter and three months of bad sleighing." So very, very little was known by the rest of the world concerning this great country.

An episode which occurred about the same time evokes a similar thought. I was walking through the buffing department in a factory when I heard an argument in progress between a big, husky, likeable Englishman, whom I knew, and a Canadian who was operating the buffing wheel beside him. Just as I arrived at the scene, the big cockney settled the argument, whatever it was, by saying, "What difference does it make? We owns you." Two world wars and our own country's stature have led to a much more enlightened appreciation of the status of Canada.

FOR SOME TIME a course for me at the University of Toronto had been under consideration. It was difficult to decide what undertaking in life I was most fitted for, as so often is the case when one is young and without experience.

After discussion at home, it was decided that a law course would constitute good training, even if I decided to go into business later. There were two courses that could be followed at that time, both of which led ultimately to the Ontario Bar. One could become articled to a law firm and serve a five-year apprenticeship, which complied with one of the conditions for admission to Osgoode Hall, the Ontario Law School. The alternative, in lieu of serving the apprenticeship, was a degree in an Honour course from the University. I chose the latter and entered the University of Toronto in 1911, enrolling in the course in Political Science. I was allowed to enter my second year. My Honour Matriculation entitled me to this.

I had been advised to enter the first year course, as otherwise I would miss the fellowship of the freshman year. I found this to be the case. It was not until the end of my second year that

I really began to enjoy the associations that are so important in university life.

In my third year I was called home before the Christmas examinations, because of the serious illness of my father. In this way I missed my examinations which, in the Honour course, disqualified me for the year.

As soon as my father was out of danger, which was shortly before the New Year, I became anxious to occupy myself during the winter months until my return to the University the following year. At that time there were a number of advertisements in the papers for teachers and I had the necessary qualifications to teach, provided I could get a temporary certificate.

I answered an advertisement by the Trustees of the Village of Byng Inlet, who required a Principal for their school. The advertisement, calling for a telegraphic reply, indicated considerable urgency. In my wire replying, I listed my academic qualifications, which were quite sufficient, and stated that I was without experience but was advised that I could get a temporary teaching certificate. I did not indicate my age, which had not been asked for. I was nineteen years old.

I received an immediate wire of acceptance which instructed me to report for duty at once. I wired the time of my arrival.

The train reached the station of Byng Inlet on a bitterly cold, below zero morning in January, and a very young, beardless youth stepped on to the platform. I shall never forget the sight of the five Trustees looking all over the station platform for the incoming Principal. Never for a moment did they think that the youngster who had just stepped off the train was he. I can still see their look of disappointment and consternation as I walked up to them.

Byng Inlet was a company village. The Trustees took me over to what I later knew as the "Heated Compound", in which were located the central offices, some living quarters, and the company store. The Trustees looked at me with some pity and informed me that they had discharged the previous Principal because his pupils had locked him up in the wood-box. It was a three-room school with two assistants. The Principal had in his room several classes, including the Matriculation class—some forty-five pupils in all.

The Trustees were obviously very concerned about the difficulty of maintaining discipline. I assured them that I was confident that I could do this, particularly as I had been an officer in the militia for several years.

Their attitude was one of doubt and concern as they took me over to the school, introduced me to the two assistants, took me into my room, introduced me to the students, and then left me to my fate.

The class included students of other nationalities as well as Canadians. Some of these were at least as old, and taller, than I. I opened the drawer in the desk and found it contained a list of the students' names, and a strap. Snickers went around the room as I studied the list of names. The murmurs became louder and louder. It soon became clear that trouble was in the offing. In appearance at least, I still did not pay any attention to the disturbance, which was rapidly becoming a small commotion. Nevertheless I was keeping my eye on the students while I tried to determine who were the ringleaders. By this time the whole room was in excellent humour. Finally, one big lad in the far corner of the room decided to test the accuracy of his aim by heaving a book at one of the children in the front of the class.

I looked up suddenly and asked the lad who had thrown the book for his name. He told me, with a show of defiance. Calling him by his first name, I told him to go out into the hall which was off the back end of the room. He did. I took the strap out of the desk and walked out of the room into the hall. There stood my young friend, half a head taller than I, with a broad grin on his face. I took off my glasses, put them in my vest pocket, and told the lad to hold out his hand. Much to my surprise, he did. The grin disappeared and I sent him bawling back into the room.

I do not think any teacher could have had a more pleasant and trouble-free time than I had while teaching at Byng Inlet. The students were eager to learn and soon realized that, in some forms of mischief at least, their Principal was about four laps ahead of them.

We took long trips on snowshoes on breathless sub-zero days, when the snowshoes sang on the powdered snow, and the houses in the village resounded with the reports familiar to anyone who has lived in weather from twenty to fifty below zero. We travelled by dogsled along the ice-covered Magnetawan River, and fished through the ice where the river empties into Georgian Bay. When the ice left, we took canoe trips up the river and beyond its lower rapids. My father's shotgun still rests somewhere on the bottom of Deadman's Rapid, where our canoe upset with, fortunately, the loss of equipment only.

WHEN THIS PLEASANT TERM was over, I returned to Stratford. For me the six months had been interesting and profitable and for the students, I hope, a useful experience. The students presented me with a pair of paddles when I left. The Trustees who saw me off at the station were in a much happier frame of mind than they had been when they greeted me on my arrival.

Instead of resuming my studies at the University, I decided to go into business with my father as his assistant. The summer of 1913 saw my introduction into the manufacturing business in a company which made builders' hardware and furniture trimmings. My father was one of the pioneers of this industry in Canada.

I lived in Stratford now, and a vacancy arose in the 27th Lambton Regiment which was offered to me. I accepted, and was transferred to this regiment with the rank of captain.

In May of 1914 Sarnia was made a city, a ceremony which was to be graced by the presence of His Royal Highness the Duke of Connaught and his daughter, the charming Princess Patricia. The Guard of Honour was to be supplied by my regiment, and, as its senior captain, I was to have the honour of training and commanding it.

The rural militia regiments of that time, whatever other qualifications or virtues they may have possessed, were weak on ceremonial. It was, then, a problem to produce a properly turned out and trained Guard of Honour for such a momentous occasion.

It required the combined resources of National Defence Head-quarters, Military District No. 1, and our regiment, to provide the necessary red tunics and white helmets, together with the correct number of officers' uniforms, with their white piping and braid, for the three officers and the one hundred N.C.O.s and other ranks who constituted the Guard. In most rural regiments the officer was required to equip himself at his own expense and his uniforms usually consisted of one or two khaki drill and a blue undress for the mess. They did not include the red tunic with piping required for ceremonial occasions.

I went to Sarnia two weeks before the day of inauguration and had the men equipped and fitted with proper uniforms. I then embarked on an intensive period of training. By the end of that time we had a presentable Guard of Honour which paraded well and could present arms smartly and with precision for the Royal Salute.

My instructions were that I was to have the Guard at the station in Sarnia when the train backed in with His Royal Highness and the Princess, that the Royal Salute should be given as His Royal Highness stepped on to the platform, and that I would get further instructions after His Royal Highness had inspected the Guard.

The train backed slowly into the station on the minute. His Royal Highness the Duke of Connaught stepped on to the plat-form, followed by the lovely Princess Patricia, smartly gowned, and wearing a large picture hat. The command was given, "The King" was played, and His Royal Highness proceeded to inspect the Guard of Honour. After the inspection was over, he was very gracious and complimentary, saying, among other things, that the Guard was commanded by a "very young officer".

The officer from whom I was to receive my subsequent instructions then came over to me and I was greatly concerned to notice that he had apparently been celebrating the inauguration of Sarnia somewhat prematurely. When I asked him what my further instructions were, he simply waved his hands at me and said, "Follow the Duke." My suspicions were confirmed as to the condition of the officer.

However, orders were orders. I was given an itinerary and

throughout the day we posted ourselves at various points along the route indicated, dutifully presenting arms in accordance with my instructions each time the Duke and his party passed by. I think His Royal Highness would have agreed that he never had so many salutes from the same Guard of Honour on any other occasion in his life.

The comedy ended when we gave the Duke his final Royal Salute as he left on the train that evening. However, everyone seemed to think that this assiduous attention helped greatly in making Sarnia a city.

I said earlier that the rural regiments of the Canadian Militia were usually "weak on ceremonial". The expression reminds me of a delightful story told me by a very human man some years later.

In connection with my official duties during the second World War, I was at the Overland plant in Toledo, where the famous jeep was being built. This firm was also developing certain prototypes to the requirements of the Army Technical Development Board of Canada. I was invited to join the guests at a dinner being given in honour of General Knudsen, whose services had been made available by General Motors to the United States Government in order to assist and expedite over-all production in the U.S.A.

After the function, the General invited a few of us to his suite. General Knudsen, over six feet tall, struck me as being a man with a warm, human understanding. He had a humorous twinkle in his eye, and radiated common sense, directness and efficiency, some of the qualities which contributed to the great success and honours that were his. He told us that he had arrived in the United States from Denmark many years before as a young boy and, after working in a foundry in Buffalo, had gone to Detroit and started to work with Henry Ford at the time when the latter had just conceived the idea of building a motor car.

The General spoke of the early years with Henry Ford in terms of great admiration for his erstwhile employer. At the inception of the manufacturing business, he himself spent a great deal of time in the very small plant while, as he put it, "Henry spent considerable time at the bank." He traced the successful growth and progress of the enterprise through the years until finally it became world-renowned. Then, he said, "Henry began entertaining celebrities from all over the world."

On one occasion, a group of celebrities was assembled at dinner and the conversation revolved about the subject of world politics. Knudsen could see that Henry Ford was getting more and more restive as the conversation proceeded. As Knudsen put it, "Henry was always a little weak on geography."

Finally, weary of making little contribution to the conversation, Ford announced firmly, "The Ford Company is producing thousands of motor cars per day." "That," as Bill Knudsen said, "really floored them all!"

PART TWO

INTELLIGENCE OFFICER

CHAPTER II

THE FIRST CANADIAN CONTINGENT

THE DECLARATION OF WAR on August 4th, 1914, when I had just turned twenty-two, meant that the responsibilities which I had undertaken when I had become an officer five years earlier must now be carried out.

Together with others of my regiment, I volunteered for active service. I left home on August 10th to gather together the officers and men from our regimental area and make arrangements for entraining with them at London. We finally received our movement orders, which were to proceed to Valcartier. In the turmoil of mobilization certain arrangements, particularly relating to food en route, were not only vague but, as far as our unit was concerned, non-existent. I was in command of the contingent from the Lambton Regiment, nearly two hundred strong, when we entrained at London. We worked out the train schedule as best we could, estimating our time of arrival at Valcartier, and then wired ahead to the mayors of the various cities en route, requesting that arrangements for food be made against our arrival. I am happy to say that this was done, and we were among the first to arrive at Valcartier Camp. Here we had to make the best of the arrangements as we found them. The Camp was still being laid out and areas and tents were allotted to the units as they arrived. Some thirty thousand men were finally under canvas and intensive training was begun.

Shortly before the end of September, about the time the first contingent was scheduled to leave for overseas, a great many rumours were in circulation as to who was to be included in it. It was understood that some ten thousand officers and men would be left behind at Valcartier.

The contingent that I had brought from London had become part of the First Canadian Infantry Battalion, which at Valcartier was greatly over-strength. It was obvious that about one-third of its strength would be left behind when the first contingent sailed. Much to my dismay, I was informed by the adjutant, who was a very good friend of mine, that I was included in the list of those to be left behind. The reason given was that my name was Hahn. I felt badly hurt and distressed to hear that I was to be left behind for no reason other than my German name.

Although young, and without connections that I could think of to intercede on my behalf, I decided upon a step that had a definite influence upon my entire career. I made up my mind to see Colonel Sam Hughes, who was then Minister of National Defence, and who, I understood, was somewhere at the Headquarters of Valcartier Camp. I walked several miles from where our battalion was quartered until I found the Headquarters and the offices of the Minister of National Defence.

With very mixed emotions, I walked into his waiting-room. In this room was a secretary and a white-haired gentleman who apparently had also come to see the Minister. The secretary went in and announced this gentleman. I heard a voice roar, "Didn't I tell that damned old fool to stay at home!" The "damned old fool" was ushered in, however, and there ensued a loud set-to between them that was distinctly audible in the ante-room. Apparently the white-haired gentleman was a colonel from the Maritimes who was very anxious to go overseas. He was also a friend of the Minister of Militia. He had evidently been told that he could not go overseas on account of his age, but that his services would be utilized in Canada. The colonel apparently refused to take "no" for an answer to his request. The interview finally ended on a very friendly basis.

This explosive prelude did not augur well for the interview that I was seeking. Finally I was ushered in to the presence. I saluted, was told to sit down, and was asked curtly what I wanted. I told the Minister that I had brought a unit to Valcartier with the intention of going overseas, and that I had just been informed, on very good authority, that I was one of those to be left behind because I had a German name. I felt extremely hurt and I wanted to go with the first contingent.

The Minister asked me a number of questions. In the midst of the questioning, two senior officers of the Headquarters Staff at Valcartier were announced. I was told to remain seated. They came into the room and told the Minister about the formation of a Machine Gun Brigade that was to accompany the first contingent overseas. The Minister was very pleased at this announcement; I can still see him leaning across the desk with both hands in front of him as though he were firing a machine gun and saying, "We'll mow them down." Then he turned to the two senior officers and told them to "run along": they saluted and left.

The Minister continued his questioning of me. Then, without any comment, he told me to report back to my unit.

The following afternoon, I was called before my Commanding Officer and quite properly given a first-class calling-down for having gone to see the Minister without passing through the proper channels. He confirmed the fact that he had intended that I should be left behind with the others, but that he had received instructions that I was to report to Headquarters at Valcartier Camp.

The message which the adjutant showed me had come through from the Minister. Even now I blush to recall its contents. The Minister had forgotten my name, and the message read, "The smart young officer from Stratford who had an interview yesterday afternoon is to report to Headquarters immediately."

I did not know until some years after the war that immediately after my interview, the Minister had picked up the telephone and called the late Mr. George Dingman, the owner of the *Stratford Herald*, who was good enough to provide the Minister with the information which resulted in my transfer to what ultimately became the Headquarters of the First Canadian Contingent. At Headquarters I was attached to the Staff where my duties were mostly concerned with Intelligence.

THE ORGANIZATION of the units that were to comprise the First Canadian Division had now been completed at Valcartier and preliminary training carried out. The infantry were armed with the Ross rifle which had been designed and produced in Canada.

This rifle, a magazine, bolt action type, weighed nearly eleven pounds without its bayonet, and on the ranges at Valcartier had proved to be a weapon of considerable accuracy. However, the straight pull action of the bolt, a type different from that used by the armies of the other major powers, proved later, in the field, to be its undoing.

By October 1st, the First Canadian Expeditionary Force had moved from Valcartier to Quebec, and to the strains of "It's a long long way to Tipperary" embarked upon the thirty-two transport ships which comprised the first and largest convoy of its kind ever to cross the Atlantic. This first contingent, the survivors of which became known as the "Old Originals", marched with confidence, great enthusiasm and a somewhat sober gaiety to their embarkation point. We little realized how few of this great band of volunteers would survive the trials and horrors of nearly five years of trench warfare, nor that our battles, in the main, would consist of many bloody engagements for limited objectives gained at a shocking cost in casualties.

Divisional Headquarters were aboard the *Franconia*. I think the initial stages of our movements are best indicated by the following extracts from the newspaper published on board our ship, two days before our arrival at Southampton:

FRANKONIABLAETTER

Printed and Published on Board

H.M. Troopship "Franconia" Quebec to ——

Vol. I No. 1 Tuesday, Oct. 13, 1914. Phone Ocean 23

First and foremost let it be stated that we are the aristocracy of the fleet.

This is written in no snobbish spirit. Personally, I have never had any ambition to ally myself with the aristocracy. But it must be admitted that being with the Headquarters' Staff has its advantages. It means that we are on the best ship, that we have more and better food and that the nurses are with us—or, we are with them. The nurses maintain an admirable balance. Were it not for them everyone would probably hate the sight of everyone else, by this time, and long for a few moments of solitude. Thus, being with the aristocracy, pro tem, mixing with the comme il faut and pommes de terre, so to speak, has advantages.

The weather has been phenomenal, unprecedented—the ultimate desire of all who look upon the sea as a rapacious parasite, that snatches meals that have scarcely had time to settle comfortably. There has been nothing that could claim relationship with a storm, even by marriage. The good ship rolled a bit for a couple of days, but even the weakest stomach could not rise up and protest.

For almost a week the troops had been pouring down to the docks at Quebec when we, on September 29th, sought out the *Franconia* and took possession. All the following day was spent in loading the ammunition and stores. We cast off at night and when Thursday came we were far down the river. The *Eureka* slipped out from Father Point about noon and took off the pilot and the letters that the prudent had taken time to write and after this short delay we continued.

All that day the wooded shores of the St. Lawrence slipped by. Routine work was begun. The various units were drilled and given physical exercises. The gymnasium was opened, the course of lectures started and the games on the sun deck were discovered. Night drew about the lone vessel ploughing her way through the gulf.

Then came the morning and we gazed through the cabin port-holes and discovered that we had reached the rendezvous. The great fleet had gathered. The greatest force that ever crossed an ocean was collected there in placid Gaspé Bay. The cruisers, grim and grey, were anchored at the east end, and scattered over the sunlit waters were the transports, including the *Canada* with the troops from Bermuda. Falling back from the shores were the wooded hills of Gaspé and down their flanks tumbled the gleaming white cottages of the settlers.

The following morning saw the arrival of Col. Sam Hughes, with Col. McBain, Mr. E. H. Carrington and the Minister's secretary. Standing on the bow of the tug, the Colonel shouted farewell words of encouragement and goodwill and in response was cheered again and again by the troops.

Night came and a touch of grim reality was added to the great adventure by the curtaining of all the port-holes. The deck lights were not lit and the only signs of life all over the wide basin were the winking signals as the messages were flashed across the waters, shimmering under the moon. On Saturday, October 3rd, the fleet sailed from Gaspé, about four in the afternoon.

Lectures, parades, games, dancing and concerts were incidents of the days and evenings. The commandant, Col. Williams, each day made his inspection and the officers of each unit did all they could to make the men comfortable.

The only really exciting happening of the voyage occurred on the morning of the first Monday at sea. The ship was startled by the "man overboard" signal. A rush was made for the port rail and far out above the great roll of the waves could be seen a head, pitifully small. The man had fallen from the *Royal Edward*, the ship directly ahead of us.

The man was rescued by a boat lowered from our ship, which on reaching the water was found to be without a plug. This incident, as may well be imagined, caused orders to be issued for the complete inspection of all life-boats carried by the ships of the convoy.

We proceeded in three columns designated X, Y, and Z, escorted by five cruisers of the Royal Navy. The crossing was an exceedingly smooth one, the ocean being like a millpond for the entire trip. The day before we sighted land we were met by a battleship of the Royal Navy which greeted us off the starboard quarter of our convoy with a message from her signalling projector. In Morse code the message spelled out the words, "Welcome, Canadians".

While it is not quite clear to what extent the existing mobilization scheme was used in Canada at this time, it was nevertheless no mean achievement to have been able to land an infantry division, a cavalry brigade and all the necessary equipment in the British Isles in less than two and a half months after the declaration of war. Much of the credit must go to the Minister of National Defence, who ended the war as Lieutenant-General Sir Sam Hughes, K.C.B.

THE INTENSIVE TRAINING that fall through to the early part of February, 1915, was carried out in the mud of Salisbury Plains. There the Division was placed under a British Commander, Major-General E. A. H. Alderson. The senior officers of the Divisional Staff, as well as the Brigade Majors of each of the three infantry brigades, were staff officers provided by the British Army. During this period of training and organization, in an effort to improve the efficiency of the Division, an entirely new departure from the British Staff organization within an Imperial Division was made. The Canadian establishment was expanded so that the Divisional Staff added to its Headquarters a General Staff Officer Third Grade, and each Brigade Staff added a Staff Captain. The duties of all these additional officers were to be confined exclusively to the organization and functioning of Military Intelligence. This innovation was later extended and each battalion allotted one officer exclusively to Intelligence work. These additions to the various Staffs were responsible for the very complete Intelligence organization that existed in what later became a Canadian Corps of four Divisions, and which contributed to its successes. As for myself, I remained on the Headquarters Staff of the First Canadian Division, still concerning myself with Intelligence matters.

I had leave on two occasions before my departure for France. The first time I went to Portsmouth where permission for me to visit the Naval Dockyards had been granted. They were of great interest to one who had never before been in a naval yard. I witnessed the hoisting of fifteen inch guns aboard one of the battleships. I also asked if I could see a submarine, and was told that there was a French vessel lying in the yards at the time. My naval escort took me over to where this submarine was moored. The conning tower was open and upon our hailing the vessel, a young Frenchman with a big beard, who turned out to be its commander, stuck out his head. The British naval officer advised the French commander that an officer from the First Canadian Contingent would like to go below. I was greeted with great enthusiasm, taken below and shown the mysteries of a submarine. Its torpedoes, tubes, methods of propulsion under water and surfaced were explained to me by the French captain.

I was surprised that the British naval officer did not come below with us, but there seemed to be some sort of courtesy understanding, even though we were allies, that naval officers did not go aboard one another's ships unless specially invited.

During my second leave I visited Brighton, where I had my first flight in a plane. It was an open pusher-type, rather a ramshackle contraption, that was capable of about eighty-five miles per hour, and I was very thankful that this wood and wire struc-

ture held together until we landed. Later in France I was to
make low-altitude reconnaissances over enemy territory in the old
R.E. 8's, which had a speed of about one hundred miles per hour.

I was greatly interested when Sir Hiram Maxim, then a distinguished looking gentleman of seventy-five with flowing white
hair and beard, came to have tea with us at our mess. After tea,
I sat enthralled and listened with wide-open eyes as he described
his many inventions, the first of which was a pair of irons to be
used for curling hair. He was, however, most famous for his
invention, in 1884, of the Maxim gun, the first reliable automatic
weapon to be produced. The memory of this meeting with Sir
Hiram is of more than ordinary interest to me. Twenty-five
years later I was to head a company that was said to be the largest
individual producer of machine guns in the British Empire during
the second World War. The same company was to design the
first belt-fed automatic cannon.

Before we left England, together with the other members of
the Staff of the First Division, I had the honour of being presented
to their Majesties King George V and Queen Mary. On the
same occasion we met Earl Kitchener, who was later lost on a
cruiser in the North Sea, and Earl Roberts of Boer War fame.

We were to leave England early in February from the Port of
Bristol. On arrival at Bristol, we found our ship, *The City of
Benares*, and embarked on it. We were ready to sail when it was
discovered that a few men had not returned from shore leave,
and a patrol was hastily organized to sweep through the lower
Port of Bristol to round up these men. The time arrived when
the patrol was supposed to have completed its sweep and returned
to the ship. Some fifteen minutes after our scheduled time for
sailing, it became apparent to us that the patrol had lost its way.
I was ordered to go ashore, to keep in the vicinity of the docks
and see if I could expedite the return of the patrol to the ship.
I was told that if by any chance the patrol should come aboard,
two short blasts would be blown on the ship's whistle, when I
was to return immediately.

After hurrying around in the adjacent area for about a quarter
of an hour, I heard the two short blasts. I hurried back to the
dock. To my horror I found that the moorings had been cast

off and the ship was standing twenty feet off the dock, but not under way. My arrival had been anticipated. As soon as I rushed on to the dock one of the huge loading cranes dropped its hook and swung it towards me. At the same time I was instructed through a megaphone from the ship to step on the hook. I did. I was then hoisted and swung on to the fore deck amidst the cheers of the troops on board.

Thus began the journey from England to France.

WE HAD A VERY ROUGH PASSAGE particularly in the Bay of Biscay. Many of us echoed the sentiment later portrayed in one of Bruce Bairnsfather's famous war cartoons, where one terribly seasick British Tommy crossing the Channel on leave asked his companion, who was in a similar condition, "Why didn't we 'old this 'ere war at 'ome?"

The First Canadian Division arrived at Saint-Nazaire in France on February 13th, 1915. It was the first formation in France that was not a regular division of the Imperial Army and it was the eleventh division of the British Army to arrive there.

Our trip across France was uneventful. We traced our way across the country on our maps and tried out our academic French on the startled inhabitants. The Staff of the Divisional Headquarters proceeded on the first train so that we could set up facilities necessary for the detraining arrangements behind the Neuve-Chapelle-Armentières sector, where the First Canadian Division was to be located to receive its initial experience in the trenches.

Various officers of the Divisional Staff were allotted certain hours at the railway station, and on the second night I was assigned to my tour of duty as detraining officer. Instructions were very simple. I was given a schedule of the incoming trains, together with the name of the unit carried by each train. As a train arrived, I was to locate the Commanding Officer's car and hand him the instructions as to the area to which his unit was to proceed. I was then to report that each unit had moved off to its destination. The trains rolled in. In each case I found the Commanding Officer, handed him his instructions, the troops fell in, and moved off into the night.

About the middle of the night another train rolled to a stop. I found the car where the Commanding Officer was sitting with some of his staff. I saluted, informed him who I was and handed him the instructions from the Division. After he had read them, he announced that he was quite prepared to move his men immediately if they were required to fight, but he had too much regard for their comfort to move them at that hour of the night for any other reason. He went on to say that he would billet them in the village where they were detraining and then move them off to their destination in the morning. Young as I was, I was disgusted by this grandstand exhibition obviously staged to impress his staff. I informed him that all other units had moved off as instructed and that it would be necessary for me to report his compliance, or non-compliance, with the instructions which I had handed to him. He repeated in a loud voice that he would not move till morning, and that I could report this to whomever I liked.

The unit detrained, moved into the village, billeted there for the rest of the night and proceeded in the morning. The other units following rolled in during the night, formed up, or limbered up in the case of vehicles or guns, and moved off to their destination.

The recalcitrant Commanding Officer was duly disciplined for his behaviour. It is interesting to record that he was one of the first officers to be sent back from the Front.

In order to give the Canadian Division battle experience, small sections of the troops were moved into the trenches and sandwiched in between seasoned British regiments. This same procedure for their initiation into trench warfare was then followed by companies, and later by battalions. Finally, the First Canadian Division took over its own sector of the Front. It soon became apparent that the Canadians were adaptable and they very quickly became accustomed to the routine of stationary warfare.

We saw the preparations for the battle of Neuve-Chapelle which was planned by the British on our right flank. We watched the movements of the troops to the forward areas and the concentration of artillery for the battle that was about to take place.

The enemy for some time had employed in the field a forty-two centimetre, approximately fifteen inch, Howitzer. We had heard a good deal about this weapon before our arrival in France, and we found that the British were now about to employ for the first time an answer to this enemy weapon, a new fifteen inch Howitzer which was promptly nicknamed "Grandma", and which we heard was to be installed in the sector on our right. A few of us went over to witness the installation of what was then regarded as a monster of destruction, and for some days we watched it being laboriously mounted in the emplacement which had been prepared to receive it. With great anticipation and great expectation, we assembled behind this wonderful new weapon on the afternoon when it was to be fired for the first time against the enemy.

Standing behind the gun, I watched the shell which weighed a ton being slowly hoisted and moved into the breech. With all the enthusiasm of youth I could no longer contain myself. I turned to a grizzled-looking old veteran standing beside me and asked, "Are they going to fire the gun now?" The old war-horse, looking at me with disgust, replied with no little sarcasm in his voice, "No, they're just seeing if it fits."

By this time the powder charges were being placed in the breech and the breech closed. After a further delay, we were told to keep our mouths open. The operators were ready to fire the gun electrically by pressing a button.

A terrific explosion followed. Standing directly behind the gun, we could see a black streak as the ton projectile hurtled towards the top of its trajectory. Seconds later a column of smoke arose some miles in the distance as the shell detonated on or near the target.

After this round had been fired, however, "Grandma" was not pointing in the same direction. We soon found that it took considerable time to bring her back into alignment after each round had been fired. The big fifteen inch Howitzers used by both sides, as well as the twelve inch naval guns mounted on railway trucks, were useful mainly for their effect on morale. Later in the war our Headquarters, situated ten or more miles behind the Front, were shelled a number of times by big naval rifles fired from railway sidings, but in every case the shells exploded in fields adjoining the village in which we were located.

At this stage of the war the equipment was relatively simple. The fighting equipment of the Canadian infantry soldier consisted of the Ross rifle and bayonet, and his rounds of ammunition. Steel helmets and gas masks were as yet unheard of. Hand grenades of the crudest construction, largely improvised in the field, were still being used and when you lit the fuse to throw a grenade made out of a jam tin, or started the fuse of another type by tapping the percussion cap against your heel, you hoped that this instrument of destruction would not explode in your hand. We later received issues of a limited quantity of the Mills hand grenade, which proved to be extremely efficient.

The enemy already had his famous "potato masher", consisting of a container of explosive the size and shape of a small can of fruit, with a wooden handle about eight inches long screwed into one end. This handle was used to throw the grenade after the string had been pulled which started a five and one-half second fuse burning.

I have many reasons to remember this type of grenade. I am something of a collector and when I look now over the many odds and ends that I brought back with me, I find one trophy of particular interest in this connection. I was walking along the front line in the summer of 1916 in a trench system called the "Bird Cage", in front of Ypres. Here the lines were so close together that we used to heave hand grenades into each other's trenches. Just as I stepped around the corner into a trench bay, a potato masher landed in it. I jumped back around the corner into the bay that I had just left and, with heart pounding, waited for the explosion that did not come. After a few minutes, the runner with me and I decided that it was a dud and as we went through the bay I picked it up. We moved along the line for a short distance, and then I unscrewed the handle and took out the detonator. I discovered that the humorist who had thrown this friendly token had inscribed upon the handle in indelible ink "Greetings from the Fatherland", together with his name and address in full.

CHAPTER III

ACTION IN FRANCE

IT IS NOT MY PURPOSE to attempt a record of the First Great War; its events have been completely and ably documented in many volumes. I shall recount only such episodes and experiences as are still impressed upon my memory and which during my lifetime have had a marked influence upon my judgment and actions.

The Battle of Neuve-Chapelle took place on our right flank and was concluded with meagre results at the cost of very heavy casualties. The famous Princess Patricia Regiment, which was composed of soldiers who had seen active service, and which had arrived in France before the First Canadian Division, was engaged for the first time in this battle, and acquitted itself with great distinction. Our own Division, early in April 1915, was transferred to the famous—or infamous—Ypres Salient, which protruded in front of the city of Ypres in the form of a semi-circle and was considered to be the gateway to the ports of the English Channel. We took our position in the line with a British Division on our right and a French Division on our left flank.

In the twelfth century, Ypres had a population of two hundred thousand and was larger and more influential than London. Over the centuries its importance and influence had waned and by 1916, with a population of a hundred and eighty thousand, it was mostly famous for its wonderful Cloth Hall, whose turrets, towers and carved archways had already been badly damaged during the first bombardment in the autumn of 1914.

I was riding into Ypres along the Pavé Highway flanked by high trees on either side, while the second great bombardment of the city was in progress. It was the first but not the last time that I saw refugees—women and children, the aged and the infirm

—leaving their homes and possessions behind them, taking with them only what they could pull or carry, driven to an unknown destination and future by the same lust for power of some individual or group which has been recorded with the regularity of a repeating decimal since history has been written.

Divisional Headquarters were at Brielen, north-west of Ypres. Shortly before our arrival in this sector the first regular daily Divisional Intelligence Summary to be published in the British Army was inaugurated by our Division.

In the early afternoon of April 22nd, while I was in Ypres during what appeared to be a relatively quiet interval, I was startled by the noise of an incoming 15-inch Howitzer shell which by this time we could easily recognize. The sound was similar to the roar of an incoming express train, followed by a terrific explosion in the square of Ypres. A column of smoke and debris rose some four to five hundred feet in the air in the vicinity of the Cloth Hall. This seemed to be the signal for an artillery bombardment which became general along our entire Front. I dashed back to Divisional Headquarters as the shelling increased in intensity. Shortly after five o'clock, word was received that gas had been released, particularly on the front of the French Division on our left flank, and first reports indicated that those who had not been killed by the initial release of the dense clouds of greenish, yellowish fumes were retiring in complete disorder in an effort to escape the poisonous, choking gases, which we knew to be chlorine.

I was sent forward to reconnoitre. I soon encountered the retiring elements of the native French Division, most of them without their weapons, many of them in a state of collapse or near collapse from the effects of the gas. They were gasping out, "Le gaz! Le gaz!" as they staggered by me. Although the sharp odour of chlorine was very evident, by this time it was sufficiently diffused that it no longer caused any great distress.

It was clear that there had been a complete break-through on the left flank of our Division, which was tenaciously holding its own lines, and that a gap extending over a mile existed on our left.

After making my report at Divisional Headquarters that night

I was instructed to take a company of cyclists and establish them
on the bank of the Yser Canal. The Yser Canal ran in a direction
north by west from Ypres, and the bridges, starting from the city's
most northerly limits, crossed the canal at intervals of about half
a mile, and were numbered one to four. I was to establish my
cyclists at No. 4 bridge, which was the last still held by us north
of Ypres. My instructions were to mine the bridge, hold it, and
if the enemy advanced to the canal, to blow it up should the
position become untenable. I rode down at the head of my small
column and we arrived at our position, sustaining two casualties
and the loss of my mount from shell-fire as we neared the bridge.

When the canal was constructed, the earth had been thrown
up on the western bank. This formed a ten-foot mound which
paralleled the canal. There were some rifle pits along the top
of the mound and, on its reverse slope, a few dugouts that afforded
protection against the almost continuous shell-fire to which we
were to be subjected. The bridges were pontoons, built by the
engineers and only wide enough for a single line of vehicular
traffic. All these bridges, No. 4 in particular, were receiving special attention from the enemy in his attempts to prevent reinforcements from crossing the canal.

We dug ourselves in between remnants of French and British
units. Before our Division was withdrawn from this sector, we
had elements of forty-two different battalions fighting under the
command of our Divisional Commander. The battle raged
throughout the night. The gallant stand of the First Canadian
Division that day, and in the days that followed until May 4th
when the Division was relieved, aroused the admiration of our
allies. It came, too, as a stunning surprise to the enemy, who
had jokingly referred to us as "The Canadian amateurs", and in
other terms even less complimentary, when we first made our
appearance in France.

The position at No. 4 bridge became almost untenable as it
was kept under intermittent fire during the daytime and heavy
harassing fire at night. In spite of all the precautions we could
take, we were suffering continuous casualties. It was considered
by Headquarters that the place was sufficiently hot to require a
relief every forty-eight hours. On the occasion of the first relief,

being very young and foolish, I had the men relieved and returned the officer, sending back word that I was now thoroughly familiar with the area and its vicinity and that I should prefer to stay at my post until the Division was relieved. I did not realize at the time that I would endure this for nearly two weeks.

On the fourth day, about eight o'clock in the morning, a regiment of French infantry started moving in from behind us along the road that led to the bridge. Up to this time they had been concealed from direct observation by the canal bank. When they reached the road that ran parallel to the canal about a hundred yards behind us, they left the road and swung into an adjoining field, where they settled themselves on the ground in close formation.

A French officer came to where I was located and advised me that the troops intended to cross the bridge in broad daylight, deploy, and get into the communication trenches, through which they would move into the front line ahead of us. After they had assembled, they planned to launch an attack at four o'clock that afternoon. The attack was to be supported by two batteries of French seventy-fives, that in the meantime had pulled into the field behind us, and other supporting artillery. About an hour later, a German plane flying at a very low altitude in front of us, spotted this concentration and dropped a stick with a white light at each end, which floated to the ground in a horizontal position.

Within the half-hour, the enemy opened up with a terrific bombardment directed against the area of the bridge, shelling the canal bank and the fields in the rear. From my position on the top of the embankment, on looking behind me, I saw direct hits beginning to register in the midst of the French regiment less than two hundred yards away. Suddenly the French seventy-fives, which were limbered up, galloped on to the road leading to the bridge, crossed the bridge fifty yards on my left, swung their guns into position on the opposite canal bank and unlimbered. Their horses and riders dashed back across the bridge. The two batteries immediately opened rapid fire upon the enemy front line directly ahead of us, which consisted of a heavily sandbagged trench with its rectangular machine gun emplacements clearly visible at intervals.

By this time the French regiment was moving out towards the road leading to the canal and breaking across the road that ran behind the canal. The fire was very intense and the regiment was suffering casualties that, fortunately, were not as severe as one would have believed with the heavy bursts of shrapnel and high explosive which seemed to be dusting the ground all around the men.

As I was watching them cross the road behind me, a shell struck one of the trees lining the road and exploded about forty feet up the tree shearing it off. Two Frenchmen dropped to the pavement. They were both dead when I went over to them after the bombardment. So were a number of others lying in the vicinity.

During the same interval, a whizzbang had gone through the rifle pit less than two yards to my left, passed through the chest of a Tommy who never knew what hit him, and then exploded as shrapnel some distance behind us.

The French regiment had moved rapidly across the bridge into the communication trenches and then up into the front line trench, from which they were to make their assault at four o'clock that afternoon. In the meantime, the horses belonging to the French battery had again dashed across the pontoon, the guns were limbered up, and withdrawn across the bridge. They located themselves in the fields behind us preparatory to supporting the afternoon assault and went into action with their guns spread apart at wide intervals. Fumes and smoke from what appeared to be an enemy direct hit would completely envelop one of the French seventy-fives and its men crouching behind its shield. But the bright, spurting flash of the gun would defiantly stab through the greyish-black cloud, and I knew that some of its heroic crew had survived the burst.

I shall never forget what happened that afternoon, and I shall always remember my thoughts when I saw the tragedy that followed.

A desultory fire consisting mainly of bursts of overhead shrapnel was carried out by the French guns, supported by some other guns, against the heavily sandbagged fortified trench with its menacing machine gun emplacements. This pitifully ragged and

ineffectual fire, which could not be called a bombardment, produced no visible destruction. It continued until four o'clock.
Then I saw the gallant Frenchmen clamber out of their trenches
in their blue coats and red trousers, and start their advance across
No Man's Land toward the German lines. The enemy behind
the still undamaged machine gun emplacements sprang into
action. The guns began spitting their noisy staccato of death
into the advancing men. In the face of this heavy fire the French
went down like ninepins along the entire line. The few bewil-
dered survivors gallantly pressed forward until they too were
sprawled upon the field with the rest of their regiment. It was
hard to believe that I was witnessing reality.

After the first few days, during which the Canadian troops
were heavily and almost continuously engaged, it became apparent that the Ross rifle was proving unsatisfactory. The men
whose lives depended upon reliable weapons were complaining
that the Ross would jam when used under conditions which
required rapid fire and that it was impossible, when the rifle
became heated, to open the bolt, even by standing the rifle up
on its butt and driving the heel down against the bolt lever.

We had concrete evidence of this dissatisfaction. In the midst
of the battle we found that many of our men had discarded their
Ross rifles and had armed themselves with the British Lee-Enfield
which they had either picked up in the field of battle or, as we
soon learned from official complaints, had "borrowed" from British troops in the vicinity. It was quite common to see units, or
portions of units, moving along and find some of the men
equipped with the long Ross rifle and others with the Lee-Enfield.

Tests were held using ten Ross rifles and ten Lee-Enfields and
rapid fire trials were conducted. It was found that on the average
the Ross rifle would jam at thirty rounds rapid, and the Enfield
could carry on sustained rapid fire without jamming until an
average of a hundred and ten rounds had been reached. The Ross
rifles were withdrawn and such troops as by this time had not
"borrowed" Enfields had the standard British rifle issued to them.

The First Canadian Division had been supplied with mounts,
and horses for their guns and vehicles from the various re-mount
depots. During the battle of Ypres, we saw the picturesque Al-

gerian Cavalry for the first time. The men in their flowing robes
were mounted on small, spirited chargers. During and after this
action we noticed that some of these small, fine looking Arab
chargers had somehow become part of the establishment of the
First Canadian Division. It was evident that the handsome animals appealed to the lovers of horse flesh in our Division and
had been "borrowed" from the Algerians. By this time the
Canadians had established a reputation as competent foragers.
Their position in this regard was never challenged until the
arrival of the First Australian Division.

As I have already said, it would be difficult to find a greater
assortment of troops than those which I visited on my daily patrol
along the bank of the Yser Canal. We were dug in alongside
units of the French, Turcos, Zouaves, British, and elements of the
Lahore Division from India, as well as dismounted units of the
Algerian Cavalry.

There was very little to relieve the horror in the environment
of death and destruction in which I lived for the following two
weeks. More attacks were launched on our immediate front.
These were accompanied by the discharge of gas, but by this
time we had learned to protect ourselves to some degree by cre-
ating an improvised filter. We tied around our faces wet handkerchiefs or several layers of cloth which we had soaked with
water from our water bottles or by other means, and breathed
through these crudely fashioned masks.

All this time we were anticipating further attacks. We
realized that some days must pass before adequate and effective
reserves could arrive in our sector. Every available man was in
the trenches and we hoped that reinforcements would arrive in
time. Rumours, as always in war, were flying thick and fast.
There were two cockneys in the rifle pit on my right and during
a lull I overhead them discussing the possibility of help arriving
in time. I heard one tell the other that the Commander-in-Chief
of the British Army, Sir John French, had just had an interview
with "Papa" Joffre, the Commander-in-Chief of the French
Army. According to this intrepid warrior, French had said to
"Papa", "Look here, you old ——, you had better get some troops
up to Wipers, bloody quick."

A few days later, a regiment of Turcos moved undetected to the bridge, crossed it and quickly disappeared in the communication trenches in front of me. Some distance farther on, they left their trenches and started to take a position in extended order. Their real objective was never clear to me, for as soon as they deployed, they were subjected to an artillery bombardment which, as often happens, caused them to close up from their flanks towards the centre. In a very short period they were massed in close formation and were receiving direct hits from heavy Howitzer shells as well as whizzbangs. Suddenly I saw some of them break out, throw away their weapons and start running towards us. In a few moments the entire unit was streaming towards us and was soon at our rear. It was a most demoralizing experience to witness this rout and one can easily conjure up what could have occurred if it had taken place in the centre of a general assault.

Stringent orders prohibiting looting had been issued. These were mainly for the benefit of the city of Ypres, from which by this time all civilians had been evacuated. The attacks had subsided during the days preceding May 4th, and late one afternoon I saw my batman returning from the direction of Ypres. He walked up to me holding a handful of rather elaborate looking walking sticks. A quick-witted Irishman, he thrust an ebony cane with a curved silver handle into my hand before I could make any comment. Then, looking in my eyes, he saw a suspicion and a question being formed. "Where did you get these?" I asked. He saluted smartly and said, "Sir, these were given to me by the Mayor of Ypres."

While I had every reason to suspect that the Mayor of Ypres had left the city many days before the arrival of my batman, I was not in a position to prove this, nor did I make a serious effort to find out whether his statement was fact. I still have the ebony cane with its curved silver handle and I still prefer to cherish the delusion that it once carried with it the compliments of the Mayor of the famous city of Ypres.

During the final days of this engagement, my acquisitive batman did perform a real service by picking up a riderless horse which was wandering aimlessly along the road behind our rifle pits. Its owner had obviously been wounded, as the saddle was covered with blood and a Lee-Enfield with its stock cut off by a shell splinter was still in the saddle bucket. The horse, a small, gentle chestnut, had been slightly wounded in the near rear leg, presumably by a splinter from the same shell. We kept him some distance behind the canal in a farmer's barn which had escaped the shelling. We were relieved by the Fourth British Division on May 4th and I rode my new mount which I had named "Wipers" with a new rifle and the presentation cane from the Mayor of Ypres in the saddle bucket. I found Headquarters for our Division at Nieppe. "Wipers" remained my mount until I was severely wounded in September of the following year while with the Eighth Canadian Infantry Brigade. When I returned to the Front, I assumed duties on the General Staff of the Third Canadian Division, and "Wipers" remained with the Brigade until the end of the war.

The Field Marshal Commander-in-Chief of the British Army in France, Sir John French, Earl of Ypres, in his despatch to the Secretary of State for War at the War Office in London, reporting upon the battle of Ypres, included the following sentence: "In spite of the danger to which they were exposed, the Canadians held their ground with a magnificent display of tenacity and courage, and it is not too much to say that the bearing and conduct of these splendid troops avoided a disaster which might have been attendant with the most serious consequence."

In the test of their first battle, against troops whose life-long training had been war, Canadians had proved that they were superior to an enemy abundantly supplied with every weapon and agent for destruction known at that time. The First Canadian Division, consisting of twenty thousand men, had suffered over six thousand casualties. What particular qualities had enabled these troops to make this battle the most important feat of arms yet recorded in the annals of Canadian history? The majority of these troops had been civilians, drawn from all sections of Canada and from every conceivable occupation. In the main they were completely inexperienced in the art of warfare.

Canadians have inherited their traits from a background that

is chiefly English, Scottish, Irish, French and German. They
have inherited, too, the adaptability, stability, the courage and
determination which they so gallantly demonstrated in this action.
Their stand won immediate recognition for the First Canadian
Division and enhanced the prestige of our country.

THE DIVISION in the following months participated in the attacks
against Festubert and Givenchy. These attacks, again with limited objectives less than half a mile in depth, were made against
heavily wired and strongly constructed trenches. By this time
it was patently clear that we did not have ammunition in sufficient
quantities to conduct the war properly. The main supply of shells
available for the artillery consisted of the ball shrapnel type which
burst in the air, the shell velocity projecting and spraying the
ground with the half-inch lead balls with which the shell was
filled. This type of ammunition was effective against troops
advancing in the open; it was completely unsuitable for the
demolition work which the artillery was required to do in destroying enemy wire and trenches, in preparation for an infantry
assault. High explosive shells which detonated on hitting the
ground, whose fuses could also be set for air bursts, became the
urgent requirement for the type of warfare with which we were
confronted.

It requires little imagination to envisage the heavy losses sustained by the First Canadian Division in these attacks. One of
our battalions engaged at this time, through lack of sufficient
ammunition of the right kind to prepare for its advance, lost
twenty out of twenty-three of its combatant officers.

At the Front we had had it forcibly brought home to us that
the decision in the field was more than a matter of which side
possessed superior, or more weapons. Conducting the war on a
side that had to ration its shells, against an enemy who daily
presented us with tangible evidence of far greater resources,
made us realize soon that an important factor in obtaining the
decision would be who could win the race in expenditure of
ammunition. Even to me, a young officer in my twenty-fourth

year, it was apparent that adequate labour facilities behind the lines were at least as important as the military considerations.

We were faced then by an enemy who twice in my lifetime was to demonstrate that he knew the advantage of preparation. On both occasions he had assembled vast accumulations, not only of the munitions required, but the reserves of raw materials necessary for their manufacture as well. This enemy entered both wars so organized and prepared that the immediate and effective mobilization of all his national industries and resources was assured. How great was the disparity in the first World War was determined after its end, when it was found that the Central Empire was producing 250,000 shells a day, a production ten times that of the allies.

This condition, apparent to us all, and costing untold lives, made a profound impression upon me at the time, and even more so when I saw it continue tthroughout the following year. I was first wounded in an enemy attack which was preceded by a four-hour bombardment, while for nearly three hours of this period our guns stood silent for lack of ammunition.

Our situation then was best expressed by the French Premier, Georges Clemenceau, who said, "England did not want war. It must be said once more to her credit, and alas! to her confusion, that she was not prepared for it."

This statement would be fair only if "England" were taken out of it and the words "all peace-loving nations" substituted. We would then have a fairly accurate assessment of the state of mind and the lack of preparedness of all the peace-loving nations who have had wars thrust upon them since the turn of the century.

BY THE SPRING of 1915, the Second Canadian Division was already crossing the Atlantic, this time in single ships and not as a contingent. After a training period in England, it arrived in France in September, 1915, and joined the First Division at Ploegsteert Wood. The Canadian Corps was then formed under the command of Lieut.-Gen. Sir E. A. H. Alderson, K.C.B., and I remained attached to his Staff. Major-General Currie was placed in command of the First Division and his Brigade was taken over by Brigadier-General Lipsett. I later had the honour of serving on the Staffs of both of these distinguished officers.

The Second Canadian Division on its arrival in France was under the command of Major-General Turner, V.C. Two years later, while convalescing from wounds received at the Battle of the Somme, I was attached to the Staff of the Canadian Military Headquarters in London, then under the command of General Turner. At that time I engaged in a small prank, which I shall record later and for which I hope the gallant General will forgive me should he read this.

During the fall of 1915 the trench systems were improved and Canadian troops showed a marked aptitude and ingenuity in their patrol work in No Man's Land. Trench raids were inaugurated by the Canadians at that time. There was no prospect of an offensive on our part before the following spring. The rainy season started in October and only those who experienced this first fall and the following winter in the mud and filth of the trenches can realize the hardships that had to be endured. Colonel W. G. MacKendrick joined us here and his outstanding direction of road construction for the Canadian Corps resulted in his being taken by Army Headquarters. He became well known as "Roads" throughout the British Army and was awarded the D.S.O. He was later, for many years, a director of our companies and a warm friend.

One of the great problems that confronted us was to keep the troops dry and comfortable when they were relieved from their tour of front line duty. The facilities that existed behind the lines for bathing the troops were of the crudest. In the area which we occupied we found use had been made of a few breweries in which some beer barrels had been cut in half, but these arrangements provided only a limited supply of hot water. There was no organized arrangement for handling the clothing and underwear of the troops.

With one of the Administrative Officers of the Corps Staff, I visited one day a number of these improvised bath-houses. As we inspected a starch factory in which two hundred men a day were being bathed, I made the remark—as I thought the following day, foolishly—that there should not be the slightest difficulty in organizing the facilities of this factory to handle a brigade of 5,000 men a day.

I thought nothing of the remark at the time, as I was still carrying on under the instructions of G.S.O. 2 of the new Canadian Corps, although we had mainly routine work under the conditions then existing. Next morning, however, I was sent for by the Administrative Head of the Army Corps and confronted with the statement that I had made the day before. He asked if the facilities could be increased to the extent that I had indicated. I replied that it was both possible and simple. I was then informed that the General Staff would release me from my duties for the time being and that I was to proceed with the organization of a system of bath-houses in the Canadian Corps area with the greatest possible speed.

I sent a convoy of lorries to nearby Bethune, which on its return delivered two hundred beer barrels to the starch factory. These were cut in half, producing four hundred bathtubs, which were placed on the spacious floor of the factory. I had the engineers pipe steam from the boilers into the large vats standing in this room, which we kept filled with water from the adjoining canal. Four hundred pails, towels and soap formed the rest of the equipment, and within the week we were bathing a brigade per day as planned, running through four hundred men every half-hour.

This created a new problem. We had planned to issue the men with fresh underwear after they had bathed, and we now had to create proper laundry facilities with a sufficient capacity to carry this out. I had available at the time a motor cycle with a sidecar, and the driver would dash me around from one village to another. With the help of the local authorities, I soon was able to organize the laundry problem.

There still remained two other problems. The first, how we could rapidly dry these large quantities of underwear; and secondly, how we could sterilize the men's uniforms while they were being bathed.

The first problem was the most pressing, as there was no use in providing baths for the men unless we could then issue them with clean, dry underwear. We used existing buildings and had long drying sheds constructed by the engineers in the back areas as well. These units were shelled occasionally, but fortunately little damage was caused. But we soon found, as we hung up the clothes to dry in the buildings or sheds, that in spite of the heat provided by stoves that we had bought or commandeered, the air soon became saturated with moisture and the drying process was slowed down considerably. In order to provide proper circulation for the drying sheds, I was authorized to proceed to London there to see Major-General Sir J. W. Carson, K.C.B., who, with his Headquarters at the Cecil Hotel, was in charge of all purchasing and supplies for the Canadian troops. Max Aitken, who later became Lord Beaverbrook, was at our Headquarters that day and offered to drive me to the Channel. He has probably forgotten how we stopped the car en route while I oriented a map and gave him his first lesson in map reading.

I arrived in London that afternoon and was ushered into the presence of General Carson, a very distinguished looking white-haired gentleman who, I believe, was one of Canada's leading industrialists of the time. He asked me what I wanted and I explained to him what our problem was, telling him that we required eight 36″ suction fans, complete with gasoline engines and other accessories. I had a feeling, while I was telling the General why I wanted fans of particular sizes and their functions, that he did not clearly understand what I was talking about. However, he listened very kindly and attentively, jotted down a few notes, and finally, with a wave of the hand, said, "They are authorized." I jumped on the packet boat and was back at our Headquarters the following morning. The suction fans, with their gasoline drives and all their equipment complete to the last detail, arrived the next day.

We installed the first unit in one of the smaller sheds. It produced a suction in the drying hut that reversed the draft and pulled all of the smoke into the hut, until the speed was reduced to provide a flow of air at the rate we required.

We now had a complete solution of our drying problem. Dr. Amyiot, a brilliant Canadian scientist whom I called in to solve the vermin problem, soon sketched up a steam chamber in which the uniforms of the troops could be placed while they were bathing. On live steam being let into the chamber, the uniforms were disinfected.

Working with the engineers, I had designs completed for a bath-house to use showers, which required less hot water than tubs. Five of these were constructed in the Corps area together with sufficient laundry and disinfecting facilities to handle ultimately over fifty thousand pieces of laundry and clothing per day.

We now had a standard design for a bath-house complete with its disinfecting chambers, which permitted the rapid construction of these units in any location. To provide steam, I made use of threshing machines which we hired or commandeered in the back areas and dragged along the Pavé Road to their destinations by lorries which were supposed to proceed at a very low speed in order to prevent the rivetted boilers from leaking all over when they arrived.

That winter the luxury of these hot baths and all that went with them was looked upon with some envy by the British Divisions and I was called in to Headquarters and told that Sir Herbert Plumer*, the Commander of the Second British Army, was going to inspect three of the Canadian Corps baths. I arranged the inspection so that he would end up with our very latest and newest model, which we planned to put into operation the day preceding this inspection.

On the appointed day, I met the Army Commander and some of his Staff at the first bath, which he inspected, then proceeded ahead of him to greet him on his arrival at the second establishment. I then left for the newest model that was to receive the final inspection. Upon my arrival here, I was somewhat taken aback to find everything in perfect order, troops going through as scheduled, with one exception. The threshing machine had arrived the day before and the engineers told me that the driver of the lorry which had hauled it over the Pavé Road for some twenty-five miles had not followed the instructions he had received about the slow rate of speed at which the machine was to be drawn. He had apparently galloped quite gaily with this machine over the rough Pavé Road. On firing up, it was found

* Field Marshal Lord Plumer, G.C.B., G.C.M.G., G.C.V.O.

that there was hardly a rivet in the boiler that did not complain about the rough passage by leaking water and blowing steam in all directions as the pressure rose. The engineers had done a first-class caulking job during the night, but the boiler was still voicing its protest when Sir Herbert arrived.

In spite of my concern, we both had a good laugh over the incident and I was asked to draw up a report on our system, including our blue-prints for the bath-houses and laundries, and to have our Corps forward these to Second Army Headquarters. This was done and the following year shower baths for use behind the lines became a standard part of British Army equipment.

In February of 1915 I turned over these bath-houses and all the arrangements that went with them to an officer who was designated "O.C. Baths, Canadian Corps", and I returned to my former duties on the Corps Staff.

It was in the same month that I happened to pick up a copy of the London *Times* which we received in the field. On glancing through it, I was dismayed to note that someone in Canada had questioned the propriety of my serving on the Canadian Head-quarters Staff. The reference in the *Times* was very brief and stated that the matter had been raised, apparently in the Canadian House of Commons, and had drawn a very vigorous reply from the Minister of National Defence.

Since I did not know what it was all about, and since this was the second occasion on which my having a German name had been raised, the story in the *Times* caused me great embarrassment. I was deeply hurt that this matter should be raised after I had served in the field.

I addressed a letter to the Corps Commander, attaching the clipping from the *Times*. I stated that under the circumstances, if my presence on the Staff was causing any embarrassment whatever, I wished to be relieved of my duties and would be prepared to serve in whatever manner my services could best be utilized.

On the following day the General sent for me. When I appeared before him, he greeted me in the most kindly fashion. I could see my letter lying on the desk in front of him. He looked up at me, picked up the letter and said, "Hahn, do you know what I think of this? Treat it with the contempt it deserves."

Then he tore up the letter. I returned to my duties greatly heartened.

It was not until I returned to Canada that I found out what had happened. I very much appreciated not only the remarks of the Minister of National Defence, but an editorial in the London *Free Press* as well, which had been kept for me, together with other editorials relating to the same subject. The editorial in the *Free Press* read as follows:

CAPTAIN HAHN

Major-General Hughes makes a striking reply to the Ottawa *Journal*'s editorial "problem". The *Journal* asked if a German should be the chief of the intelligence branch of the Canadian department of war. The major-general's answer is that he wishes he had a Dominion full of such men: that their detractors might far better be engaged in following the example of men of the type of Capt. Hahn, the intelligence chief in question. It turns out that Capt. Hahn is not German born, though of Teutonic descent.

There are some concrete facts that sustain the attitude of Sir Sam. For example, thirty-eight Canadians of German origin have been killed in the war in defence of Canada and the British Empire. There are hundreds of men of German origin who are fighting side by side with their fellow-Britishers in the cause of liberty. These men have either yielded their lives for Canada or stand ready to do so. "Greater love hath no man than this: that a man lay down his life for his friend." As for Capt. Hahn, he has been decorated with the Military Cross and mentioned in despatches by the British officers in the field for bravery.

"This is not a war of race, but a war for liberty," says the major-general. Do we grasp the meaning of this? Do we understand that it is primarily liberty for which we are fighting? Do we know that if Germany wins we will lose all, no matter what our nationality?

Capt. Hahn comes from Stratford. He is at present in the trenches.

IN THE FIELD, Staff officers were appointed within the Canadian Corps usually by promoting Staff officers from other formations to fill a vacancy when one occurred, or by appointing officers who had been "learners" to fill the junior Staff vacancies. Learners were officers who were considered potential material for Staff duties. These were drawn from the different units and attached for instruction to the Canadian Corps or Divisional Staffs. Later, when the Canadian Corps included four Divisions, Staff learners were also attached to some of the Brigade Staffs.

The Staff under a commander had two main divisions. The General Staff with its Intelligence Division was responsible for the planning and conduct of the field operations: the Administrative Staff, as the name implies, was charged with the responsibility for all problems relating to personnel and supply. Learners were attached to both of these branches, depending upon their suitability, or if they were considered suitable for either branch, upon the inclination of the officer concerned.

As I was always more interested in the function of the General Staff, I was given the opportunity of continuing my training under both the General Staff Officers, Operations and Intelligence, of the Canadian Corps.

It was then the custom for the Generals in our Corps to make their request for a Staff officer or learner by name. In April, 1916, I was informed that I was considered to have had sufficient training to be given a Staff appointment. I anticipated an appointment with great eagerness.

It frequently occurs in life that we have to take a decision between two courses, and sometimes this decision is a very difficult one to make. This happened when I was advised that my name was being considered for appointment by two commanders, each of whom had a vacancy on his Staff. Of the two Staff positions, the senior one was on the Administrative Staff. The other was as a Staff Captain, Intelligence, for the Eighth Canadian Infantry Brigade.

Each commander had his own particular foible, and that of the General Officer commanding the Third Canadian Division was to invite any officer who was being considered as a prospective Staff officer for his Division to lunch and a game of checkers.

A few days later I was invited to have lunch with General Mercer, commanding the Third Canadian Division. After lunch I was not surprised when I was asked to sit down to a game of

The Globe, Toronto

H.R.H. THE DUKE OF CONNAUGHT INSPECTS
THE GUARD OF HONOUR

The Guard was furnished by the 27th Lambton Regiment. After the inspection His Royal Highness said, among other things, that the Guard was commanded by "a very young officer". Everyone seemed to think that the assiduous attention of the Guard of Honour to the Duke helped greatly in making Sarnia a city.

INTELLIGENCE OFFICER

I left home on August 10th, 1914, a young inexperienced lad. I returned to Canada in June, 1919, a much matured man, whose black hair was already greying at the temples. These photographs were taken on the same spot five years apart.

ON THE YSER CANAL

This photograph of myself was taken in one of the rifle pits along the top of the canal by the officer who came to relieve me. It is among the last taken at the front. Two days later the possession of cameras was forbidden and their use in the trenches was made a court martial offence.

checkers with the General. The General won, but I apparently caused him enough trouble to be invited on the following day to fill the vacancy existing on the Staff of his Eighth Brigade.

Following my inclination, I advised the Corps Commander that I would prefer to continue in General Staff work and would be glad to fill the appointment on the Staff of Brig.-Gen. Victor Williams, then commanding the Eighth Canadian Infantry Brigade. I assumed my new duties and on the 31st of May our Brigade moved into the line and took up a position in the Ypres Salient, in a section of the line in what was known as the Sanctuary Wood Area.

Brigade Headquarters was in the embankment of Zillebeke Bund, a triangular lake with its base something over a mile south-east of Ypres. At its apex, about a mile farther east, the village of Zillebeke was situated. From Headquarters we could see our front lines on the crest of the ridge and halfway between this crest and Zillebeke village was a beautiful copse of trees along the edge of a small creek that ran from the copse into Zillebeke Bund. This patch of wood, about an eighth of a mile square, was soon nicknamed Maple Copse.

The front line trenches were about three hundred yards apart, and we were greatly concerned when Colonel H. J. Lamb, C.M.G., D.S.O., from the General Staff of the Corps, arrived at our Headquarters at the Bund on the afternoon of June 1st, bringing with him an aeroplane photograph taken that morning which showed that a trench had been started by the enemy during the previous night, virtually in the middle of No Man's Land. This confirmed other information which we had received from the Brigade from whom we had taken over, that there had been a great deal of activity behind the enemy lines, all indicating an impending offensive. Our reserves and divisional reserves had been disposed in accordance with these reports, and the artillery, though during this period ammunition was still severely rationed, had received additional supplies in response to their urgent request.

The digging of an assembly trench by either side in those early days was considered the final preparation immediately preceding the assault. I was sent up to the front line after having viewed the photograph and was instructed to keep in touch with the battalion commanders and send back reports to Brigade Headquarters.

When I arrived in our front line, I was confronted with a most unusual sight. As far as I could see along our front, shovelfuls of earth were being thrown out of the assembly trenches and here and there the head and shoulders of a soldier would appear above the trench as he heaved out his shovelful.

Our artillery had already registered on the assembly line and a short, sharp bombardment, which was limited to only ten minutes on account of the ammunition shortage, was opened upon this line at five-thirty that afternoon. The enemy immediately responded as usual with a volume of fire on our lines considerably in excess of ours. It was clear that it was now not a question of whether the enemy was going to attack, but purely a question of when.

I stayed in the front line all evening and through the night, sending back reports. At three o'clock on the morning of June 2nd, I received a message from Brigade Headquarters instructing me to return at once and, if the General was asleep, to awaken him.

I returned to Brigade Headquarters some two miles behind the front line, awakened the General and made my final report. I said that all indications pointed to an enemy assault at daybreak. To my horror, General Williams told me that the Divisional commander, General Mercer, would arrive at Brigade Headquarters about six o'clock in the morning, as they considered that if the attack had not been launched by that time, it probably would not take place until the morning of June 3rd.

I suggested that, as I had been in the forward trench system all that afternoon and night and knew every inch of the line, I should accompany them on their visit. I remember General Williams saying, "Hahn, you have been up all night. You turn in", words that probably saved my life.

I turned in. At seven o'clock that morning I was awakened by heavy bombardment that developed along our entire front, together with heavy counter battery shelling directed against our batteries. Our own Headquarters were receiving a very healthy dusting. I jumped up and rushed into the Brigade office, to find that the Divisional Commander and our Brigade Commander had left an hour or so before, which meant that by this time they were already in the front line system.

An SOS from our troops had gone up, asking for artillery support and our guns were replying to the enemy fire. Within half an hour all communications were cut and our entire front line and Maple Copse were completely enveloped in fumes and dust from the terrific sustained bombardment and drum fire of the enemy.

Our Brigade major was a British officer who somehow or other refused to believe that this was a major attack. The bombardment by this time, with its frontal and enfilading fire on our rear from both sides of the salient, was the most violent to which we had yet been subjected.

By eight-thirty in the morning our own guns were almost silent, and the terrific concentration of enemy artillery continued to batter our trench system into a complete shambles. Some of our men who had been in support positions in Maple Copse had drifted back to our Headquarters and reported that every leaf had been blown off the trees of the Copse, the trunks splintered, all shelters there completely destroyed, like everything in the vicinity, and that our two sacrifice guns had been put out of action. The enemy troops had not yet made their assault. Nothing was known of the fate or the location of the two commanders.

I requested permission to make a forward reconnaissance and set out along the edge of Zillebeke Bund, through the village. There I ran into a first-class concentration of shelling and lachrimatory gas. I joined one company of a battalion in support that was moving in extended order from the village to dig themselves in just west of Maple Copse. By this time the enemy had occupied the crest of the ridge and as the four runners and I left and dashed across into the Copse, we were subjected to some rifle and machine gun fire, fortunately inaccurate.

The Copse was a mass of leafless, splintered tree trunks and had a breastwork consisting of a wall of sandbags along its south side, facing the curve of the top of the ridge, some two hundred yards above it. The ground was so soft that it was impossible to dig and there was no parados to protect this breastwork from the splinters of the shells as they exploded against the tree trunks or on the ground behind them.

It was grim behind the breastwork. The battalion commander, Colonel Baker, was soon mortally wounded and the second-in-command, Major Draper*, who later in the war commanded a brigade and after the war became Chief of Police of Toronto, and Dicky Rhodes†, the adjutant, were included in the list of casualties before the afternoon was over.

We ran up and down the breastwork, firing over the top from different places to give the enemy an impression of strength. By the middle of the afternoon nearly three-quarters of its defenders had been killed or wounded. Most of the casualties were caused by the heavy artillery and trench mortar fire that was concentrated on the Copse. The man on my right was killed, and a few moments after, an overhead high explosive shrapnel burst and clipped off the end of the nose of the man on my left. I was bandaging up his nose to the best of my ability when I felt on my left shoulder the impact of a sledge-hammer from a splinter from another overhead burst which knocked me down on top of the casualty whose wound I was attempting to bandage. I received attention from one of the few remaining stretcher bearers still on his feet. On taking off my tunic, I found that the splinter, which had struck me on top of my shoulder, had passed along through the muscle of the back and emerged some four inches lower. These two holes were patched up with gauze and tape.

The two messages, each with double runners, which I had sent back during the course of the afternoon had fortunately arrived safely at Brigade Headquarters, and those of us who were left behind the breastwork withdrew under the cover of darkness, using the small brook which ran back towards Zillebeke Bund, carrying out such casualties as were still living.

Our Brigade, or what was left of it, was relieved. Only eight

* Brigadier-General D. C. Draper, C.M.G., D.S.O. and Bar, Croix de Guerre.

† Colonel W. Rhodes, D.S.O., M.C.

hundred out of thirty-two hundred men survived this attack, and this number included many walking wounded.

We had no idea of the fate of our two generals until the following day when the enemy wireless announced that a Divisional Commander had been killed and a severely wounded Brigade Commander was among the few prisoners who had survived. It was later confirmed that Major-General M. G. Mercer, C.B., had been killed in action and that our Brigade Commander, later Major-General V. A. S. Williams, C.M.G., had been severely wounded and was a prisoner.

This battle again made me realize the loss of life that was occasioned through lack of sufficient ammunition, and that we were still a long way from being able to obtain a decision.

THE WOUND which I had received was of a light nature and required only daily dressings. The remnants of our Brigade were inspected a few days later by the General Officer commanding the Second British Army. After this I had ten days leave in England. When I returned, the Brigade was being brought up to full strength under the command of Brigadier-General J. H. Emsley, C.B., C.M.G., D.S.O., who had fought with great distinction and had been severely wounded in the Boer War, where he had earned the nickname of "Gentleman Jim".

All the ground that was lost on June 2nd was again in the hands of the Canadian Corps by the middle of July. While our Brigade was in the trenches my duties took me daily into the front line system where we maintained the closest liaison with the battalions. I was particularly concerned with the intelligence that was being accumulated every day from front line sources of information. These reports originated in the main from camouflaged observation posts which were sited in the most suitable positions in the front line trench system. I also interpreted for the Battalion Commanders and the Battalion Intelligence Officers the most recent aeroplane photographs of the enemy territory opposite their immediate front.

I spent many nights out on patrols with the Battalion Scout

Officer in the eerie No Man's Land between the front lines. Often my heart stood still when we heard the crack of a flare pistol in the enemy front line trenches; I felt certain that we were under observation as the star shell ignited in the air. No Man's Land was brightly illuminated and as we hugged the ground, I awaited the burst of rifle or machine gun fire which was the penalty of discovery. Every object in No Man's Land, as we crawled from crater to crater, conjured up visions of an enemy patrol. I was fortunate enough never to be intercepted by a hostile scouting party.

One night, however, six of us had concluded our patrol and had entered a sap which extended from our trenches into No Man's Land. The end of this trench was held by a post of four men. When we had proceeded about twenty yards along the sap, we heard the explosions of two potato-mashers near the post. We rushed back and found that apparently we had been trailed by an enemy patrol which we had not seen. When they saw us jump into the sap, they decided to throw the two bombs, which exploded outside the trench. The area was immediately illuminated with star shells fired by both sides. I have no doubt that certain tree stumps and shadows between our lines were given a thorough going over by the small arms fire that followed.

The Daily Intelligence Summary was inaugurated in the field by the First Canadian Division. In time it developed into a very complete résumé of all pertinent information. This was collected from front line sources and included reports from the observation balloons in the rear areas, as well as information obtained through the examination of prisoners and captured documents. All of this went to senior formations which channelled forward information relating to the enemy and his activities in front of the sector that we were holding.

The instructions of our Corps Commander were that he did not wish to find at any time any "sign of levity" in the reports. He also specified that all reports were to be limited to statements of facts and under no circumstances to include what we called "an appreciation". No deductions were to be made. There was a good reason for this. Appreciations of the offensive or defensive intentions of the enemy could best be made by the Intelligence

Staffs of senior formations. It was properly considered that a conclusion could not be drawn from an isolated incident no matter how significant it might appear. It was true that when the great mass of information available to the senior formations was assessed as a whole, definite trends were usually indicated. Occasionally, some humorist would make a comment or include a remark that did not conform to the ban on levity, and we sometimes closed an eye to efforts that we found particularly amusing.

In the days before steel helmets, the enemy went into the front line wearing a forage cap the shape of a pill box. Each cap had a circle of metal or cockade on either side of it. Each cockade carried three colours in concentric circles. One was always red, white and black, the colours of the Imperial German Army; the other might be any combination of colours and represented the regimental colours. Occasionally, observers picked up one of these pill box caps in their telescopes.

I remember reading a report which stated that "one of the enemy had been seen in a trench (and gave the map location) wearing a pill box forage cap which had on one side a red, white and black cockade, and a green, yellow and heliotrope cockade on the other (some hat)." This got through as far as Canadian Corps Headquarters. The Intelligence Officer there was called in by General Alderson, the Corps Commander, who said that while he did not understand the significance of the expression "some hat", he knew that it was not good English, and he considered that this report contravened his instructions regarding levity in the summaries.

One other incident which has amused me through the years was a report which I received from a front line observation post, which included in the Intelligence Summary of the day, "At 4 p.m., at A 2.2, C 1.4, (a map location behind the enemy lines) a train was seen proceeding south with smoke issuing from its funnel. At the same time, and at the same place, a train was seen proceeding north with smoke issuing from its funnel. It is strongly suspected that there is a double track at this place."

We picked up a great deal of movement behind the lines from our observation posts, which were usually equipped with twenty-power telescopes. In the last year of the war, when our attacks resulted in deeper penetrations, I had a fifty-power telescope installed which enabled me on various occasions to determine whether I was witnessing the movement of our own or enemy troops. In the summer of 1916, however, activity on our sector was still slight, and both sides indulged in a type of harassing fire that often caused great consternation to troops who thought they were moving undetected and out of range behind their lines. An artillery officer was located in one of our front line observation posts from which a direct telephone line had been run to his battery. If we had noticed troops moving in certain well-defined areas up to a couple of thousand yards behind the enemy lines, one or more of the guns of the battery would register on this point at a time when no movement was taking place. After registration had been completed, if movement was then observed at this location, the artillery officer in the observation post would simply order his guns, which we designated as "sniper guns", to fire.

It seemed amusing to watch a startled enemy run for cover as the shells exploded about him during an otherwise extremely quiet day. It was less amusing when we were on the receiving end of this kind of entertainment, particularly when, caught in the open, we knew that there was someone looking at us through a telescope and at the same time instructing his No. 1 or No. 2 gun to fire, and when we knew that shells were already screaming on their way towards us.

A good deal of mining and counter-mining was also going on in the area. This was particularly hair-raising work. Both sides were shoving out tunnels, starting from their front line trenches. They passed underneath No Man's Land and were engineered and designed so that charges of high explosive could be placed beneath the opposing line. These were then blown during a major attack or sometimes to support a trench raid or reconnaissance in strength.

The engineers who directed and undertook this extremely harrowing and dangerous work were called the Sappers and Miners. Being susceptible to claustrophobia, I still shudder when I think of crawling out under No Man's Land into these tunnels where our listening apparatus picked up the noise of the enemy's picks and shovels, as they counter-mined in our vicinity. It then became a case of "who would blow first" to cave in the other tunnel.

We were always on the alert for any new weapon or shell employed by the enemy. Any piece of new equipment was usually sent back to Divisional or Corps Headquarters to be examined and recorded. The enemy at this time had come out with a trench mortar shell which we called the "oil-can". We did not know the details of its construction, but we had often seen it hurtle through the air when fired into our trench system, and were familiar with the devastating blast and explosion which followed.

One bright, sunny afternoon that summer, Major Pearkes* and I were walking along our front line trenches. The Major's courage was already well established in our Corps. Some time before this, I was told, he had been taken out of the front line with the handle of an enemy potato-masher protruding from his skull. Fortunately the injury was not as serious as was at first indicated, for after the handle was extracted, he was soon back in the line again. He later won the Victoria Cross and other decorations. On this day everything appeared peaceful and quiet. Suddenly we heard the dull explosion of a mortar in the line opposite us and looking up, we saw an oil-can hurtling end over end. It appeared to be dropping on top of us. We flopped to the bottom of the trench. The oil-can hit with a dull thud behind the parados of the trench in which we were lying. This was one of the many occasions when I wondered what permitted my heart to continue beating during that terrifying second when we awaited the heavy blast that probably would have buried both of us. However, it did not come. I stood up rather shakily and looked over the back of the parados. There was the oil-can intact, including a very convenient handle on the top with which to pick it up. This the gallant Major did, hoisted it over the parados, and without further ado proceeded to unscrew the evil-looking contraption that we knew must contain its detonating action. When this was unscrewed, we removed the detonator we

* He served in the second World War and is now Major-General G. R. Pearkes, V.C., C.B., D.S.O., M.C., Croix de Guerre.

found inserted in its end. I heaved a great sigh of relief. We took
the detonating device apart and found that it consisted of a sharp,
weighted firing pin set in an oscillating spring which was released
after it was fired from the mortar. This detonating device was so
designed that when the oil-can hit the ground, the impact would
cause the weighted pin to oscillate between the springs, and the
point would set off a cap in the detonator.

We decided that we should take this trophy to Brigade Headquarters and send it back to the Division, as we felt they would
be greatly interested in it there. Between us we lugged the fifty-
pound specimen back through the trench system to Brigade
Headquarters where we walked into the Brigadier's shelter and
dumped it on the floor beside him. We were greeted with a roar
of "Get that out of here", but the Brigadier quickly realized that
it had been disarmed. We called Divisional Headquarters, who
informed us they were interested only in its dimensions and
weight, and told me to "bury it".

As the oil-can had stunted my growth and probably shortened
my span of years, I decided that that was not good enough. So
I took it out into the field and with a cold chisel and a hammer
proceeded to take it apart. It consisted of a tin canister fifteen
inches high and eight inches across. It had a heavy wire handle
at the top end such as one finds on an ordinary pail. Its metal
top was crimped over wood, and through the centre of this wood
projected what seemed to be the nose of an obsolete shell from
which we had unscrewed its detonating device.

I chopped out the wooden top which was about one and a
half inches thick, and found that the detonator had been screwed
into an old type of shell which formed the centre of the oil-can
and that this shell was seated upon the head of a loaded potato-
masher. The space between the obsolete shell and the can itself
was packed with half-pound bags of T.N.T., and to add further
diversion to what already seemed to be a sufficiently interesting
and effective piece of merchandise, bits of three-quarter inch iron
rod were packed in between the bags of T.N.T. The designer
of the oil-can must have been a very disagreeable person. This
oil-can reposes in my home with other trophies of World War I.

At this time we had with us under the Corps command a unit

called "The Canadian Railway Troops", commanded by a very beloved character who was nicknamed "Foghorn" MacDonald*. He was an expert when it came to constructing railways, and he and the unit did excellent work in providing transportation to our forward areas. However, he had never been trained as a soldier and was unaccustomed to the relationship of military formations one to another. He had a profound disdain for the ceremonial connected with military life. On one occasion British Army Headquarters put through a call for the Canadian Corps Commander. They were wrongly connected and got instead the redoubtable "Foghorn". British Army Headquarters were more than puzzled when, on inquiring if they were speaking to the Canadian Corps, they received from "Foghorn" the reply, "Hell, no. We're just a bunch of sub-contractors."

* Lieutenant-Colonel J. B. MacDonald, D.S.O.

CHAPTER IV

THE SOMME AND AFTERWARDS

THE FOURTH CANADIAN DIVISION had arrived in France and in October, 1916, became part of the Canadian Corps.

The Battle of the Somme was initiated by a British attack on a twenty-five mile front on July 1st, 1916, after very intensive artillery preparation. This large scale operation was intended to relieve the enemy pressure on the French lines at Verdun. The costly offensive turned out to be a "Verdun in reverse", resulting in terrific slaughter, and achieving through the summer months a series of limited objectives.

In the beginning of September, 1916, the Canadian Corps was moved south to the Albert area where we were to participate in what was by this time quite properly described as the "blood-bath of the Somme".

By the time we had arrived on this front, early in September, the British had advanced to the ridge just above Martinpuich. This position afforded observation over the enemy held area of Courcellette and the Thiepval Ridge to the west.

I have always had the greatest admiration for the fighting qualities and heroism of the British soldier. In this action we took over a sector of the front line from these stubborn troops who had displayed all those qualities of bravery, endurance and determination which have made Britain what she is.

Brigade Headquarters were located in a gravel pit behind Pozières, which had just been captured. On September 13th, I was informed that our Brigade was to attack at daybreak on the morning of the 15th, and that for the first time tanks would be used to support the attack. My instructions were to establish an observation post in or near the jumping-off trench and to make arrangements with the attacking battalion to have prisoners brought into my post immediately following the attack. It was vital to determine whether our attack had been a complete surprise, and particularly whether the enemy had any warning or information about the new weapon of war.

I spent the day familiarizing myself with the front line trench system and selecting a suitable position for the observation post. I sited it about a hundred yards to the left of "Tom's Cut", the main communication trench, in a supporting line which paralleled the jumping-off trench and was some seventy-five yards behind it. This site was on a slight rise and provided an excellent view across the No Man's Land between the opposing lines into the immediate enemy front line trenches and well into and beyond the final objective of the attack.

I went back to Pozières that night and stayed in a deep dugout which had been captured the day before. Here I slept on the floor, having as companions three very dead Germans who had been killed earlier in the engagement on the previous day. This dugout was to be put into use as an Advance Battalion Headquarters on the following day. I had cause to remember it later.

During the night my runners had built a splinterproof shelter that was to be my observation post as well as their own shelters in the parapet of the trench. I went up at daybreak and spent the day in this post, making certain that all my location points in the enemy lines had been properly oriented. These were to be used in the reports that I would send back during the action.

I sent messages back to Headquarters during the day. Eight runners were dug in beside me. Our telephone line, laid overland, usually lasted only a short time after the beginning of an engagement and the dust and fumes of battle rendered our helio signalling lamp ineffective. C.W. wireless sets had come into use but were not yet available for distribution to brigades, and these were the days before walkie-talkies. Runners, then, were the most reliable, though costly, method of getting back vital messages from the front line observation posts. My instructions were to return at four o'clock on the afternoon of the 15th unless I received a message to the contrary.

The night of the 14th seemed to indicate only normal front line enemy activity. With us the excitement was intense, particularly before the assault when I could hear the movement of our men assembling as quietly as possible in the jumping-off and support trenches. Shortly before dawn, I heard an ominous rumbling and clanking coming from the rear: in spite of desultory fire from our artillery, which had been timed to drown the sound of their approach, we could hear the tanks moving up for their first assault.

Just as day was breaking, two of these monsters rumbled and clanked over the trench on either side of me. On my right I saw a male tank with its little two pounders; on my left a female moved, armed only with machine guns.

I was looking at my watch and counting off the seconds. Less than a minute later, at zero hour, the whole front began to shake and rock as the light guns spat the rapid fire of their creeping barrage and the thunder of the heavy guns indicated that their shells were roaring towards the selected targets and concentrations in the enemy rear areas. The men, bayonets fixed, were clambering out of the trenches.

There was sufficient light now, and I could see the row of tanks with the line of our men behind them, moving across No Man's Land at a walk. The light guns had laid down a creeping curtain of white shrapnel air bursts which extended to the right and left as far as I could see. The shells were exploding over the moving tanks and virtually over the heads of our men, driving their charges of ball shrapnel into the enemy trenches, and dusting up the ground. The enemy were calling for the support of their own artillery by firing frantically SOS rockets from their trenches, and these multi-coloured balls flared into the air. Before the enemy guns could lay down their shells on their own SOS lines, our tanks and men had reached the enemy front line trenches some two hundred yards away. Great clouds of dust arose around our tanks which seemed to draw most of the enemy machine gun fire. I saw very few of our men go down. The tanks by this time had rolled relentlessly over the enemy front line and our bombing crews, hurling Mills grenades, moved laterally along the outside of the German trenches with that speed which is the only assurance of survival. Their bombs were exploding with precision in the trenches ahead of them as they carried out their rapid and devastating attack.

I could see numbers of the enemy jumping out of the trenches and surrendering. What was most important to me, two prisoners were now being escorted back across No Man's Land. I was talking to them eight minutes after zero hour. They both confirmed that the attack was a complete surprise and that they had received no warnings about the possible use of tanks. As far as they knew, no anti-tank defences were in existence in their area. This message was sent back by double runners with five minute intervals between them, as by this time the enemy shell-fire was very intense and our front line area was being raked by machine gun fire.

One of the two prisoners spoke English fairly well. He had been shot through the arm. I asked him why he had not surrendered; he said he was completely dumbfounded by the tanks. When our troops appeared on the top of his trench, he had intended to drop his rifle and throw up his arms but, as he put it, "One of your fellows simply went bing-bang."

Throughout the early morning I watched the tanks and men progress to their objectives. Shortly after the capture of the enemy front line system, I saw three of our men dropped, one after the other, as they were returning across No Man's Land. We discovered three German snipers in a shell-hole two hundred and fifty yards to our left, one of them using a rifle with a telescopic sight. The runners and I engaged and eliminated this group in a quick and spirited exchange of shots at the cost to us of one serious casualty. We were very lucky with our runners during the early part of that day, but not so fortunate later on.

I sent back reports throughout the day. When I saw that our positions had been taken and consolidated, I started back along what was left of Tom's Cut to the Advance Battalion Headquarters now established in the dugout in Pozières. On my arrival I found a message from Brigade Headquarters which said that the morning's attack would be exploited and the second attack would be launched at six o'clock. I was to return to my observation post and report results. The operation orders for the attack were included with my instructions.

By this time the troops that were to launch the second attack had been passing through Pozières. As I left the dugout to go back to my observation post, I moved along the trench filled with troops going forward to the attack. It was a bright, clear day, and this movement had been observed from Thiepval. We immediately came under very rapid and concentrated fire from the enemy guns situated there. The fire was so accurate and intense that my runner and I jumped out of the trench and ran overland. This was fortunate for us. I later learned that one company suffered such severe casualties that it was not able to participate in the attack.

It was now apparent to the enemy that a second attack was about to be launched, and a very heavy general fire was concentrated on our forward area. By this time I was back in Tom's Cut, which had been very badly flattened out by the bombardment during the day and offered little shelter, and we were again among men moving forward along the trench. We had to pass through several heavy barrage points established by the enemy. A short distance ahead salvoes of heavy shells were exploding in and about the trench. These groups of bursts were coming in at half-minute intervals. The troops would wait and, as each salvo exploded, would rush through.

We waited for our salvo. As a group of us rushed through, the enemy became unpredictable and strayed off his thirty second interval. I went down from a shell splinter that hit my tin helmet and knocked me sprawling. What caused me the greatest concern at the moment was a terrible feeling of bareness and exposure, as the splinter had knocked the tin hat off my head. I was not hurt and I hastily retrieved my all-important protection. This was warning number two for that day. In the morning with the opening barrage, I had been hit by a spent shrapnel ball from one of our own "shorts". I was glad to find that my runner had traversed the barrage point without injury.

I finally reached my observation post and six runners were able to get through and join me later.

The objective for the second attack was the village of Courcellette and the establishment of a post on the left flank. Five blue rockets fired in rapid succession were to be the signal that the flank block had been established.

I looked at my watch as it ticked towards zero hour. I heard again the thunder of the barrage and saw the deadly line of shrapnel shells bursting twenty yards apart. The barrage was hugged by our advancing line of troops and I could see them on this bright September evening moving into and through Courcellette and towards the left flank of their final objective. By eight o'clock I had sent back two messages indicating the progress of the attack and the positions reached.

Some of our men had moved into their final objectives, and I awaited the rocket signal. At ten minutes past eight I saw three blue rockets fired, which indicated that the post had been established on the flank. I was not concerned that the signal had not been completed, as two other rockets could easily have been lost. My own observations, confirmed by check points and prismatic bearings, indicated clearly that the final objective was now in our hands.

The four runners and I now proceeded to take our equipment out of the observation post, as our home-made director boards and telescopes were still not in plentiful supply. I decided to return to Advance Battalion Headquarters and then to Brigade. I planned to site a new observation post the following morning, provided our Brigade continued to be engaged in this action.

As our objectives for these attacks were still limited and we had not yet penetrated to sufficient depth to affect the enemy guns, hostile artillery shelling continued to be extremely heavy and was concentrated on all the possible approaches to our front line area. We moved out of the observation post along the short trench into Tom's Cut, or what was left of it. By this time it was completely flattened out by the enemy bombardment. We were moving rapidly back along this trench: darkness was just beginning to fall and the sky was illuminated by the flashes of our own and enemy guns. The continuous drum fire was still so heavy that it caused a constant pressure on the ears. It would have been necessary for a shell to explode very close at hand before one would be aware of the noise of its explosion.

Suddenly I heard a burst that must have been very near the four runners following at my heels. I had started to turn when an exploding shell a few yards to my right enveloped me in a shower of sparks. I felt again the sledge-hammer impact as I spun around and fell face downward on the bottom of the trench. I lay there powerless to move and conscious only of the warm gushing of blood.

Two HOURS passed. My clouded mind could not comprehend why my runners did not come to my assistance. I did not realize that they too were stretched out in the trench behind me and that only two of us were to survive. I was dimly conscious of each heavy impact and explosion as other shells struck the ground in my vicinity. By this time nothing much mattered.

I heard someone moving near me. I was partially turned over and a voice said, "He's dead." I was told afterwards that I weakly and profanely contradicted this statement. I was loaded on a stretcher and the two bearers—those gallant and most unrewarded of all men—began to carry me back. On occasion, when a close H.E. burst or the bright flash of an overhead shrapnel seemed about to eliminate us all, they quite properly ducked, and once I rolled off the stretcher. On being put back again in the darkness, my pistol lanyard caught over one of the handles and its slip-knot tightened itself around my neck. A feeble protest secured my release from this discomfort.

I was taken back into the deep dugout at Pozières in which I had slept a few nights before and which was now used as the Advance Battalion Headquarters of the regiment under the command of Colonel Lockhart Gordon, D.S.O. Colonel Gordon is now dean of Canada's accounting profession. He still remembers that when what was left of the body was brought down into his dugout, the Battalion Medical Officer predicted that shock and loss of blood would not permit me to reach the ambulance alive. By this time I could still hear, but my vision was blurred. I was vaguely conscious of light, of the murmuring of voices above me, and of being again lugged up the steps of the dugout.

I was loaded on an ambulance and arrived back at the Casualty Clearing Station in the immediate rear. There it was considered that I was too weak to be moved and that a drastic operation was necessary, which should be undertaken further back. Two days later I was put on a hospital train for No. 20 General Hospital at Camiers. Here I was placed in a hut which, I later found out, was called "The Danger Hut". It had twenty beds, and only severely wounded casualties were admitted. I learned later that less than half of the patients who entered this ward survived. This was before the days of blood plasma, but the treatment and surgery available were excellent. The surgeon of King George V, Major-General Sir G. H. Makins, G.C.M.G., C.B., examined each patient with the other surgeons, and he was constantly in attendance in a consulting capacity in our hut. He and a Dr. Harkness decided that it was unwise to risk the shock of an operation at this stage and I was advised to send for my parents—which was a privilege of all patients in the Danger Hut. As they were in Canada, they could not have arrived in time if the operation were unsuccessful and I felt there was no use causing them more anxiety.

On September 19th, my parents received the following official cable:

Sincerely regret inform you Staff Capt. James E. Hahn Infantry Officer reported admitted to No. 20 General Hospital Étaples September 17th gun-shot wound severe. Will send further particulars when received.

While I did not know the context of this message, I knew the official telegram would be disconcerting. I thought confusion would be the best antidote, and I sent a message which they received on the following day. It read as follows:

Wounded. No danger. Don't worry. Address me Savoy Hotel, London. Love.

I am glad to say that this and my other cables, which followed hard on the heels of official cables stating that I was still on the danger list, accomplished at least some of the purpose I had in mind.

The young Canadian lad in the bed on my left, shot through

the kidneys, died the first day, and was replaced by a casualty who had received a ball shrapnel in the brain. After he had been brought in from the operating room, as he was coming out of his anaesthetic, I was horrified to see him suddenly sit up erect in bed, shout for the orderly, and collapse. At first he was quite irrational and would cry out that the Canadian beside him was going to kill him. When I left some six weeks later, he was lucid most of the time although he still occasionally ordered a gas mask inspection. He also became sufficiently rational to discover the deception that was practised upon him, as he always received water instead of the spirits which he demanded and which, of course, were not permitted to a head patient. He bade me a very cheerful farewell when I left.

I watched the officer on my right die. He was paralyzed from the waist down from a shot through the spine. After he had been tapped with rubber hammers, he was advised that he had only a few days to live. This turned out to be the case.

Across from me a fine looking Englishman, shot through the throat, had fits of agonized coughing which could not be controlled until he collapsed in a faint. It was a wound from which it was thought he would recover.

In the bed across the room they had brought in what was left of a soldier who had had a shell explode virtually beneath him, causing the loss of both feet and forearms as well as numerous shrapnel wounds in his body. I shall never forget the look on the faces of his parents as they sat beside him day by day in the Danger Hut. His courage was boundless and he survived an ordeal as excruciating as any man could be called upon to suffer.

It was impressed upon me in this hut, lying on my back able only to turn my head, that we should always give thanks for good fortune. A similar sentiment was expressed to me many years later in India by the aged and distinguished Governor of the Central Provinces, an old friend of Gandhi's, who knew our continent well and who told me at his palace near Nagpur that the prayer of all Canadians should be, "Dear God, do not take away from us the burdens that we have."

For the benefit of any doctors who might have had the patience to read thus far, my operation among other things included the ligation of the right internal iliac artery and the removal of a gluteal aneurism in the right hip. All I can remember is that I had very little interest in life for a considerable time and I knew that I must be very ill when even the faint strains of music which I loved coming from the other huts of the hospital bothered me. I also remember my great delight when I was allowed my first boiled egg.

I WAS SENT BACK to England towards the end of October. After spending a short time in the Royal Free Military Hospital in London, I was returned to Canada for three months' leave. I arrived home just in time to spend a very happy Christmas with my parents. Before the end of the three months' period, I received instructions to attend a Medical Board. As I was still lame and was likely to remain so for some time, I was certain that I would be boarded as medically unfit and retained for service in Canada. My friends were all at the Front and I had no desire to finish the war in Canada. I therefore decided in the middle of January to return to England without attending the Board. I bought my own ticket to sail on February 4th, the day after the German declaration of unrestricted submarine warfare.

I arrived in England after an uneventful voyage, uncertain as to my reception when I reported to Canadian Military Headquarters at Argyle House in London. However, Sir Richard Turner was very sympathetic. I told him that I wished to get back to France as soon as possible. I was then appointed to the Staff of the Director of Organization.

I located quarters in Bayswater. On a good many mornings I had breakfast there with Baron Heyking, who was then the Russian ambassador to Great Britain. It was an experience for a youngster who had been taking a course of political science in Canada to be able to acquire information about Russia from such a source. The Baron was very interesting and communicative. Coming as I did from democratic Canada, I was shocked beyond belief at the Baron's answer to one of my questions. I had asked him, "What about your masses in Russia?" He dismissed the question lightly, saying, "They are just cattle." I had not believed it possible that a native of any country could refer to his compatriots in such a manner. The Baron did not appear to have the slightest suspicion that the Russian Revolution was only three months away.

There were air raids in England at that time and their effectiveness can best be judged by the fact that there were all told one hundred and ten zeppelin and air raids which caused an average casualty of ten civilians and three soldiers per raid. Compare this with the 298,000 casualties of all kinds in England alone during the second Great War. The possibilities of annihilation if man's greatest stupidity, war, cannot be prevented in the future, would appear to be great.

I was sent to Hastings to take over as Acting Brigade Major during the leave of the Brigade Major stationed there. In Hastings I was most unhappy with all the ceremonial and paper work which were part of the operation of a base camp. My main recollection of this camp was a letter that was minuted on to me by a bright young learner, who went to France and was killed there shortly after his arrival. The letter was from Mrs. ——, who stated in effect that her husband, Private ——, No. ——, had received a long sentence for drunk and disorderly conduct. She wrote that he had been a good husband and his record showed that he had been a good soldier. As she was about to become a mother, she earnestly requested that the sentence be commuted or substantially reduced. The officer's comment on Minute 2 was: "In view of Mrs. ——'s condition, it is strongly recommended that some, if not all of it, be cut off."

About this time I received a letter from the Staff Captain of the Eighth Brigade who had been trying to locate some of my effects, particularly my automatic pistol and prismatic compass, which had been lost in the shuffle after I had been wounded. I give an extract from his letter which I found entertaining:

The B.M. made up a very amusing code embodying many of his pet expressions for in our sector we are supposed to be very careful what we say on the phone. We have notices on our phones which say, "Be careful what you say on this phone; the Germans can hear you." The joke is that *we* can't.

On my return to London I found that several vacancies had been allotted to Canadian officers for the Staff course to be held at Cambridge University. I had heard of this course, which was available at intervals to sixty officers drawn from all parts of the British Empire. My application was accepted. I found it an excellent course, and I do not believe I ever put in longer hours than I did while I lived at Clare College at Cambridge University. At the end of the course it was announced that two groups would be notified to report before the General Officer Commanding: those who had done well and those whom it would be necessary to inform that they were unsuitable for Staff work. I received a summons and was happy to find that I was included in the first group.

I returned from this course to my duties at Canadian Military Headquarters. Shortly afterwards I attended an investiture at Buckingham Palace, where I had the honour to receive the Military Cross from King George V, who put a lame Canadian officer very much at his ease.

A letter had been received at our Headquarters from the Hon. R. B. (later Lord) Bennett, who at the time was Director General of National Service. To minimize the difficulties which would arise in establishing Canadians on their return to Canada after the war, the authorities at Ottawa wished to obtain certain information from every officer and man serving in the field, whether with a Canadian or other unit or in hospital. The authorities required information about occupations the men would be interested in after the war. I was assigned the task of organizing a scheme to provide this information. After working out a plan, I visited all the Commands in England and the Headquarters of all Canadian formations in France so that they would be conversant with the scheme and afford me their fullest co-operation. To carry out this work I was given a white pass which enabled me to shuttle back and forth between France and England as required. It is interesting today to look at the two Orders promulgated in this connection. One was issued by Major-General R. E. W. Turner, V.C., K.C.B., D.S.O., commanding the Canadian Forces in the British Isles. The other, issued by Field Marshal Sir Douglas Haig, G.C.B., G.C.V.O., K.C.I.E., Commander-in-Chief of the British Army in France, included the following: "Capt. J. E. Hahn, M.C., Canadian Headquarters, has arrived in France ... G.O.C. Armies, Lines of Communication, and Directors and Heads of Departments and Directorates will afford him such assistance and facilities as he may require."

With this type of support, the work was done with expedition. When I turned in my report on 17th July, 1917, satisfactory results had been obtained.

During my convalescence in England while engaged on the various tasks assigned to me by Canadian Military Headquarters, I had missed the months of detailed preparation by the Canadian Corps for its brilliant and successful assault against Vimy Ridge, which was captured on April 9th. This was the only major engagement of the war in which Canadians participated where I did not serve with the Canadian Corps in the field.

On one of my trips to France, I was attached to Tenth Corps Headquarters as a result of arrangements made through my friend, Colonel Mitchell*, who went overseas with the First Contingent and was in charge of Second British Army Intelligence. The Tenth British Corps was to be on the left flank of an attack to be launched by Australian, New Zealand, Irish and Welsh Divisions against the Messines-Wytschaete Ridge. To prepare for this attack, over five miles of tunnels had been constructed leading from our trenches underneath the Ridge. From the Ridge the enemy had complete observation over our front and rear areas. These tunnels led to twenty-four mines, some of which contained charges of twenty-five tons of T.N.T., which had been pushed by our troops underneath the Ridge. Nineteen of these mines were ready at zero hour on the morning of June 7th. From Mount Kemal I witnessed the blowing of the Ridge, the culmination of the largest mining operation carried out during the war. The sight of the yellowish glow of nineteen volcanoes erupting, seemingly slowly, towards the sky and overhanging the ridge with a pall of smoke and dust, together with the heavy rumbles of their explosions added to the crescendo of the barrage, was an unforgettable and terrifying spectacle. I made a

---

* Brigadier-General C. H. Mitchell, C.B., C.M.G., D.S.O.

reconnaissance into the remaining shambles at zero plus two hours. It was no surprise to find that the Ridge was in our hands.

When I returned to Canadian Military Headquarters in London, I was informed that there was to be an election in the Province of British Columbia and I was instructed to arrange that all British Columbia troops overseas should have the opportunity of casting their ballot. I worked out a scheme with the Agent General for that Province at British Columbia House in London and completed it by the end of July. I was then told that Canada was to have a General Election and in view of the experience I had had with the National Service Card scheme and the British Columbia election, I would be put in charge of the arrangements which would enable all Canadians in the British Isles and France to cast their ballots.

I had returned to England with the intention of getting to France as soon as I was fit. Running a General Election seemed to me to be the last straw. That night, using my white pass, I crossed to France on the packet boat and proceeded to the Second Echelon Canadian Headquarters which was the rear channel of the Canadian lines of communication located on the north coast of France. At seven o'clock in the morning, I called up the Corps Commander, General Currie, knowing him to be a very early riser, and asked if I could come to Corps Headquarters to see him. He replied that he would be very glad to see me if I could dash up immediately, as later in the morning he was leaving Headquarters to be knighted in the field by King George.

I told the Corps Commander that I wanted to get back to France. As I was still very lame, he wondered if I would be able to stand the racket. I assured him that I would and asked if he would request my return to France. Such a request from the Corps Commander would not be refused by Canadian Military Headquarters. I was told that a message would be sent that afternoon. I asked the Corps Commander if it could be taken as understood that my visit had not taken place: he laughed, and concurred.

The next morning in London I was called in to Sir Richard's office. He held in his hand the message which was a request by name for my return to France. He also asked if I would be able to stand service in the field, as I was still lame. I assured him that I would be able to and that it was my desire to return to the field. If a very gallant soldier and gentleman* should by any chance read this, I hope he will forgive this deception.

THE FOLLOWING DAY I returned to France and reported to Canadian Corps Headquarters. There I learned that I was to be attached to the General Staff of the Third Division, commanded by Major-General Lipsett.

During the next two months I attended several courses in the field which were invaluable to me. As the Operation Orders or plans for battle employing the various arms were drawn up by the General Staff, it was fundamental that these officers should have the greatest possible familiarity with the functions of the weapons that they were causing to be employed, as well as a thorough knowledge of their destructive powers and limitations. I had already attended several of these courses, but I took a refresher in machine gunnery. During this training I sat in a sandbagged hut located on the edge of a beach on the north shore of France. Here I watched the effects of a machine gun barrage fired from some two thousand yards at our rear, as the bullets kicked up spurts and splashes on the beach and smooth sea in front of us.

We learned many things from a short course in tanks. One of the problems remaining at that time was how to provide a satisfactory system of ventilation that would clear out the combination of gun and gasoline fumes. This was sometimes very concentrated. On a subsequent attack a number of men were transported in tanks with orders to establish themselves on reaching a certain objective. On their arrival, however, it was found that they were so incapacitated by the fumes that they could not carry out their instructions.

I attended the gunnery course with General Lipsett. I remem-

* Now Lieutenant-General Sir R. E. W. Turner, V.C., K.C.B., K.C.M.G., V.D.

ber standing with him with our backs against a haystack while a battery of eighteen pounders fired from behind and over us in order to demonstrate the difference in effectiveness between ball shrapnel and instantaneous fuse high explosive. These rounds were fired at rows of dummy wooden targets two hundred yards in front of us. Both of us hoped fervently that we would not have any "shorts".

One of the most interesting courses I attended was the flying course. There was a very limited allotment for this, which was held at Bertangles, and only one vacancy was available for our Division. The General considered that the General Staff Officers should draw for this vacancy and I made the lucky draw. The course lasted for ten days. We were up each day and were instructed in every type of mission, reconnaissance, aerial photography, bombing, close support work, and other tasks with which the Air Force was normally occupied. The slow, single-engine planes were constructed of a light, flimsy framework, covered only by a thin fabric through which a hand or foot could easily be pushed. The structure was held together by a series of guy-wires and represented the advanced design of the day. This was the era of the R.E. 8's, the Sopwith Camels, the Bristol Fighters, and the D.H. 4's.

I had watched aerial activity grow from the time of our arrival in France, when the number of planes on both sides was still very limited. Prior to our arrival, engagements had been fought between planes where rifle or pistol fire was exchanged. I witnessed many aerial combats between and during engagements. It was always horrible to see the occupants of a burning plane leap out of it to their death. Parachutes had not yet been developed which could be used from aeroplanes. We did have parachutes that were used by the crew members of the stationary observation balloons, if they were forced to jump out of their baskets when their balloon was set on fire by incendiary bullets or shell-fire.

One evening, shortly before the war ended, I saw a German plane pinned in the cross-beams of our searchlights at about five thousand feet. Then I saw a stream of tracer bullets from one of our night patrolling planes and heard bursts from its machine guns. The enemy plane caught fire. Its crew jumped and I witnessed parachutes being employed for the first time from an aeroplane.

The aerial bombs used during the first war were very light, most of them weighing twenty pounds. Later, what was considered to be a "very heavy" bomb was produced which weighed sixty pounds. From time to time we would be subjected to what the enemy described as "very important bombing raids" against our trenches. These consisted of a force of twenty or so planes, dropping ineffective cargoes of light bombs against a trench system. The performance was very noisy, but produced little actual damage. Towards the end of the war, when large bodies of troops were moving in the open, particularly during the night, some damage and casualties were caused by enemy aerial bombing in our front and rear areas.

On several occasions later I made low-flying reconnaissances over enemy territory and witnessed the yellow rhythmic flashes of the enemy anti-aircraft guns as they concentrated their disconcerting but ineffective attention on us, although in the old R.E. 8 reconnaissance plane we were flying at less than a hundred miles an hour. We also received a good deal of attention from enemy machine guns on the ground.

On these flights, I sat behind the pilot. As I was unable to identify quickly enemy planes which we encountered, the pilot and I arranged a simple signalling system. If I spotted a plane whose identity I doubted, I was to tap him on the back and point towards it, as conversation was difficult in the open plane. If it was one of ours, he would signify by waving his hand in front of him; if it was an enemy plane, he would point at my Lewis gun which was mounted on the swivel seat on which I was sitting and I was then supposed to go to work. Fortunately there was only one occasion, after I had tapped the pilot on the back and pointed, when he turned and with emphatic gestures pointed to my machine gun. The enemy plane dived at us from above and the bursts of its tracer bullets spat by us as they described their parabolic trajectory. These mingled with the equally ineffective bursts from my Lewis gun. This encounter took place as we were returning from a reconnaissance over Meri-

court and nearing our own lines. The pilot dived rapidly so that
we would have the benefit of protecting fire from our own front
line trenches. Fortunately for our slow R.E. 8 and the one fright-
ened member of its crew, the enemy broke off the engagement.

EARLY IN OCTOBER the Third Canadian Division was in a rear
rest area. We were having tea in the mess when the Corps Commander, Sir Arthur Currie, arrived and said to the Divisional
Commander, "Lipsett, we're for it." We all knew this meant we
were to participate in the battle for Passchendaele which had been
under way, and which had by now obtained a reputation not
much more savoury than that of the Somme. Due to the rains,
the area was a muddy bog and the terrain which had been completely devastated by shell-fire was pock-marked with shell holes
so dense that the craters of many were touching each other.
These made life even more difficult and dangerous for advancing
troops, as the shell holes were full of water and many wounded
men, falling into the mud or shell holes, were drowned.

Before we had finished tea, the Corps Commander disclosed
that the Canadian Corps was immediately to start taking over the
sector occupied by the Australian Corps. Major attacks were to
be launched by our Corps on or about the 20th of October.
The Corps Commander told us that he had received information
about that area which was far from satisfactory. It related to the
progress that had been made and the cost in casualties to date.
Colonel J. L. McAvity, D.S.O., and I were instructed to proceed
to British General Headquarters, from there to Army Headquarters, and on forward to the Australian Corps. After discussing the
general situation with the officers of these senior formations, we
were to proceed up to the front and make a reconnaissance on the
front of the Australian Division in the line. We were to bring
back all available information concerning the Passchendaele operation and make such recommendations as we saw fit, based upon
the discussions we would have and on our own observations.

Messages were dispatched by the Corps Commander to British
Army Headquarters through the proper channels. Within the

hour we had received a reply that we should go direct to the Headquarters of Sir Douglas Haig and that by the time we reached there all other necessary instructions would have gone forward to the formations concerned.

We arrived at General Headquarters that evening and were taken into the map room where recent operations and future objectives were explained to us. Everybody seemed quite happy about the progress that was being made. Further attacks with very limited objectives were scheduled to take place almost every two or three days.

The following morning we proceeded to Army Headquarters, where the story was much the same although the reports we received were less enthusiastic than those of the previous evening. We then went to Australian Corps Headquarters. Here the atmosphere was completely devoid of any suggestion of enthusiasm. Criticism was very bitter on the cost of the operation that the Australian Corps was carrying out against the heavy enemy concentration of both troops and artillery over a terrain where movement was next to impossible. The chief complaint was that sufficient time was not allowed to cut the heavy enemy wire entanglements and a great many casualties were incurred before the opposing trenches were reached as our troops tried to penetrate the wired defences. We were informed that the First Australian Division was attacking at daybreak the following morning, and we received permission to visit the attacking Division that night. Here we encountered the same bitter comments.

The attack the following morning was for a limited objective. We started our reconnaissance shortly after zero hour, and found many Australian dead hung up in uncut wire, confirming the information we had received. We had a particularly rough morning, but managed to get back to Australian Advance Divisional Headquarters and finally back to Australian Corps, where we had left our car.

We drove back to our own Third Divisional Headquarters with our report. We had not discussed this very long with General Lipsett before he bundled us into his car and told us to come back and tell the Corps Commander exactly what we had told him. When we arrived at Corps Headquarters, we went over our report with Sir Arthur Currie. I could see him getting more and more restive as our tale unfolded. Finally he rose and, banging his fist on the desk, said that he would not attack until the preparations were sufficiently thorough and complete to ensure the success of the operation. He added that he would so inform the Army Commander. We took over the front on October 18th, but we did not attack in accordance with the schedule which was originally set for us.

Although the working parties were subjected to continuous deadly harassing shell-fire, roads were constructed in order to permit the movement of troops, guns and supplies. Infantry officers and observers from each battalion that would take part in the projected attack were stationed in the observation posts of the gunners. The artillery wire-cutting programme was carried out until those infantry officers were satisfied that sufficient gaps had been made and maintained in the enemy wire to permit the passage of their attacking troops. The delay and the thorough preparation enabled the Canadians, although the attack started ten days later than scheduled, to push the enemy off the ridge. After bitter fighting, Passchendaele and the ground beyond was in the hands of the Canadian Corps by November 10th.

This period was a very difficult one for me. Those of us who in preparation for and during the battle travelled over the dreadful Moozelmarke-Meetschele Road under constant shell-fire will never forget walking over our own dead lying half-buried in the liquid mud. As I was still quite lame, it was a problem to negotiate this terrible terrain, but youth has great powers of endurance and resilience, and in spite of many exhausting days I was now getting stronger and more agile.

IN DECEMBER, 1917, I was appointed G.S.O. 3 on the Staff of the Fourth Canadian Division, commanded by Sir David Watson, and I was now engaged on the operational side of General Staff work, which is concerned with the planning and conduct of battles. In this work my experience on the Intelligence side of the General Staff stood me in very good stead.

The Germans launched what turned out to be their last major offensive in March 1918. While the Canadian Corps as such was not directly engaged, the First Canadian Motor Machine Gun Brigade was thrown into battle and fought with great distinction in the delaying rear-guard action. For a time it seemed that one or more divisions of the Canadian Corps might become involved. The Canadian Corps Commander, however, was concerned with the possibility of our Corps being split up. He felt very strongly that one of the major reasons for the success of the Corps was that it had been able to fight with all its divisions together as an integrated unit. His suggestions and representations resulted in the Canadian Corps remaining intact.

Our own Division was engaged in strengthening the defensive positions on the south of Vimy Ridge, as we anticipated that the enemy offensive might be directed along the Souchez Valley in an effort to turn our right flank. During the following days I spent considerable time on the south shoulder of Vimy Ridge, where, together with our Engineer officers, we laid out with tape the positions that were spitlocked each night, and subsequently dug into the trench systems that were constructed to protect the south flank of Vimy Ridge in the event of an enemy drive along the Valley.

One day, while engaged in this work, we received a salvo of high explosive and gas shells which fortunately caused only three casualties. I was one of those completely enveloped in clouds of sweetish-smelling phosgene gas before we could get on our gas masks. Again I went out on a stretcher, but forty-eight hours' rest eliminated the possibility of any further reaction from the gas, which acted on the heart.

The enemy offensive failed and was finally brought to a standstill. By the end of May we were located in a rest and training area behind Arras. The atmosphere was still particularly sensitive to a possible continuation of the enemy offensive, and we had been equipped with the maps and information in case we were required to counter-attack in that sector.

A German batman had been captured on the front south of Arras who, during his examination, had stated that he had heard his officers discussing an attack which the enemy was planning to execute within a few days' time. This information was relayed to us and we were advised that the Fourth Canadian Division would be used to counter-attack, should the enemy succeed in capturing the sector said to be their objective. The British were holding this front by means of a series of connected strong points and I was instructed to get together the Battalion Commanders and certain members of the Brigade Staffs. We were then to proceed some thirty miles to the front and reconnoitre the strong points with which we would be concerned if a counter-attack were required by our Division.

I had two London buses report at Divisional Headquarters during the night and had laid out the reconnaissance so that all officers taking part would be picked up at designated times at certain rendezvous in their respective Brigade areas. The trip was so planned and routed that we would debus as close as possible to the lines at the south end of the sector and then move along the communication trenches to the most southerly strong point.

The schedule was timed so that we would reach this strong point at daybreak. The buses were then sent to the northern part of the sector and instructed to meet us at a given rendezvous at five o'clock that afternoon. We had had breakfast before we left and carried a very light lunch. I acted as pilot, seated beside the driver of the leading bus. Dawn broke on what turned out to be a very beautiful and quiet June day. We reached the front line system and moved all morning from one strong point to another, had a bit of lunch, finished the rest of our reconnaissance in the afternoon, and then came out of the line and met the buses which were awaiting us at the appointed rendezvous. I again sat with the driver of the leading bus and for the return trip by means of my map directed the route he was to take back into our Divisional area.

When we left the front line rear area, one of the officers opened the sliding window behind me and suggested stopping at the first canteen to pick up some wine for their mess. Passing through the first village, I stopped the buses and the officers loaded a number of cases of port aboard. Then we resumed our journey. Shortly afterwards the window at my back was again opened and one of the officers passed out a bottle of port and suggested my joining them in a drink.

As I was still a complete teetotaller, I declined. I thought no more of it and continued to direct the buses into our Divisional area. When we stopped at our first rendezvous within the Brigade area where its officers were to be debused, I was horrified, on opening the door, to have two of these officers fall out of the bus. Upon making an inspection of both buses, I found to my consternation that the port had played havoc with many members of our reconnaissance party. For a moment we could not understand what had happened, for while most of these officers, whom I knew very well, took a drink, they were all seasoned soldiers and it was apparent that something had gone radically wrong. The majority had taken one drink and no one had taken more than two. However, the combination of a very hot and strenuous day, very little food, and the result of being confined in the enclosed bus, apparently enabled one or, at the most two, drinks of port to produce devastating effects.

It was by this time eight o'clock in the evening and the much advertised offensive was to take place the following morning. I was advised by officers whose advice upon matters of this nature was much more expert than mine that the effect of the port would pass off very quickly, and that I need not be concerned if the offensive should develop in the morning.

I returned to Divisional Headquarters with a very anxious feeling, but I did not tell the Divisional Commander, as I felt he would probably be unnecessarily alarmed. As it turned out, the attack did not develop. It was afterwards known in our Division as "The Batman's Battle".

CHAPTER V

THE LAST PHASE

THE CANADIAN CORPS COMMANDER was advised in July, 1918, that our Corps was to be one of the spearheads of an attack, which was to be launched on the morning of August 8th. We were told that this attack was to be the beginning of a general offensive that would develop and be maintained along the entire front in an effort to reach a decision that fall. Since the element of complete surprise was considered one of the prerequisites to ensure the success of the attack, the moves were so timed that the assembly of the Canadian Corps in the concentration area would be completed immediately preceding the attack.

As the appearance of the Canadian Corps in a new sector always indicated potential trouble for the enemy and a possible offensive, means were taken to provide him with misleading information. Two battalions of our Corps were sent to the northern sector together with sections of our Signalling Corps. The enemy was provided with wireless messages which enabled him to identify the Canadians. Canadian clearing stations were also sent into this area and enough tanks to be sufficiently obvious to enemy aerial reconnaissance concentrated near St. Pol.

I was given a most interesting assignment by Sir David Watson, our Divisional Commander. It was vital that the impending attack should not be disclosed by the appearance of the usual reconnaissance parties in the front line system of the Australian Corps, which we were to relieve immediately prior to the attack. I was therefore to proceed to the Australian Corps where arrangements had been made for me to stay with the right Australian Division in the line. From there I could send back all available information relating to this particular front that would be required for our attacking troops. By this time the Canadian Corps had developed the Intelligence file. This enabled us to provide complete information, including maps and aeroplane photographs, of an enemy sector about to be attacked. This file was issued down to companies and batteries so that all units and formations would have all known information regarding the enemy, and would have an opportunity to acquaint themselves prior to the attack with all data relating to the front on which they were about to become engaged.

I spent a very interesting ten days "incognito" on the Australian front and lived in the mess of the right division of the Australian Corps. Only certain members of the Divisional Staff were aware of the reason for my visit. I removed all Canadian emblems from my tunic and was ostensibly with the Australians to exchange methods of procedure on front line Intelligence. I was thus able to accumulate the information which I required and to fix certain orientation points in the enemy back areas so that time would not be wasted in the observation posts when, two days before the attack, some of our officers visited these posts in order to acquaint themselves with the terrain ahead of them.

The movement and concentration of the Corps was carried out with precision and without incident. For a few days before the attack, we had several of our bombing squadrons flying up and down the enemy front just before daybreak, to ensure that on the morning of the assault the drone of their motors would drown out the noise of our tanks moving forward to the assault.

On the morning of the attack, before zero hour, I was standing with Major-General L. T. Lipsett, C.B., C.M.G., commanding the Third Canadian Division, on the edge of a gravel pit in which his Advance Divisional Headquarters were located. This able commander was unfortunately killed just before the end of the war. The Third Division was the right attacking division of the Canadian Corps and our Division, the Fourth, was likely to be employed to leap-frog or attack through the Third Canadian Division on the following morning, if the opening offensive proved to be successful. Prisoners were to be brought back to the gravel pit, where we urgently required to know if the enemy had been taken by complete surprise. In the darkness we could hear the planes droning overhead. About four o'clock in the morning we heard the tanks move by us. We began looking at our watches with the aid of a flashlight as they ticked to 4.20, the zero hour. The crescendo of our guns was followed by the enemy counter-action. Interrogation of prisoners brought by sidecar to the gravel pit disclosed that they had been taken by surprise and all reports began to indicate that we were moving ahead on schedule towards our first objective. The final objective for the day was the Blue Line some seven miles in advance of our jumping-off position in the morning.

After sending back the initial information, I went forward to make a reconnaissance on the right flank of the attack, with the dual purpose of reporting on the progress of the battle and of familiarizing myself with the ground over which our Division would be required to attack on the following day. During this reconnaissance, I encountered a rather tragic scene. I had passed beyond the Green Line, some two miles inside of enemy territory, and my runner and I were moving along over slightly rolling terrain. As we walked into a slight draw, we saw ahead of us one of our tanks out of action, and found on reaching it that it had received two direct hits on its side. These had killed its crew and created a bloody shambles inside the tank. Looking up the slight incline to our right some sixty yards away we saw three guns of a battery of German howitzers in their pits on the reverse side of this slight slope. The fourth gun had been pulled out of its pit and turned around; its depressed barrel was still levelled at the tank. We walked up to the battery site, around the guns, and found what seemed to be all the gun crews dead, some lying around the gun and the others near the gun pits. They had all been machine gunned. We walked in front of the battery and saw the tracks of another tank which apparently had been moving parallel with the ill-fated tank in the draw. The entire crew of the enemy battery, while occupied in pulling the one howitzer out of its pit and intent upon engaging the tank moving on their right, had failed to notice the approach of the other tank, which was armed with machine guns. Its tracks showed it had moved directly towards the enemy battery firing as it approached. It had then swung off to the right in front of the pits, turned and continued forward in the attack. I opened the breach of the gun still laid on our tank, and found as I expected that it had been loaded ready to fire its third round.

Since we were now about to proceed into an area where there was considerable small arms fire, the runner and I each picked up a Mauser carbine and a couple of bandoliers of ammunition from the dead crew members and continued our reconnaissance. I brought this carbine back to Canada with me and it reposed in my gun room as a war trophy for over thirty years. I finally had it re-stocked and fitted with a telescopic sight and used it as one of my light rifles when big game hunting in India.

By evening all reports indicated that the Blue Line, our final objective, had been reached and that we were in contact with the Australian Corps on our left and the French on our right. The Canadian Corps Commander arrived at Divisional Headquarters that evening and plans were discussed for the attack which our Division was to launch the following morning. We were to leap-frog through the Third Division. The attack was to be launched from the right end of this line resting on the Amiens-Roye road, which was the dividing line between the Canadian Corps and the French, who were to coordinate their attack with ours. All reports seemed to indicate that the Blue Line had been reached, yet there seemed to be some uncertainty as to the position of our right flank and our liaison with the French. At the end of the conference, the Corps Commander suggested that this situation should be clarified and I was instructed to make a reconnaissance so that I would arrive at the Blue Line before daybreak. I was to confirm our own position on the Blue Line and ascertain where our right flank joined up with the French. Our Division was to move through the Blue Line at eleven o'clock the following morning, the 9th.

I left Headquarters shortly after midnight and proceeded by car to the rear of a wood situated about half a mile behind the Blue Line and several hundred yards north of the Amiens-Roye road. We dashed without lights along this road, which was receiving some scattered attention from the enemy. and reached the rear of the wood. From here I planned to proceed on foot to the Blue Line. I sent the car back. When I entered the wood,

I found it was full of our troops. I found the Battalion Commander and he was most emphatic that we had not reached the Blue Line. He said that his men were dug in at the front edge of the wood, and as far as he knew, these rifle pits constituted our front line position. He had been trying to establish contact with the French on his right, but had been unable to do so and patrols which had just come in from in front of the wood had not established contact with the enemy in the open fields that stretched half a mile ahead, where the right anchor of our Blue Line was to have been located.

It was now apparent that the right flank of our line was some half a mile to the rear of the Blue Line and that farther to the north we joined the Blue Line, as the village of LeQuesnel, one of our final objectives, was being heavily shelled by the enemy.

This was most disconcerting in view of our impending attack. I felt it imperative to find out exactly what the situation was in the wood touching the Roye road some half a mile ahead of us. I asked the Battalion Commander to establish definite contact with the French on our right while I made a reconnaissance of the area in front of us.

Several of our tanks were still burning in the open fields between the two woods. I started to move rapidly across this open area. We had traversed two-thirds of the distance between the two woods when suddenly the sky to my rear and right was split with the flashes and thunder of guns, and to my horror, on looking behind me, I saw in the light of the coming dawn the flashes of the explosions of a creeping shrapnel barrage. This barrage ran south to my right from the Amiens-Roye road and its line seemed to begin nearly half a mile to the south and rear of our positions in the wood behind me. We rushed to the shelter of the nearest tank and in amazement and consternation watched not only the creeping barrage as it moved in our direction to the south of the road, but saw German SOS rockets fired from the wood less than two hundred yards in front of us and from German front line positions south of the road. To the noise and flashes of the French barrage was added the thunder of the German guns laying down their fire on their prearranged SOS line. The enemy apparently knew that we were holding a line in the wood behind us, as their shells commenced screaming over our heads and exploding along the edge of the wood which we had just left. With great dismay we watched the French barrage creeping closer and closer to us on our right. We could see the lines of French troops advancing under their protective curtain of shrapnel. Up to this time they did not seem to be encountering any serious difficulty in their advance.

A railway embankment ran slightly to the right and some distance behind the enemy held wood. As the French lines started to approach this embankment, they encountered very heavy machine gun fire and I saw a good many men go down.

It was now nearly six o'clock in the morning, and it was obvious that our men should not move in broad daylight from the position we held in the rear across the open fields, when it was evident that the wood on the Amiens-Roye road, which was supposed to be our right flank, was still held by the enemy.

The French by this time were digging themselves in south of this wood and the main road. We got back to our own wood as the enemy ahead of us were too occupied with the French to waste any of their attention on us. I immediately proceeded to our Advance Brigade, commanded by Brig.-Gen. Victor Odlum, C.B., C.M.G., D.S.O., whose reputation as a commander and for personal gallantry made his name a legend. I advised him of the situation which we both considered precarious to our Division. With the dispatch for which he was so well known, he immediately moved units of his Brigade to the south of the Amiens-Roye road, advanced through the new French held front to a position to the south of the enemy held wood, and then struck north so that the Blue Line came into our possession. The attack of our Division which followed at eleven o'clock was a complete success.

The Canadian Corps continued to be engaged in this area until August 19th, and by then had advanced to a depth of nearly fifteen miles. By this time we were fighting over the trench systems of 1916. Here the old wire was completely overgrown with grass. This enabled the enemy to put up a most stubborn resistance by means of dense concentrations of well sited machine gun positions which were very difficult to locate.

At one time during this action our Advance Divisional Headquarters were located in a culvert under the road. I had just returned from the forward area on a day in which we had been very heavily engaged, and Sir David Watson showed me a message which had come through from England, offering me a senior appointment on the General Staff of a Canadian expedition which was about to leave for Siberia. I told the General that I should prefer to continue to serve with the Canadian Corps in France until the war was finished. I did not realize that it was Major-General Emsley, my erstwhile Brigadier, who was commanding this expedition, which ultimately reached Siberia and returned after a rather uneventful sojourn in that country.

The Canadian Corps had so far seen very little of the Cavalry Divisions. These had been kept in being throughout the war with the intention that they were to be put in action when they could be usefully employed. The terrific volume of small arms fire that could be concentrated against a target at this stage of the war reduced the possibilities of using mounted men against an enemy who, although reeling back from a series of continuous blows in the last hundred days of the war, still maintained an unbroken front and continued to the end to fight a bitter rear-guard action.

In the last days of our thrust in front of Amiens, our Division was engaged to the north of the Amiens-Roye road and was having considerable difficulty in this terrain where it was hard to locate the old trench systems which confronted us. Aerial photographs did not disclose the grass-covered wire and we had made every effort to obtain maps of this area which had been fought over two years before.

Divisional Headquarters on this particular morning consisted of Sir David Watson and those members of his Staff who constituted Advance Divisional Headquarters. We were grouped around a lance stuck in the ground flying the pennant of the Commander of the Fourth Canadian Division.

I had just returned from an early morning reconnaissance of our front line system. I found that we were having great difficulty in locating and dealing with hidden groups of machine gun nests. The enemy was able to focus heavy concentrations of small arms fire from posts which were located in depth in front of us, and which were so sited that they protected each other by covering fire. Just as I arrived back and was discussing the situation with Sir David Watson and the other members of our Staff, we saw a great cloud of dust moving towards us, rising from the road that ran to our rear. This turned out to be a division of British cavalry moving towards us, coloured pennants flying and the steel of their lances glittering in the sunshine. Overhead a protective screen of planes flew back and forth and covered the advance of the long columns of mounted men. The head of the column finally drew abreast of the field in which we were located and the lines were halted. The Cavalry Commander, accompanied by several members of his Staff, rode over to where we were standing in a group watching the colourful spectacle.

They had no sooner reached us than what must have been a lone enemy reconnaissance plane spotted the cavalry column standing beside the road. Notwithstanding the heavy aerial escort, without the slightest hesitation the plane dived in and started firing bursts which kicked up spurts of dirt and dust about the head of the column. The plane was immediately engaged by our escorting planes, but they seemed unable to bring it down. For a few minutes there was a lively dog-fight with machine gun fire directed at the lone plane as it tried desperately to extricate itself. We last saw it driven almost to the ground, making its way back into the enemy territory.

The Cavalry Commander was anxious, if possible, to exploit the advance that had been made by breaking through with his mounted troops. Our Divisional Commander outlined our general position and asked me to restate the details of the reconnaissance which I had just completed, with particular reference to the difficult nature of the ground and the overgrown defences that we were encountering. On account of the hidden entanglements and the dense enemy machine gun concentrations which we knew existed, we considered that it would not be possible for cavalry to break through on the front on which our Division was engaged. When this recital was completed, the Cavalry Commander, much to our surprise, turned to the members of his Staff beside him and gave orders that a patrol was to be sent forward along the Amiens-Roye road and contact established.

Sir David Watson and I looked at each other in amazement. The reconnoitring thrusts by the cavalry in this area could not penetrate the strongly defended machine gun positions. I do not know, but I believe that this must have been one of the last actions by the cavalry. No further effort was made by the Cavalry Division to exploit a break-through on our particular section.

THE CANADIAN CORPS now became engaged in a series of battles which followed each other in rapid succession. I attended the Corps conferences with our Divisional Commander when the Operation Orders for these battles were being drawn up. My particular concerns were the timing, and distribution of the targets to be given to the heavy artillery, and working out at what, when, and where the enemy reserves would be employed for the counterattacks which would follow.

While in the forward area, during the action to which I am about to refer, in September, 1918, I picked up from one of the enemy dead a nine millimetre sub-machine gun. These had just been issued for the first time to the infantry units of the German Army. My runner and I carried this weapon, together with a metal case containing six magazines, back to our Headquarters. I fired the new weapon that afternoon and was very much impressed with its deadly short range fire power and its potentialities as an infantry weapon. Nearly twenty years later, when I urged that an automatic weapon of this type should form part of the establishment of British infantry equipment, I was told on more than one occasion that it was merely a "gangster weapon". I was more than taken aback when it was indicated from sources who should have been better informed that the fire power of a sub-machine gun was similar to that of a shot gun, and that therefore it could not possibly be considered a lethal weapon.

We were to attack the Crocourt-Quéant Line. This trench system was protected by three or four rows of wide strips of densely placed barbed wire. The trenches were well constructed and contained deep dugouts twenty feet below the ground, some of them capable of sheltering large numbers of men. These had two or three outlets to the trench. This so-called impregnable line was soon pierced after bitter fighting.

We were next moved to the Cambrai Front and the Canadian Corps followed up its successes by the capture of the previously fought over Bourlon Wood, which was first bypassed by encircling its edges with a smoke barrage. Cambrai fell, then Denain, and we found ourselves entrenched along the banks of the Canal de L'Escaut which ran south along the west side of Valenciennes to Trith-St. Léger, and then swung more or less in a westerly direction to Denain.

This canal ran along the bottom of a valley which sloped upwards to the shoulders of hills a half-mile distant on either side. The enemy had flooded the canal as a means of defending Valenciennes. The approaches to the canal from either side were covered with water in some places for nearly a quarter of a mile. Our defences and trench systems ran along the top of the hill on the north side of the canal and overlooked the flooded valley below, and the enemy-held slopes on the other side. The British joined our right flank some distance to the west and the line again swung south. I attended a conference where it was decided to turn the German flank by moving the British troops into our area and then driving south across the canal in the vicinity of Trith-St. Léger. Visibility had been very poor in the days preceding this conference and we did not have sufficiently recent or satisfactory aerial photographs of the canal and its bridges.

I was instructed to reconnoitre in the vicinity of the village and to report the condition of the bridge which crossed the canal located at the south end of Trith-St. Léger. I proceeded to the right brigade front, which was holding that particular sector of the line and had established its headquarters there. Here I was joined by "Snapper" White, the Brigade Intelligence Officer, and a Cavalry Liaison Officer who was stationed with the Brigade and who still hoped that some day there might be a Cavalry breakthrough. The three of us went to Battalion Headquarters, where we picked up the Battalion Intelligence Officer.

From our front line we studied the lay-out ahead of us and

decided that all four should move down into the valley, using such cover as was available, and attempt to reach a building designated on our maps as a nail factory and located on the edge of the canal some two hundred yards west of the bridge.

We reached the bottom of the slope and left the cavalry officer in a place of concealment on the edge of the flooded area. The three of us then waded through the water which was knee deep, towards the nail factory, now three hundred yards ahead of us. After some stumbling about in these uncharted waters, we reached the three-storey barnlike building without incident. We entered, found it deserted, and ascended to its third floor. From a window at the east end we could look straight along the canal and see the bridge in which we were interested. It was quite obvious that the bridge had been blown, and its two halves had sagged into the water from the abutment on either side of the canal. I was, however, puzzled when, through my glasses, I could clearly see barbed wire on both the concrete abutments of the demolished bridge. I told the others that we would go back to the edge of the flood, pick up the cavalry officer, move eastward along the valley on the dry ground and enter the north side of the village. From there I would make a reconnaissance of the bridge itself, as there was something about the situation that concerned me. Before we left the factory, Snapper White casually picked up a brass bugle that was lying on the floor. He said that he had learned to play this instrument in his younger days when he belonged to a bugle band.

When we had passed through the village and reached its southern outskirts, we found a high brick wall running along the left side of the road, behind which were located sizeable buildings which we later found belonged to a steel plant. A row of one-storey houses joined together ran along the opposite side of the street. We could not yet see the bridge; the map indicated that farther along, the road took a slight turn to the right and then led straight to the bridge some sixty yards in front of this turn.

Before we reached the turn, I posted Snapper White and the Battalion Intelligence Officer in one of the houses. I thought it better to attempt to reach the bridge alone by keeping as much as possible in the shelter of the row of houses on the right side of the street. This row ended about fifteen yards from the bridge and the road then took an upward incline to the concrete abutment, which was covered with coils of barbed wire. I hurried up this incline and stepped on to the abutment. A glance quickly confirmed what I had seen from the factory; the bridge was useless and there was barbed wire not only on the abutment but in front of a row of houses running along and facing the opposite side of the canal to my right.

Suddenly a helmeted head arose from behind the abutment of the opposite side of the canal. I saw one of the enemy throw a rifle to his shoulder and, before I could move, fire pointblank. Fortunately, my paralyzed and fear-stricken mind started to react when this hasty marksman began to reload. Quicker than words can describe, my automatic was drawn, cocked and fired, and my mind was already made up that my only hope lay in reaching the end house behind me. It was evident that there was an enemy post of four men situated across the canal.

The second shot fired by one of the men of this post struck the brick wall as I threw myself through the door. Fortunately I was only cut by flying brick splinters.

The three shots in quick succession brought the other two officers to the turn of the street, which was covered by the enemy post as well as from points across the canal. It was clear that the enemy was located in strength in the houses and at many other points along the canal bank, and that they had already anticipated the possibility of a flank attack.

It was about noon. The loud staccato burst of enemy machine guns situated in the houses on the opposite side of the canal filled the small room in which I was standing with a deafening noise and flying plaster, as their bursts came through the window and door of the end wall facing the canal. This fire was kept up intermittently, and the flying pieces of brick, plaster and ricochets drove me into the cellar of the house, where I stood in about three feet of water facing the open entrance. Every now and again I shook the plaster dust off my cocked automatic. By this time Snapper White's training in the bugle band began to show itself. He was blowing the Reveille and Retreat which I could recognize, and many other stirring blasts that I didn't. These must have shaken and confused the enemy as much as they did me, although I doubt whether anyone could have been more badly shaken than I was at that time, and chilled by the water.

Fortunately for us the enemy, now on the defensive after heavy defeats, must have believed, as the result of the noise, confusion and bugle calls, that we were about to launch some kind of attack. He was in no frame of mind to cross the canal and heave a couple of bombs into the house in which they had seen me hurriedly take shelter. Snapper and I kept shouting to each other, and I assured him that I was all right. The only possible way of extricating ourselves in broad daylight would be through relief arriving from the crest of the hill behind the village.

The Battalion Intelligence Officer had already gone back, contacted the cavalry officer, and instructed him to return to our front line, and advise the Commander of our predicament. We would have to stay where we were until help arrived. About two and a half hours later I heard the clatter of infantry moving into the village behind us and could hear the men talking as they mounted machine guns in positions which would enable them to place their bursts along the road leading to the bridge. A loud shout up the street from behind informed me that three long bursts with intervals would be fired up the street. At the end of the third burst, I was to come out of the house and run back until I reached the protection of the street turn behind me.

I thought this over and hoped the men in the post could not understand. We had in front of us now a very concerned enemy, and I felt certain that at the end of each burst the street would immediately come under observation and fire. I shouted back to carry on with the three bursts, but that I would come out at the beginning of the third burst and the machine gunners should continue to fire past me on the opposite side of the street.

This procedure worked. I must confess that the staccato snapping of these machine gun bursts as they spit beside me was one of the most comforting sounds I have ever heard.

It was fortunate that this reconnaissance was sufficiently thorough to reveal that the enemy was holding along the banks of the canal in strength and not, as we had believed, some eight hundred yards to the rear. As a result of this information, the flank attack was not attempted. In view of the dispositions now determined, it was considered too precarious to attempt to put bridges across the canal in this heavily flooded area in the face of a prepared and alerted enemy.

Valenciennes soon fell and our Division ended the war near Mons. We received the news in a somewhat awed and stunned silence and could not believe that what we had hoped and prayed for throughout the years had really come to pass. There was very little rejoicing among the troops in the field; too many of our gallant friends were no longer with us.

THE UNITED STATES severed diplomatic relations with Germany in February 1917. Her troops began to arrive on the Western Front in June of the same year and by the time the Armistice was signed, three American Armies had been placed in the field and over two million American troops had been landed in France.

The Canadians were never engaged on the flanks of the Americans, but we did have their officers attached to us for instruction. Shortly before the Armistice, Colonel Bagby from the Intelligence Staff of American General Headquarters was attached to our Division for this purpose and I spent such time as was available familiarizing him with our own procedure.

When the Armistice was signed, we were both due for leave and we decided to go together using his Cadillac as our means of transportation. We planned to visit the battlefield of Waterloo, from there to proceed to Brussels, as we had heard that the King and Queen of the Belgians would be returning to their capital about the twenty-first of November, after an exile of nearly five years.

We drove through the neutral zone which had been established between the opposing armies, and reached Waterloo, where we saw and climbed part way up the monument. At Waterloo a happy Belgian innkeeper who in us saw Allied officers for the first time since the beginning of the war, out of the goodness of his heart favoured us with one of the most delightful looking, but toughest steaks I have ever tried to eat.

We reached Brussels on the evening of November 20th, the day before the King was to enter the city. Our car was virtually mobbed by a rejoicing populace when we arrived. Colonel Bagby had learned that the American Embassy had already been set up in the city. We proceeded there and were given two tickets for a small stand that had been erected opposite the Parliament Buildings, from which we could witness the triumphant return of the Royal couple and their children, at the head of the Belgian and other Allied troops.

When we arrived the following morning to locate our seats on this small stand, the sidewalks near the Parliament Buildings were thronged with people. As we reached a place in front of the Parliament Buildings opposite the stand, one of a pair of long French windows was opened and we were invited to come into the building and watch the procession from inside the Parliament Buildings. We were conducted inside, where we joined a group of Belgian officials with whom we witnessed the stirring spectacle of the entry of the victorious armies headed by the Royal Family. They marched with all the verve and dash of Continental troops to the strains of martial music.

Our Belgian friends were most kind. That evening we were invited to a dinner party attended by the Minister of Finance and other Belgian notables. We were told that the King would make an official appearance on the following day to greet the Belgian public at the historic Hôtel de Ville, and we were invited to attend and witness the event. The Hôtel de Ville of Brussels is a large rectangular building with a huge court in its centre. We were to join our Belgian friends in a room overlooking this court. We arrived at the Hôtel de Ville and proceeded along the corridor looking for the door which, according to our instructions, was the entrance to the room where our friends would be. I opened the door which I thought to be the entrance to the right room and started to enter. To my consternation I found that it was occupied by the Royal Family, the Commander in Chief of the Belgian Army, and a few other dignitaries among whom I immediately recognized the immaculate Burgomaster Max, with his goatee. He was the gallant Mayor of Brussels who had continually defied the Germans during the occupation and had been imprisoned by them.

Before I realized what was happening, or could back out, the little Burgomaster had rushed forward, seized hold of Colonel Bagby and myself, pulled us into the room, and without any further ado presented us to King Albert and Queen Elizabeth. Prince Charles and Princess Marie-José were standing with them. The Burgomaster, who spoke perfect English, insisted that we stay and witness all further proceedings. The Royal Family stepped from the room to the balcony which overlooked the court below, jammed with thousands of people. People in the room pushed Bagby and me out on the balcony where we stood behind the King and Queen. I shall never forget the sight. The atmosphere was charged with emotion. The people in the square below were mad with joy and excitement, as they hailed the returned King and Queen after their long absence. Tears rolled down the cheeks of the royal couple. I do not think there were many dry eyes in the assembly which witnessed the spectacle.

As we left the room, a lady standing just outside the door dropped a rose which she was attempting to present to His Majesty. The King, a very kindly man, picked up the rose and quickly put the flustered lady at her ease.

In the adjoining room we found our friends who were amused and happy on learning of our experience.

Two of the Divisions of the Canadian Corps were ordered forward to the Rhine Bridgeheads in accordance with the terms of the Armistice, while our Division was stationed in Brussels. Here many kindnesses were showered upon us by the Belgian people. On New Year's Eve, 1918, a reception was given by Major General Sir David Watson, K.C.B., C.M.G., in the ancient and beautiful Hôtel de Ville, and this was followed by a New Year's Ball with the Fourth Canadian Division as host. Before me, as I write, is a programme of this historic event.

BIENVENUE!

Tonight the 4th Canadian Division has the honour of welcoming, in the historic Hôtel de Ville, the representatives of Europe's bravest people—our friends and allies, the Belgians.

The Officers of the 3rd Canadian Division, of the British Army and of the Australian Imperial Force, who are our guests, join with us in doing honour to the people of Brussels—the capital of the gallant little country which defied Germany—and saved the Liberty of the World.

As we dance in the year of glorious peace, which dawns at midnight, let us all join in one heartfelt New Year's wish

VIVENT LES BELGES!

This ball has often been compared with the one which was held the night before the Battle of Waterloo, and in the years which have followed I have seen many references to it.

Life in Brussels for the following five months was most interesting. Though the fighting was over, the Adjutant General and Quartermaster General's Branches were still very much occupied with their duties. The General Staff, however, had considerably less to do. We were no longer confronted with the necessity for obtaining Intelligence nor were we occupied with the meticulous detail required to work out the operation orders for the conduct of battles, or required to make the many changes to those plans later brought about by an enemy who stubbornly refused to conform to the operation we had laid out.

Although we pursued a very active round of social activities, I felt that we could employ a good deal of our time to advantage, and I suggested to the Divisional Commander that we work out some sort of university course in liaison with the University of Brussels. I myself was particularly interested in a plan of this sort. The General gave me *carte blanche* to proceed, and I found the University authorities most willing to co-operate.

A series of lectures was arranged and made available to the University graduates and undergraduates within our Division. The lectures were delivered by professors of the University, nearly all of whom conversed in fluent English, and with one exception were held in the various University buildings or museums in Brussels. The exception was one of the lectures on engineering. We were told that we would be shown a project in which Belgian engineers took great pride. This was the Canal Maritime de Bruxelles au Rupel, and we were to make a journey along the entire canal by barge. We were to meet at seven o'clock in the morning. On account of this early start, many of the officers who were to go on the expedition had come in to Brussels from the Divisional area the afternoon or evening before.

I arrived at the rendezvous some minutes before the scheduled time and found a group of Belgians awaiting us. In addition to the lecturers, there were several of the engineers who had designed the canal and a very stout contractor who had built it. In spite of my protests, the contractor, throughout the trip, insisted on addressing me as "Excellency".

The prospective students started to arrive. It was a cheerless, overcast morning and after a difficult night in Brussels, they did not seem to relish the prospect of the journey. Some forty of us went aboard a large, gaily be-flagged, open barge. At one end we found a large table on which were spread the drawings and blueprints of the canal.

The morning was not only disagreeable, but windy and one of the blueprints immediately blew overboard. From the looks and comments of the officer students, they couldn't have cared less if they had all disappeared. I strongly suspected that at this juncture most of them hoped that the barge would sink.

We finally got under way and the explanation of the reason for and the design of the canal started. I looked forward and saw a group engaged in pulling corks out of long wine bottles, and a few minutes later large trays full of wine glasses were brought aft and their contents consumed. I do not know whether the barge streamed a log, but it seemed to me that about every kilometre this performance was repeated. We had not travelled many kilometres along this canal before the entire group was in complete agreement that the canal was one of the best designed and constructed that they had ever seen, and that this was the most interesting lecture they had ever attended.

As we passed each bridge and village, we found colourful decorations and a gay crowd of people waiting to cheer us as we went by. Shortly before noon we passed a dilapidated-looking houseboat moored to the side of the canal. My contractor friend pointed this out to me and said that we had just about reached the end of our journey and would be coming back to have lunch on this houseboat, which belonged to him.

When we arrived for lunch, we entered the houseboat whose exterior completely belied its beautiful and delightfully furnished interior. Its walls were hung with fine paintings and we sat down to lunch at a table set with exquisite linen, silver and crystal. The feast that followed was in keeping with the day, and each course was complemented with the proper vintage.

After lunch our Belgian friends were very kind and complimentary in the addresses directed to their Canadian guests. I remember replying in my somewhat imperfect French and whether it was that, or whether it was the effects of some vintage, as I raised my glass to toast the broad contractor's health, I cried, "A votre ceinture!" This was greeted with a roar of good-natured laughter and the *entente cordiale* was never more so. We arrived back in Brussels just before dark. I wonder if any of those who participated in the voyage can remember any details about the canal itself other than those which I have related.

Later, as a result of the Brussels course which we initiated, the Khaki University was established and provided an educational service for all the Canadian forces during their stay on the continent and at the training centres in England, prior to their return to Canada. The instructors for these courses who volunteered their services were chaplains, Y.M.C.A. secretaries, and many others in our army who had had previous experience in the teaching profession.

I attended many delightful social events during those months. At one dinner party I sat beside Mr. Kirschen. He was the lawyer who defended Edith Cavell, the gallant British nurse who was ruthlessly executed by the Germans during the war, and he told me about his unsuccessful efforts to save her life.

Our own Headquarters were located during this time at the Chateau de la Hulpe, one of the homes of the Armand Solvays. This story would be incomplete if it did not record the innumerable kindnesses of the Solvays and their many friends to those of us who spent months in Belgium while awaiting our return to our native land.

PART THREE

INDUSTRIALIST

CHAPTER VI

HOME AND SOME ADJUSTMENTS

I RETURNED to Canada in June, 1919. I had left home nearly five years before a young, inexperienced lad. I returned still young, but a very much matured man of twenty-seven whose black hair was already greying at the temples. The Canada to which I returned was also changed.

But of one thing I was very sure: I was proud to be a Canadian. Canada's response in 1914 had been prompt and effective. Her contributions of men, money and natural resources had been impressive. Her material contributions were still mainly the products of the fields, forests and mines. The munitions of war produced by the industries of that time were large quantities of shells which ranged from the eighteen pounder to the 9.2 inch howitzer. High explosives, cartridges, fuses and shell components were also produced in large quantities, and over a hundred steel and wooden ships aggregating a total of 367,000 tons were constructed in Canada. The five years of war had resulted in increased development of our natural resources. Canadian industry had received a great impetus and now knew the meaning of standardization of products and skills.

The measure of Canada's industrial growth to the end of the second World War is clearly indicated by the vast and varied contribution (to which I shall refer later) which Canadian industry was able to provide twenty years later.

Canada's contribution in manpower during the first World War consisted of a total of 595,000 men; of these 465,000 were voluntary enlistments. By the end of September, 1918, there were 160,000 Canadians in France in the Canadian Corps and on the lines of communication, and another 116,000 in England. Canadian troops had suffered 232,000 casualties.

In the field the Canadians had proved themselves very adaptable; they were ready to adopt improvements from the British and French, and were quick to add their own innovations and improvements to the existing systems. The world had a new and fuller insight into what was meant by Canada and the Canadians. Canadians themselves for the first time began to measure the stature of their own country, which had grown significantly in the eyes of the rest of the world.

A reaction followed this war, which was the beginning of the social evolution that has been taking place ever since. There was a great deal of labour unrest which resulted in the forty-eight hour week in Britain and recognition of the trade unions. Bolshevism appeared for the first time in Canada, and in October 1918 some fourteen societies believed to be so inspired were banned by a Dominion Order in Council.

During the five years of war I had learned many things. I knew now the great folly and stupidity of war itself, and how lamentably unprepared we were for it. I saw how the pressure of battle quickly developed and brought out the inherent qualities of the individual, whether these qualities were good, bad or indifferent. The rapid replacements, ranging from private to general, which were required as the result of battle casualties very soon taught me that none of us is indispensable, no matter how much we may fancy ourselves. I learned that vanity, conceit and stupidity are never the attributes of the great, and that the most intelligent and thorough plans have to be complemented by equally intelligent and tireless hard work to bring them to a successful conclusion.

After my return home I had some difficulty adjusting myself to a civilian occupation. I decided to finish the law course which I had begun before the war. The Benchers of the Ontario Law Society offered great encouragement and assistance to men returned from overseas, and I was allowed to enter Osgoode Hall and finish what is normally a three year course by attending classes for a period of twelve months. One year was granted as an allowance for service overseas. I entered the course in September 1919, finished my second year by the spring of 1920, and then was permitted to enter the special summer course made available for returned men. In this way I completed my third year by the fall of 1920.

While attending the course at Osgoode Hall I wrote *The Intelligence Service Within the Canadian Corps, 1914-1918*. I felt that a record of the organization and operation of our Intelligence Service as it was built up to function within the Canadian Corps might be of interest. Apparently it was considered so by Major-General J. H. MacBrien, C.B., C.M.G., D.S.O., later Sir James, the Chief of the General Staff of the Canadian Militia, and Sir Arthur Currie, G.C.M.G., K.C.B., my Corps Commander, the former of whom was kind enough to write the foreword and the latter the historical résumé which served as an introduction to the book. My book was later found in the Reference Libraries of the Canadian and British Armies and was used as one of the text books on military front line intelligence. At the outbreak of the second World War, all existing copies were collected and made available to Canadian troops.

A good many books about the war were written and published after the first World War. I thought it might be interesting to suggest an exchange with some of the authors of these. As a result a correspondence developed with them and I was able to collect a most interesting library of contemporary books which contain autographs and comments of the authors. These volumes recorded the events as seen through the eyes of our erstwhile allies or enemies. Among them are books by Lloyd George, the wartime Prime Minister of Great Britain; T. G. Masaryk, the first President of the Czechoslovak Republic; Liddell Hart, the military critic; R. C. Sherriff, the British author of the great war play, *Journey's End*; Bruce Bairnsfather, whose brilliant cartoons broke through the monotony and horror of a long war and provided an occasional ray of sunshine; Arnold Zweig, author of *The Case of Sergeant Grischa*; and others. I also received volumes which recorded the activities of the other Services. I was very happy at this time to receive a beautifully illuminated manuscript of the poem *If*, long a favourite of mine, which had been autographed by its author, Rudyard Kipling.

After the completion of the special summer course at Osgoode Hall in 1921, I was called to the Ontario Bar and became a member of the Law Society of Upper Canada.

While attending Law School, I had met Dorothy McLagan at the Military Ball in Stratford on New Year's Eve, 1920. My family had moved to Stratford in 1912, but my bride-to-be was abroad that year with her family, and later away at boarding school, so that we did not meet until my return from overseas. Our fathers had known each other for many years and our mothers later succeeded each other as President of the Victorian Order of Nurses. The late George McLagan was the founder of the McLagan Furniture Company, which during his lifetime grew to be one of the largest and most successful companies in the industry. Mr. McLagan, who died in the summer of 1918, had been greatly interested in civic affairs and closely identified with the development of the city of Stratford. One of the permanent results of his many public-spirited activities is the beautiful park system which exists today, which was created and developed while he was Chairman of the Park Board of that city. His daughter became my wife on September 15th, 1921. She has been my main source of inspiration and strength during our happy years of married life.

By the time of my marriage I had become articled to the legal firm of McCarthy and McCarthy. I was fortunate to have the opportunity of beginning my law experience with that distinguished firm. I did not, however, stay very long in a profession for which I soon felt I was completely unsuited, and my association with the tolerant members of the firm lasted only about a year.

During this period I made one very undistinguished appearance at court. The list of Mr. D. L. McCarthy, one of Canada's leading counsel, was always full, sometimes to overflowing. One morning I received a call shortly before eleven o'clock. Mr. McCarthy was required to appear in Hamilton and it was necessary to secure the adjournment of a case to be heard in about fifteen minutes before the Appellate Division in Toronto. I was instructed to secure this adjournment. Completely unfamiliar with the case in question, I seized the documents, pushed them into my briefcase, rushed up to Osgoode Hall and donned my gown. I entered the room where the proceedings were being held and found myself in the presence of five distinguished-looking jurists who were prepared to go on with the hearing. At the first opportunity I arose and requested in the case of Blank versus Blank that the hearing be adjourned owing to the unavoidable absence of our counsel. One of the distinguished jurists sitting on the bench in front of me asked me whether I was appearing for the appellant or the respondent. I was completely unprepared for this or any other equally reasonable question relating to the case. The members of the Bench regarded me first with surprise, then with amusement, and finally with compassion. One of them at last remarked that as the young gentleman did not seem to know which side he was acting for, the adjournment might properly be granted. This was my first and last appearance in a court of law.

Shortly afterwards I had a frank discussion with the members of the McCarthy firm, which very likely barely anticipated an equally frank discussion initiated by them. I had come to the conclusion that I was a complete liability as far as the legal profession was concerned. I knew now that both by experience and inclination I would be better suited to and happier in industry.

WHEN I LEFT the law firm with the announced intention of entering industry, one of the McCarthy partners suggested that I go for advice to a relative of his, Sir William MacKenzie. I had an interview with Sir William, and as a result I was offered and accepted a position with the Independent Telephone Company, a corporation in which Sir William was interested. The position was that of assistant to the manager.

The late Sir William MacKenzie at the turn of the century was one of Canada's railway magnates as well as one of the country's leading industrialists and financiers. By 1922 a few radio transmitting stations with very limited range had been constructed, and crystal type receiving sets and components for their manufacture began to appear on the market. Sir William, together with several of his contemporaries, and the other interests involved, had envisaged the commercial possibilities of radio, and the Independent Telephone Company had purchased the Canadian rights to Dr. Lee De Forest's group of patents. They had brought in a supposedly leading radio engineer from the United States, placed him with this company, and by 1922 were producing radio sets which were among the first to be built in Canada. Unfortunately the management of the company, which for a great many years had been associated with another product, was unable to adjust itself to the manufacture of the new and highly technical radios. The sets had the vacuum tubes inserted on the outside of the radio cabinet and so little did the manager know about radio that, depending on the number of tubes, he referred to the sets as "two or three lamp sets". The purchasers of these sets complained that they were unable to keep them properly tuned. The engineer insisted that they were entirely satisfactory. The public disagreed. As a result, many sets were returned and a large unsold inventory was accumulated.

I have already related how as a child I was interested in wireless telegraphy. The problem of the set which would not stay tuned fascinated me. I arranged to instal several in my house in Toronto where I had set up a small radio laboratory in an attic, and here I spent a good many nights testing them. The station adjustment seemed to change every time the hand, in process of tuning in a set, moved to or away from it. In other words, the hand acted as a condenser.

As one result of these experiments, I reached the conclusion that there was no future for me with a company engaged in the manufacture of radio sets which did not work. I decided to sever my connection with it, but I was persuaded that in all fairness I should inform Sir William of my intention. I did this in an interview. He asked me why I proposed to leave. I told him. He was so interested in my account of the experiments with the radio sets that immediately he put on his hat and accompanied me to my house, where we climbed to the third floor laboratory. We spent considerable time trying to make the sets work without success. When he left that night, Sir William asked me to take no action about leaving the company until he returned from Europe, where he was going in a few days.

Before he left, however, he must have said a word in the proper quarter. The sets were properly shielded, which was all that was required to make them function. However, things had gone so badly for the company that on one occasion I was informed that they could not pay my salary. It was suggested that I take on myself the task of selling the now shielded sets on a commission basis. For some time I travelled widely throughout Ontario selling sets in all sorts of likely and unlikely places, gradually whittling away at the large accumulated inventory, and earning more money from commissions than I ever had from my salary with the company.

Partly as a result of my childhood interest in wireless telegraphy and partly because I was convinced that radio, which at that time was considered by many as a toy or fad, had tremendous commercial possibilities, I decided to enter this new and exciting field. On his return from Europe, I informed Sir William of my decision to set up my own company and he and his associates were good enough to arrange an exclusive licence for my company under the group patents which they owned. This was the Lee De Forest group. In 1923 I obtained the licence and formed the De Forest Radio Corporation in Toronto.

Lee De Forest, who commenced his experimental work in 1899, has been called the father of the three-element vacuum tube which made possible radio and, later, television. He introduced the third element into the vacuum tube and named the new tube the "audion". This invention enabled the radio wave to be modulated as it was being transmitted, and again as it was received by the radio operator. It was then converted into sound through the audio system of the receiving set.

Shortly after I formed my own company, I met Dr. De Forest. As is the habit of most inventors, he was already ranging ahead with many new ideas. In great excitement he showed me a piece of moving picture film on which he had succeeded in developing a sound track which made it possible to synchronize sound with the picture. This new invention was later called "Phono Film".

At that time we were still in the days of the silent movies; the "talking movies" followed a few years later.

In the formation of my own company my father's advice and assistance stood me in good stead. Throughout my entire industrial career I have followed his wise counsel which was always to be the controlling owner of any business in which I was engaged. His financial assistance was also most helpful when I started out on my first business venture.

THE DE FOREST RADIO CORPORATION commenced operations in very small premises in Toronto with a staff of five. I was President, General Manager, Secretary-Treasurer; I also helped to build the radio sets. When necessary, I did some of the sweeping. We imported small quantities of De Forest receivers and vacuum tubes from the American company, assembled them and put them on the market in Canada.

In addition to the many other capacities in which I was acting at that time, I also opened such little correspondence as we received. After we had been selling our sets for a period of weeks, I opened a letter from an important Canadian corporation. It was short and very much to the point. It stated that we were infringing a large and impressive group of patents, a list of which was appended. We were instructed to cease and desist forthwith in the manufacture and distribution of our sets, otherwise the corporation would have no alternative, though with regret, but to commence litigation proceedings against us for infringing their patents. Nowadays I recall with amusement that in my capacity as President of the corporation I began my answer to this very threatening document in this way:

Dear Sirs,

    Your letter has been brought to my attention.

I went on to take the position that no radio receiver could be built without employing De Forest patents. The situation, however, was not so amusing at the time; true to my army training, I sat down to make an appreciation of it.

ON THE "PHILANTE"

With my wife and family I attended the America's Cup Races of 1937. We observed the races between *Ranger* and *Endeavour II* from the *Philante*, Mr. T. O. M. Sopwith's beautiful yacht.

WARTIME VISITORS: THE DUKE OF KENT
The King's brother, who was killed in a plane crash the year following his visit,
is seen here with Harry Fearncombe (right) and "Tiny" Shannon.

I was convinced that to maintain our situation, I would require three things. First, I required a licence to manufacture under a group of valid and basic patents. That I had. I would need courage to fight back with these patents if we were molested. I was prepared to fight. Finally, I should have to have ample financial resources to be able to sustain prolonged patent litigation. My field experience had shown me that action was often imperative not only once but many times during an engagement. This situation demanded decisive action. We had the patents and the will to fight, but we were not in a position to sustain a series of long and costly suits.

Powel Crosley, Jr. was at that time pioneering the mass production of low-priced quality sets in the United States. I did not know Mr. Crosley, but the situation was too serious to worry about the amenities. I picked up the phone, called him in Cincinnati, and asked for an appointment with him.

When I met Mr. Crosley in Cincinnati, I unfolded for him the story of my attempt to set up in my own business, and how that attempt was menaced by the threat of endless and costly litigation. I asked him for assistance in meeting this threat. Mr. Crosley had his patent attorney look into the matter. A few days later, accompanied by some of his staff, he came to Toronto. We alternated our discussion of business with some hunting and fishing and at last we came to an arrangement through which my company would have the exclusive right to manufacture and sell on the Canadian market the popular and successful Crosley line of radio receivers. In confirming this arrangement, Mr. Crosley wrote me a letter in which he placed behind my company the entire resources of the Crosley Corporation in the event that we were attacked.

Armed with this document, I sallied forth to confront the Goliath of the industry which had threatened us with litigation. I was received by the President and Vice-President of the corporation and to them I outlined the situation as I had appreciated it when I first read their letter. To maintain my position, I told them, I required three things: a licence to manufacture under a group of patents; the will to fight; and ample financial resources. I had the licence; I had the will to fight. Then I took Powel

Crosley's letter from my pocket and handed it across the table to the Vice-President.

I shall never forget the scene. The Vice-President took the letter, and with an absolute poker face, read it slowly and carefully. Then he handed it over his shoulder to the President who was prowling restlessly about the room. The latter read it, threw it back to the Vice-President, and resumed his perambulations about the office. There were a few moments of silence, then the President stopped by the desk and said abruptly, "What's your proposition?"

I told him bluntly that he was probably right in his original statement that in my manufacturing operations I was infringing on some of his patents. I was equally sure that no one could manufacture a radio anywhere without infringing on Lee De Forest's patents and I had the right to these in Canada. My proposition was that we should pool our patents. An arrangement of this sort was eventually worked out which enabled both companies to manufacture and which avoided endless and destructive litigation.

RADIO SOON RECEIVED a great public acceptance. At first it was regarded by some only as a source of amusement, but it supplied some of the functions of a utility as well. The combination quickly provided an irresistible sales appeal.

Many people sensed the great public demand and realized the commercial possibilities of radio. In the early twenties over seven hundred contenders entered the manufacturing field in radio on this continent. It should be remembered that in 1922 over seventy-five per cent of the turnover in the radio industry consisted of the sale of component parts, which were used by amateurs in the manufacture of receivers for themselves. It was not until six or seven years later that this percentage was reversed, and over ninety per cent of the total volume of business consisted of the sale of complete receiving sets.

The field then was readily accessible, as it required very little actual capital to set up an assembly plant, and a great many of the so-called manufacturing operations consisted in the main of the assembly of component parts. The manufacturers who contented themselves with merchandising the assembled receivers did not incur the extensive capital expenditures required for a complete manufacturing operation. On the other hand, when more adventurous manufacturers began to make their own components, those who had contented themselves with importing and assembling found themselves saddled with an additional cost and for that reason unable to compete. This was a contributing factor to the sudden decease of many of the companies.

A multiplicity of problems confronted the rapidly expanding industry. Many businesses that had plunged into the field were soon faced with the problem of improperly balanced executive control. Some companies were operated by a management that had a good knowledge of the technicalities of the radio art, but very little business experience; other managements possessed the necessary business experience, but lacked the technical knowledge to cope with the kaleidoscopic changes and developments which the new industry underwent. The annual output of sets grew from one hundred thousand radio receivers in 1922 to three and a half million in 1929. There was a very high mortality rate among the companies which started in the new industry, as inadequate management found itself unable to cope with the annual changes in circuits and designs.

Many will remember that the radio receivers constructed in the early twenties had the appearance of a piece of laboratory equipment; later they were so designed that they could take their place as pieces of furniture in any well-appointed room. How and through what channels this new kind of equipment was to be merchandised created a considerable problem. At first no one was certain whether radio sets should be sold through music houses or through stores which distributed electrical equipment. Every possible logical and illogical outlet was used. The companies that achieved all the possible permutations and combinations of all the possible errors of the time soon took their places among the other casualties.

I have always been a very strong advocate of tabulating detailed information in such a way that it presents a visual picture.

When I was with Intelligence, we received a daily mass of information from the many departments which were set up to supply us. For example, during the sedentary type of warfare with which we were occupied during most of World War I, the calibre and map location of every shell that fell into our lines was recorded. It can be imagined how useless this information would have been if it had simply been put away in the files. We, however, created a map which we designated the "Hostile Shelling Map". Each day we plotted on this map the number of shells and their location, and by means of different colours indicated their calibre. On another map, designated "Enemy Work", we plotted daily new enemy trenches, wire, or any other new work. It is not hard to realize the visual story each map revealed and the vital information which might have been lost if all this detail had been buried in the files. A glance at these and similar maps on which were plotted all the forms of enemy activity soon indicated whether the enemy intentions were offensive or defensive.

I had no previous experience in the operation of a manufacturing business, but I did have this background. Early in my business career, General Motors published a series of booklets which showed in great detail the operation of their budgetary system and controls, and these were generously offered to anyone in industry who was interested in them. Each booklet was illustrated by a series of graphs which provided a continuous comparison of the actual operating results with the budget forecast. It did not take us very long to adapt this system to our own business. I have from that time been a great believer in a system of charts and graphs which provide a continual visual record and which show how operations are progressing and where action is required.

Like the other companies in the industry, we had our hands full in dealing with the many problems that we encountered. First and foremost was the problem of changes in design. Many of the sets put out in the first few years were transmitters as well as receiving sets, to the extent that while being tuned they interfered with the reception of nearby receiving sets. These were called "squealers". We directed our efforts to making receiving sets which were of the non-oscillating type, or non-squealers. At that time, most of the engineering laboratories of the larger companies already had equipment by which the exact sensitivity of their sets could be measured, but this type of equipment was not available to us in the first year of our operation. The first non-oscillating set that we produced had a sensitivity sufficient to receive the programmes from the nearby transmitting stations, whose range was still very limited compared with today's standards.

However, we received many complaints soon after several carloads of our sets had been shipped to and distributed in Western Canada. My dismay was complete when I received a letter addressed to the President of the Company, from a farmer in northern Saskatchewan who began his complaint as follows: "Dear Sir, I have one of your sets and the grave has nothing on it for silence." Fortunately, by the time this letter was received, we had already devised a simple method of dealing with the problem and had increased the sensitivity of our sets. We withdrew the old sets from the West and replaced them with units that were completely satisfactory.

MY ASSOCIATION with Powel Crosley, Jr. and the company which he was operating with such great success in the United States was a very happy and constructive one. About 1926 Mr. Crosley purchased the Amrad Corporation; its name was an abbreviation for the "American Radio Research Company". This company had been one of the pioneer manufacturers in the radio industry in the United States. As early as 1915 it had erected a broadcasting tower on its plant just outside Boston. Amrad was originally well financed by the important J. P. Morgan interests, and Mr. Morgan had entrusted the management to a radio operator on his yacht, the *Corsair*. It is probable that this gentleman was proficient in the Morse Code, but the owners were more than annoyed by the continual SOS's that they were receiving from him for more money, and the heavy operating expenses that were being incurred.

Amrad had secured an exclusive licence under the patents of

Colonel Mershon, one of the engineers closely associated with George Westinghouse, the founder of the American Westinghouse Company. Later, as I became better acquainted with this very delightful gentleman, he told me of his early days with Westinghouse. He was one of those aboard the train when the famous Westinghouse air brake was given its first commercial demonstration. Colonel Mershon, who had been retired for a number of years, combined the qualities of an extremely successful engineer and a very shrewd business man. In the years following his retirement he had established a laboratory in New York City where he occupied such time as he did not spend on his extensive travels on experiments with developments which interested him and which he considered were required in the field of utilities. His main attention at this time was directed toward the development of a new product which would have had a wide industrial application. This activity resulted in a by-product which was called the Mershon radio condenser.

Amrad had the exclusive licence under Colonel Mershon's patents for this condenser. It could be manufactured at a fraction of the cost of the paper condensers that were in use at the time and which had to be replaced when punctured by a surge of power. The Mershon condenser was self-sealing in case of a surge, and this eliminated both the necessity for the replacement and for a service call.

It was Mr. Crosley's belief in the commercial possibilities of this condenser, which had not yet been generally accepted by the industry, that caused him to acquire the Amrad Corporation at a time when the latter, due to bad management, was getting into difficulties. The original owners, who were not concerned by their financial losses, decided that they had had enough of the radio industry.

In the course of one of our fishing and hunting trips, I had apparently indicated to Powel Crosley that I was attracted by the possibilities of the American market. About a year after his venture into Amrad, he got in touch with me and wanted to know whether I would be prepared to acquire a substantial interest in the company, which was still having its problems. I was attracted by the broader opportunities that were presented by the proposal and acquired the interest in the company that was offered to me. I became President of the Amrad Corporation. Both Powel Crosley and I had in mind the development of the Mershon condenser to a point where it would have a general acceptance by the radio industry.

When I took over the management of Amrad and began a detailed investigation of the situation within the company, I was dismayed to find that we had just received a letter from the licensor. This informed us that for reasons of non-performance of the contract under which the company held its licence, he now cancelled the valuable agreement which had been held by the company. I discovered that Colonel Mershon was at Palm Beach, and with my wife I travelled there to see him. It was extremely fortunate for us that his action had been taken on information provided to him by a prospective licensee and contained a number of inaccurate statements. I informed Colonel Mershon that we planned to put sufficient endeavour behind his product to insure both its commercial success and the fulfilment of the terms of our agreement with him. I asked him to restore the licence to us, if upon further investigation he found that the information which he had been given was not based upon facts. This he promised to do. He made his own investigation, found that my statements were correct and, as good as his word, restored the licence to us.

Within the next two years the Mershon condenser was adopted by practically all the major producers of radio sets in the United States. It became a household word in radio, and Amrad developed a very large volume of business for this product.

CHAPTER VII

SAILING, FISHING, AND SOME BUSINESS

BY 1928 I was dividing my time between the businesses in Toronto and Boston. Our family now summered on Marblehead Neck. We enjoyed Marblehead, steeped in tradition, and the sailing lore of centuries. The painting, "The Spirit of 1776", that stirring portrayal of New England of the Revolution, hangs in the library of this quaint town.

The bar which runs out from the shore and then rises and swings north to parallel the mainland provides the natural picturesque shelter which has made Marblehead Harbour one of the great yachting centres on this continent. From our summer place "Miramar", which faced the sea on the crest of Marblehead Neck, we were able to watch the races as the seemingly endless number of classes crossed the starting line on the gun. These classes ranged from the busy little Brutal Beasts sailed by children inside the harbour, through the smaller classes and the S, R, and Q classes, to the New York 40's and the beautiful 50's. Lying at their moorings or at anchor in the harbour were the ships of the fleet, a colourful assembly which invariably included several of the large, beautifully rigged two and three masted schooners, and an occasional square rigger. The assembly of yachts during race week, flying the burgees of many clubs, provided a magnificent and unforgettable spectacle.

I was at that time a member of the Royal Canadian Yacht Club of Toronto, although my only previous experience with canvas had consisted of sailing my canoe on the frigid waters of the Magnetawan when I was a teacher at Byng Inlet. This sixteen footer, with its leg-of-mutton sail, was equipped with lee boards, and as I ventured on the river a kindly Providence must indeed

have been hovering over me to guard me from my total lack of
sailing experience.

At Marblehead I did not long resist the lure of what I consider
one of the finest of all competitive sports; soon I was looking
about for a yacht. I relied heavily upon the advice of a fine old
Marblehead sailor, the late Mr. Quiner. To his great glee, he
found a Herreschoff twenty-one foot knockabout which had been
built in 1896. We discovered that this was the old *Cock Robin*,
famous in yachting circles in the late nineties, and gave her back
her old name.

I asked Mr. Quiner how long it would take me to become a
reasonably competent racing skipper. I was somewhat incredu-
lous when he casually replied, "Oh, about ten years." How right
he proved to be!

I took off *Cock Robin*'s bronze fittings and had them all
chromium plated, much to the disgust of the yachtsmen of Marblehead, who considered that this departure from bronze fittings,
which had to be polished daily, was something in the order of
sacrilege. It was amusing to note, however, that not many years
later chromium fittings became standard equipment in yachting
circles.

We had a great deal of fun sailing the gaff-rigged *Cock Robin*.
My children (my daughter then six, and my twin sons three years
old) still remember occasionally landing under the opposite seat
in the open cockpit as we came about. At the end of our first
season we entered *Cock Robin* in the Chowder Race. A very
unskilled, but at least very persistent skipper crossed the finishing line at the tail end of a large fleet.

Regardless of her position in the fleet, the reappearance of
Cock Robin aroused considerable interest on the sporting pages.
The following extract is from a report in the Boston *Herald* of
September 1928:

Probably the most famous craft to take part in the race was the old
21-foot knockabout, *Cock Robin*, built by Herreschoff for the late
Charles S. Eaton back in the early '90's. Sailed by the late William P.
Fowle, the *Corinthian*'s second commodore, *Cock Robin* her first two
seasons out was unbeatable, having an almost perfect record of all
wins the first year. Since her racing days the *Cock Robin* has changed

hands many times and is now owned by J. E. Hahn of the Royal
Canadian Yacht Club, Toronto, Canada, a summer resident this season
of the Neck.

That fall I had the *Cock Robin* re-rigged with a new mast and
Marconi rig. As a member of the Eastern Yacht Club, the following summer I enjoyed many delightful days on the water in
the active sailing atmosphere of Marblehead.

In the summer of 1929 Marblehead celebrated its 300th anniversary. Included in the festivities was a harbour parade made
up of the yachts of the fleet which moved past the American and
British cruisers lying in the harbour during these celebrations.
Cock Robin, decked out as a villainous old pirate ship with a body
swinging from her yardarm, and manned by a murderous-looking
crew, was awarded the Cup which was the prize for her class.

Flying the burgee of the Royal Canadian Yacht Club, we again
entered her in the Chowder Race on September 15th, 1929. Mr.
Quiner was skipper. My wife, another member and I constituted the crew. September 15th held special significance for me.
On that date in 1916 I had been severely wounded and it was on
that date that my wife and I had been married. That day in a
strong nor'wester we won the Chowder Cup. The sporting pages
of the Boston papers again gave great prominence to the reappearance of the *Cock Robin*.

During the two years that I was sailing *Cock Robin*, I had
greatly admired the lines and performance of the New York 50's,
created and built in 1916 by the famous yacht designer, Mr. Herreschoff. They were seventy-two feet over all, fifty feet on the
water-line, and had a beam of fourteen feet six inches. They drew
ten feet. They were originally cutters, having a main mast of
a hundred and twenty feet, but by 1929 the 50's lying in Marblehead Neck had been converted to Marconi rig.

We decided we should like to acquire one of these 50's, and
I engaged a firm of New York naval architects to see if they
could locate one for sale with a hull which they considered sound.
They found and recommended a New York 50 which had been
ketch-rigged, and which was then located in one of the marine
yards at City Island. She had been christened *Harpoon* when
she first joined the class of fifty footers in 1916. I acquired *Har-*

poon, had her completely overhauled, and arranged for her to be delivered at Atlantic City in the spring of 1930. The trim ketch, her new chromium fittings gleaming on her white pine deck, we re-christened *Nonchalant*.

I had aboard an old New England skipper and crew. In a strong easterly breeze we took her to sea through the gap, and I sailed her rail down for the first time. After a time I handed over the wheel and went below; to my surprise I found that the bulkheads had moved nearly an inch, as about that much space was now showing above the paint line where before they had fitted snugly into her beams when she stood on an even keel. This caused me great concern and on the following day I motored down to the famed Herreschoff yard and sought Mr. Herreschoff.

I found this delightful old gentleman and explained to him that I was the owner of his old *Cock Robin* and had recently acquired one of his 50's. I told him that I was dismayed to find that when she was rail down, the bulkheads had moved. I can still see the twinkle that came to the eyes of the old gentleman as he walked over to me, patted me on the shoulder, and said, "My lad, if she doesn't do that, you get off her." I had not realized that she was so designed that the crown of the deck would move when she was heeled over and under strain. During the twenty years that I owned her, I found that although the bulkheads moved, due to the flexible design, each time when she righted herself on an even keel, they resumed positions as tightly-fitting as the day she was launched.

We sailed her out of Marblehead during the summer of 1930, and I entered the Ocean Cruise of the New York Yacht Club, which started at Marblehead and provided a week's racing. Brigadier Clarence McKee and Bill Hearst came down from Toronto for the occasion, and they, with Mr. Quiner, were the non-professional members of the crew. We raced to Provincetown, continued, after passing through the Cape Cod Canal, to Newport and Block Island, and then back to Marblehead. These races provided excellent experience against the fleet of large yachts which took part.

By the end of the races I was convinced beyond doubt that very great experience was necessary to arrive at any degree of proficiency as a racing skipper. Our entry in no way disturbed the distribution of the trophies.

Before the season was over, however, we finished first and won the trophy for second place on corrected time in the Boston Ocean Race. The course for this race in 1930 was Marblehead, Gloucester, then around the light ship at Boston Harbour, and back to Marblehead. What made this win all the more astonishing was the fact that our racing instructions blew overboard just prior to the starting gun. The race was started in a squall after several postponements. After we rounded the mark at Gloucester, we set our big spinnaker in every manner that could possibly be devised to ensure that we lost the race. Fortunately, by this time the rest of the fleet, which had witnessed this exhibition and had passed us, had become becalmed and, as so often happens under similar conditions, we carried on up and into the fleet, and were then favoured by a spanking squall which held for the rest of the race. We finished in this blow rail down, the way we started.

The following spring, with her sticks aboard, *Nonchalant* came up the Albany River through the canal to Oswego on Lake Ontario, and across the Lake to Toronto, where she joined the First Division of the Fleet of the Royal Canadian Yacht Club.

ON MY RETURN to Toronto I divided my time between the two businesses, which had both had a very rapid growth. During this period I was occasionally called upon to give addresses on the subject of radio, the new industry. I delivered one of these at the Harvard Business School in 1929. In passing, I should say that I was very much impressed with the necessity for and the soundness of this type of course, so much so that twenty years later I was gratified to see my twin sons, after they had received their diplomas at the University of Toronto, take their post-graduate degree at this school. At the time of writing, excellent courses of a similar nature are available at our Canadian universities.

Two years later I addressed the undergraduates of the University of Toronto. Recently I read again the speeches that I made on those occasions. There is little that I would change in them if I were delivering them today. The principles I enunciated then were those on which I conducted my own businesses and I am convinced that they still hold good today.

The success of any business, I feel, depends upon considerably more than the conduct of a series of successful operations. Every business must have a definite long-range objective in its relation to the entire industry. That objective should be nothing less than leadership of the industry.

It is essential to produce a good product at a fair price and to have it well and honestly merchandised. The product should be backed by truthful advertising which reflects the character of the business. The manufacturer should drive hard towards his goal; he should never depreciate his competitor.

I consider that man power is the most important asset of any business. The efficient use of capital and plant is directly dependent upon it.

This man power should be directed by a well-balanced executive staff which has the capacity for an inordinate amount of intelligent hard work. Hard work is what counts; there is no other road to success. The executive is responsible for providing well-planned and co-ordinated action. The essential qualifications of a good executive staff are stability, to keep the business on a steady course through the storm of modern competition; courage, to make the most ambitious objective possible of attainment; and vision which ranges constantly ahead of the enterprise itself.

In Canada, as elsewhere in the late twenties and early thirties, there was need for those qualities of planning and drive towards an objective; of integrity and hard work; of stability, courage and vision. We had now reached the years just preceding the great and disastrous boom of the late twenties. Business was sky-rocketing, an entirely false sense of values prevailed, and the urge to speculate seemed to have seized the public. The stock market had been steadily and rapidly rising, and every logical yardstick of values seemed to have disappeared. Very few people, when buying the rapidly rising securities, attempted to examine the assets or net worth behind the security itself. They were obsessed by the notion that the stocks would go up for ever, regardless of the intrinsic values behind the shares. I was more than concerned by this turn of events, which was only too apparent when one analyzed the balance sheet of almost any company and compared the net worth behind each share with the market price.

Shortly before the inevitable crash, which took place in October 1929, my wife and I were invited aboard a yacht which dropped anchor in Marblehead harbour. During that week I received a very flattering offer which, had I accepted it, would have made it necessary for our family to leave Canada and live in the United States. My wife and I discussed this over the week-end and came to the conclusion that, although the ultimate financial return would probably not be as great, we should prefer to live out our lives in Canada. We so informed our friends.

Some of the reasons upon which we based our decision may be of interest to the reader. It was our opinion that Canada, a young and virile country with enormous resources and an attractive future, could provide the means to satisfy the most hopeful ambitions. The possibilities of our country were only beginning to be understood; but with my experience in living and carrying on business in two countries, I was already aware of a solidarity in Canada, a distinctive method of living and a wholesome attitude in industry which it would be extremely difficult to find anywhere else in the world. That was my opinion in 1929; it remains the same today.

It seemed almost as though fate were approving our course of action. Very shortly afterwards I was approached by Mr. Richard O'Connor, the able President of Magnavox Corporation of California. This company was one of the pioneers and one of the largest manufacturers in the loud-speaker field, and a major supplier to the radio industry. Magnavox had become interested in the Mershon condenser and felt that it would like to acquire control of this product, which was now well established in the industry. They felt that the combination of the speaker and the condenser would place them in a leading position in the accessory field. The negotiations which followed resulted in the Magnavox Corporation acquiring the Mershon products by means of a very satisfactory share exchange. Both these companies had remained in a solvent position in spite of the crash, and the head office and the plants of the Magnavox Corporation were established at Fort Wayne. Mr. Richard O'Connor continued as President, and I became Chairman of the Board and remained so until the early thirties.

By 1932 all Canadian business had been seriously affected by the depression. Our company, in common with others in the new industry, was faced with many difficulties. The volume of business was greatly reduced and the competition for such business as was available was severe. Radio sets were offered at such a low price that the entire industry suffered very heavy operating losses. Many dealers during the boom period had sold sets on greatly extended credit terms and we suffered additional heavy losses when some of these dealers went into receivership.

I had made the cardinal error, while money was readily available, of not obtaining additional financing necessary for our rapidly expanding Canadian business. This would have provided sufficient capital to take care of the heavy losses that we had to sustain during the prolonged and severe depression. It was a mistake that I did not repeat later in my business career. The entire radio industry suffered greatly during the depression. The main independent Canadian company among our competitors was having problems similar to our own, but complicated by the fact that it depended upon an American company for its designs. When the American company went into receivership, the Canadian company lost the engineering facilities which had provided its designs. The directors of the company got in touch with our organization. It is not necessary here to go into all the details by which one healthy business was created out of two which had serious ailments. Arrangements were effected which enabled us to cut the overheads, arrange for the most efficient use of key personnel, and maintain the products of both companies.

As a boy I spent many a day on the banks of the River Nith, which flows through New Hamburg. I would sit holding the bamboo rod, intently watching my line and its float, which was lying lazily on the surface of the slow-moving water, awaiting that bobbing motion which indicated that a shiner, a sucker, or perhaps a catfish, was toying with the worm-laden hook dangling in the water near the bottom of the river. Sometimes I was one of the many lads of the village who fished for the carp that congregated in a large hole, forty yards in diameter, which had formed just below the dam. There was a small opening between the edge of the river and what we called the "carp pond". Occasionally a youthful fisherman would manage to flip one of these ugly fish on to the bank or beach. Anyone successful in landing an especially large one would have his prowess recorded in the New Hamburg *Independent*.

Curiosity as to what might have accumulated in the carp pond finally proved too much for the inhabitants of our village. The local engineers calculated that the fire engine, of which the village was very proud, should be able to pump out the pond in three hours. Accordingly, the narrow entrance from the pond into the river was dammed and one morning a large and enthusiastic gathering watched the fire engine begin its heroic efforts to pump out the carp pond. Everyone hoped that no fire would be inconsiderate enough to break out elsewhere in the village which would require the services of the pump and volunteer fire brigade.

The calculations of the engineers did not allow for the seepage through the dam, or for the springs which fed the pond. Late that night, by the light of bonfires, the fire engine was still striving bravely and a good deal of the bottom of the pond had been exposed. There still seemed to be an apparently inexhaustible supply of water flowing into its centre, however, and there also seemed to be a number of carp in the water struggling for existence. It was now considered that the honour of the fire engine and brigade had been completely vindicated, but that the amateurs who had made the calculations should find their vocation in other professions.

It was a particular treat when my father and mother drove me

Bob Warren

WARTIME VISITORS: THE PRINCESS JULIANA
Another royal visitor was the Princess, now Queen, Juliana of The Netherlands shown here talking to Dr. Lome and the medical staff. The Princess was gracious, charming, and alert.

WARTIME VISITORS: THE EARL OF ATHLONE
His Excellency, the Governor General, himself an old soldier, is shown here aiming and firing a Bren gun. The Bren was the first automatic weapon ever to be manufactured in Canada.

out into the country to the farm of one of our friends. Here we fished for the beautiful little speckled trout that would dart out from the shadows of the water-cress, strike the worm-baited hook on the end of the bamboo rod, be flipped out of the water on to the edge of the field and finally end up at home as that delicacy known as "pan-fried brook trout".

My boyhood was spent in a district where I learned to love the art of fishing in its simplest forms and where to us fly fishing was an obscure and mysterious method employed by a few very old gentlemen in other parts of the country when they went on their fishing expeditions. Yet fly fishing, as well as other forms, was to become one of the great pleasures of my life, here and in many other parts of the world. I am not alone in this predilection. On expeditions about the world I have seen fish-hooks formed from bone, shark's teeth, mother-of-pearl, tortoise shell, and even some of gold which many years ago were used by certain tribes in South America.

In my later youth I indulged in the other forms of fishing for which the waters of Ontario are well known, and had my early experience with bass in the waters of Georgian Bay, and with pickerel and muskallunge which were plentiful in the waters of the Magnetawan. While fishing in these waters, I was initiated into the art of trolling and plug casting. When still a young boy, I received on one occasion a Shakespeare reel—a name which was then, and still is today, considered a hallmark on reels and fishing tackle. Many years later I included this line of products in my postwar manufacturing programme.

During the war a great many men had in the back of their minds a picture of some place which they would like to revisit if they were fortunate enough to survive the campaign. My hope for the future was to revisit the waters of the Magnetawan where they flowed into Georgian Bay. This hope I realized, for immediately after visiting my parents, Captain Jack Mitchell, M.C., and I had a welcome rest and excellent fishing in the peaceful waters where I had canoed and fished before the war.

In the middle twenties my wife and I took a motor trip through the Province of Quebec, where friends of ours provided some very excellent trout fishing. By this time I was learning to use a fly rod and was in that stage which a delightful friend of mine from India best described many years later on his first day fly fishing for salmon at my camp on the Matapedia. When I met him as he came off the water the first morning and stepped out of the boat, he said to me, "I would not have believed that so many things could happen to only ten feet of line."

On leaving our friends we continued our trip through Quebec and down the lovely Matapedia Valley. As we were driving on the road which runs along the east shore of these waters, we passed some inviting looking pools which I felt should be a likely shelter for some kind of fish. Accordingly, we stopped at one of these, and I put up my trout rod and went down to the river. I made a few casts in a manner which should have been sufficient to raise the suspicion of any respectable fish. Apparently, however, the fish in this pool had never before seen a fly presented in this way and to my surprise I rose two fish which seemed to be, and in fact were, very large salmon. They fortunately did not take, as otherwise I would have lost a trout fly together with its leader. I went back to the car elated and told my wife, who had been reading, about this adventure. A short way along the road we stopped for gasoline, and I recounted my experience to the station attendant. He was somewhat taken aback, for I had been trespassing. He told me that these waters were all owned or leased and was surprised that I had not been seen by one of the river guardians, whose duty it was to protect the lessee against trespassing. The attendant told me that if I had been caught, I probably would have been fined. On reflection he added, "It still would have been a hell of a lot cheaper than belonging to the Club." I have been fortunate enough to spend the later summers of my life where the river flows between the wooded hills which form the beautiful lower valley of the Matapedia and then joins the magnificent waters of the Restigouche.

My trips across Canada in connection with my business activities revealed to me not only the beauties of the East, but the grandeur and magnificence of our Western Provinces as well. My wife and I soon became initiated into the sport of fishing for the British Columbia spring salmon known as Tyee (Indian for big fish), which abounds on the British Columbia coast. At

Campbell River on Vancouver Island we attempted to qualify for the buttons awarded by the Tyee Club for fish of different weights which are caught on tackle falling within the limits specified by the Club.

These Tyee salmon will not take the fly, but only a spoon or a plug. When hooked and played, they do not leap out of the water like Atlantic salmon, but make long, powerful runs and occasionally surface and break water with a great swirl. Even the most ardent fly fisherman who has hooked one of the powerful fresh Tyee on regulation equipment will respond to the exhibition of power, speed and endurance displayed by these magnificent fish. I believe the record on the rod and line now stands somewhere in the seventy pounds, although considerably heavier fish have been found in the nets of the commercial fishermen.

The British Columbia Cohoe salmon does take the bucktail fly and this sporting fighter is capable of performing above and below the water as well as under the boat. It provides excellent sport at Campbell River and later in the fall at Cowichan Bay while the runs are on.

On one visit to British Columbia, Air Vice-Marshal L. F. Stevenson, C.B., C.D., and I flew up to River's Inlet about 250 miles north of Vancouver on a plane which we had chartered. We admired the ingenuity of the bush pilot who found his way through the heavy cloud formations and dense fog, and finally succeeded in breaking out through a hole in the clouds. We were, however, very relieved to feel our pontoons touch down on the water.

A great number of fish had congregated at the mouth of the small river which flowed into this long inlet twenty miles from the sea. Here we saw seal doing some fishing on their own, and the tracks of bear where they had come down to the river's edge to scoop up salmon from among the many now moving up the river. We had several days of excellent fishing.

I have always been fascinated and quite unable to understand why salmon will strike at a spoon or a plug as they congregate in the salt water at the mouth of the river and yet will not look at bait of any kind once they start moving out of the bay and up into the fresh water of the river. We fished in this narrow river, with salmon breaking surface and rolling all about our boat, and did not succeed in obtaining one single strike.

Most of our fishing was done from a twelve foot skiff and "Steve" and I took turns at rowing while the other trolled. On the last day, while it was my turn to troll, instead of using my regulation Tyee tackle, I rigged my small three-ounce glass bait casting rod with a four inch salmon reel which held nearly four hundred yards of six-thread linen line. As I trolled with this outfit, using an eight inch single hook spoon, I wondered what would happen if I hooked a large fish. I soon had a strike which seemed to indicate that I had hooked one of the smaller Tyee; all doubt was dispelled when one of the first runs by this fish tore off nearly a thousand feet of line. In the distance I saw the swirl of what must have been a sizable specimen.

An hour and twenty minutes later we were a mile and a half farther down the inlet. Steve had handled our little skiff in such a capable manner as to give evidence that he might achieve the same distinction in the Navy as he had done in the Air Force. By this time I had the large fish close to the boat, but was unable to do much with him on the little rod which had by this time assumed the shape of the letter U. The performance continued for some time, till I told Steve I would attempt to swing him in close enough for the gaff. I had with me a belt life preserver which could be inflated by discharging the two carbon dioxide cartridges which it contained. Just as the fish swung in towards the gaff, Steve remarked, "Damn your soul, remember that the life belt is for the two of us." I then witnessed as neat a gaffing job as I have ever seen. The fifty pound Tyee was deftly swung over the gunwale of the boat and ended up underneath the two seats. To my surprise, the little glass rod which had taken all this punishment, immediately after the pressure had been released, sprang back into its original position without the slightest sign of a set. It still looked as though it had been used to bring in the small fish for which it had been designed.

On my trips to British Columbia I had the opportunity of fishing in the crystal-clear waters of the lakes which nestle in the mountains at an altitude of nine thousand feet near Sunshine Lodge, which can be reached after a climb by motor car from Banff.

The one fishing incident which I shall never forget occurred while my wife and daughter and I were spending a few days at Jasper, after visiting our sons who, during the second World War, received part of their army training in British Columbia. I had often heard of beautiful Malines Lake, far up in the mountains at an altitude of nearly six thousand feet. Its waters were well known for speckled trout. The trip to Malines Lake Chalet necessitated a climb by pack-horse, and I decided to go alone there for a day's fishing.

I started out in the morning by motor from Jasper, and soon arrived at Medicine Lake. I crossed this small lake by motor boat and found a guide and a pair of pack-horses waiting at the far end of the lake. We had a somewhat tortuous climb of about seven miles along the valley and gorges of the Malines River till we arrived at the lake, a beautiful sight, nestling in the mountains whose peaks still extended several thousand feet up into the snow. The Chalet was at the end of the lake from which the Malines river flowed and began its rapid, precipitous and thunderous course down the valley and gorges along which we had just ascended.

The Chalet was not properly staffed or operated during the war. I found there the wife of the schoolmaster guide who had met and conducted me from the lake on the pack-horses. There was apparently one additional assistant, but no one seemed too familiar with the locality.

The only other guests were an American couple who were going to the far end of the long lake to take some coloured movies. The teacher, who was helping out as best he could, told me he was completely unfamiliar with the fishing in the lake but was given to understand that there was one location where trout could be raised. He told me that while I was changing into my waders and fishing outfit he would place a boat at this location and would take me out to it just before he left with the party of photographers. After changing, I went to the water's edge and he took me out to a boat which he had anchored at a point where the Malines River began its flow out of the lake. He told me to cast from this position and if I was not successful, to row in and to try along the edge of the lake.

I was as much interested in the scenery as any fishing that the waters might provide. I spent some time casting, changing flies from time to time, without any success. Then I decided that I would move in and wade along the shore to see if I could raise a fish there. I went forward to the bow of the boat and hauled up the rope which held the anchor. I had no sooner broken out the anchor, which turned out to be a large rock lashed to the end of the rope, than the boat began to move; almost as quickly, one of the oars, which had been shipped and which apparently did not fit the oar locks, fell into the water. I jumped into the seat and took two or three strokes with the other oar in an effort to overtake the one that had fallen overboard. To my horror, the boat shot over a smooth glissade, which indicated the sharp drop of water as we entered the river mouth. The boat began to spin and I suddenly grasped the full significance of the thunderous roar that we had heard from time to time in our ascent along the river as we passed the various waterfalls of the Malines which dashed and thundered on the rocks below.

The experience that by this time I had gained on the water saved my life that day. The boat was in white water, spinning like a top, and my only hope of not being dashed over the first fall was to stop this careening boat, if it was possible. I rushed to the bow, let over the rock anchor, and slowly paid out the rope, hoping against hope that the anchor would find bottom and hold. It touched, and as the rope tightened and I slowly payed out more, the boat finally dragged to a stop twenty yards from the left shore and only a short distance from the top of the gorge from which the water of the first falls plunged and thundered to the rocks a hundred feet below.

I pulled off my waders, stripped to my shorts, and decided if the boat should move that I would jump into the torrent and make an effort to reach the shore. I was at a point where the river was flowing between two high banks; a fairly stiff breeze had sprung up and was blowing downstream. I lay down on the bottom of the boat to reduce the sail area and, using a tree on shore as a marker, watched it, hoping that the anchor would hold. I knew that I would be missed sooner or later and that help would arrive.

I lay there for nearly two hours. At last I saw the two women from the camp come rushing along the river bank towards me. They told me later they had missed the boat at the mouth of the river and feared the worst.

When they reached the shore opposite the boat, I shouted and told them to go back to the camp and bring the pack ropes from the horses on which we had made our ascent that morning. They were also to bring my tackle bag which contained some of my larger reels. They disappeared; twenty minutes later they were back again with the equipment I had asked for. I told them to knot together the pack ropes, which they soon did. I then asked them to find my largest reel, which was a salmon reel loaded with a forty yard casting line and a hundred and fifty yards of backfill. I instructed them to take the end of the casting line, pull it and the backfill off the reel, double the line and cut it off the reel. The double line was then tied to one end of the pack rope, while the other end was tied to a tree on the bank. I called to them that I would try to cast a small lead weight to the shore with the light fly rod which I had in the boat with me. If I succeeded, they were to tie the trout line on to the end of the salmon line. I cast for nearly twenty minutes before I was able to put the small lead sinker across the wind on to the bank at the edge of the torrent. I was relieved each time I cast that I did not start the boat.

I then told the women to climb partly up the bank and I held the rod high above my head and reeled in the doubled salmon line as they fed it to me. I need not say how quickly I lashed this on to the bow of the boat. Then I pulled in the double salmon line as they payed out the tied pieces of pack rope. The heavier line formed a big bow in the rushing waters as I pulled it in towards the boat. This strain was all that was needed, and the boat started to move. However, I had soon pulled in the end of the pack rope and the women on shore had quickly taken in the slack and fastened the other end with a turn around a tree. My boat described an arc and reached the shore without swamping.

In normal times a boom is always in position across the mouth of the Malines River in order to prevent what might have happened to me on that day. During the war, however, the camp was used very little and the boom had not been swung across the river.

Some time later I received one of the very few letters that I have been discourteous enough not to answer. It contained a bill from the company which rented the boats at Malines Lake for the ill-fitting oar which had been lost.

IT IS DIFFICULT to realize that the main propulsion equipment on the armed vessels up to the middle of the nineteenth century consisted of sail, and that steam was still auxiliary motive power even as late as the American Civil War. In the British action at Sebastopol in 1855, one of the most formidable ships in the engagement was a British man-of-war launched only six years previously, which carried only sail.

Citizens who had the means and the desire to build yachts a hundred years ago had a patriotic motive for doing so. Their activities provided data on design and rig and technical improvements in the construction of the ships themselves, which ultimately contributed to national defence. The many yachting organizations created a formidable auxiliary to the armed services each time the security of the nation was threatened. Many of the conventions associated with yachting, now taken for granted, hark back to the unofficial recognition bestowed upon yacht clubs in tribute to their continuing and essential part in the fabric of national security. That is why we still find uniforms for yachtsmen, flag etiquette and gun signals for colours, and the many customs, privileges and rituals for yachts, which give yachting a significance that sets it apart from other aquatic sports.

The founding of the Royal Canadian Yacht Club in Toronto is best described by its archivist, C. H. J. Snider, the distinguished yachtsman, writer, and Canadian authority on ships that sail and have sailed the seas.

Founded in 1852, when yachting was a practical experimental field for naval science, and Trafalgar, only forty-seven years away, was an event still well within the memories of many original members, the

Royal Canadian Yacht Club was conceived and born in the tradition of service; a tradition which has never left it.*

The history, record and contribution of this Club, known the world over, are expressed in "The Annals of the Royal Canadian Yacht Club", a labour of love recorded by its archivist. In the first World War four hundred and fifty of its members were active in Canada's armed forces, of whom fifty-nine did not return. In the second World War, five hundred and one of its members saw service in various parts of the world, and of these twenty-three had sailed their last race.

In 1931, I started to race *Nonchalant* in the First Division of the Club. In this Division were the 92 foot ketch *Oriole*, owned by the late Commodore George H. Gooderham; the 66 foot schooner *Yolanda*, sailed by the great skipper of international fame, Commodore Norman Gooderham; the beautiful 60 foot cutter *Gardenia*, sailed by that crafty yachtsman, Commodore E. K. M. Wedd; the 72 foot schooner *Chimon*, owned by Mr. F. M. Ellis; and later the 72 foot sloop *Metina* from Rochester. The last two of these were skippered from time to time by the fire-eating, hard-driving internationally known yachtsman, the late Commodore Aemelius Jarvis, who presented the Club with the two magnificent mural paintings which can be seen at either end of the yacht club ballroom.

During the war, while going around a very complicated front line trench system, I had often wished that I possessed the uncanny sense of direction which seems to be part of the natural equipment of some people. I always had to find my way on my map through any trench system, while some companion who kept his map folded in his tunic pocket seemed to know exactly where he was at any given time. I soon learned that some yachtsmen were able to spit over the rail, take a glance to port or starboard, look up and down the luff of the sail, take a couple of sniffs, and by this procedure make a very accurate assessment of weather, wind shifts or fairings. Even if the compass was pointing in the wrong direction—which it never did—such men

* *Annals of the Royal Canadian Yacht Club, 1852-1937*, by C. H. J. Snider, Club Archivist. (Rous & Mann, 1937)

seemed to know exactly where they were. I was not one of them. Lacking those qualities of a natural born racing skipper, I felt that something must be added if I were to fulfil Mr. Quiner's prediction that it would take me ten years to become a proficient skipper. The added ingredients were good organization and a first rate crew. I was pitchforked into the races of the First Division with a yacht which, if properly sailed, was fast in fresh weather, and at a disadvantage only in light weather, due to her reduced sail area and changed rig. For the first few years at least the competing skippers had a Roman holiday with *Nonchalant* and me, but we had a great deal of fun. I sailed over our spinnaker, and in one race after another I was outsailed by yachtsmen who knew every trick of the game. I felt that only through persistent practice with a well-organized crew was there any hope for me to pick off the flags that were awarded for First, Second, or Third. The crew of *Nonchalant*—all of whom melted into the services at the beginning of World War II—worked hard in an effort to capture some of the flags and trophies. We raced each year assiduously for the points for the Club Championship of our Division in the Triangle and cruising races, and for the Championship in the First Division of the Lake Yacht Racing Association, the annual event on Lake Ontario in which yachts from all the clubs on the Lake compete.

It was hard and disappointing going as far as the trophies were concerned, but the hard-working crew which formed the afterguard enjoyed the pleasure of sailing and the trap shooting off her decks, as well as the racing.

Aboard the *Nonchalant* we carried a paid crew ranging from two to four, none of whom was allowed to touch the helm while a race was in progress. On triangle races we carried a crew of eight to ten and on long races of twelve to fourteen, divided into port and starboard watches which were on and off every four hours. The crew, other than the professionals, were members of the Royal Canadian Yacht Club and were called Corinthians.

During one of the L.Y.R.A. races held at Kingston, Len, in charge of my paid crew, particularly distinguished himself. He was a born sailor, as agile as a monkey up forward, and always ready to be hoisted to the top of the mast on the bosun's chair.

Like most of the rest of us, he had one particular weakness, which, I well knew, was destined to break out once during each sailing season. On such occasions, according to him, after stern refusals on his part, he finally—but only under terrific pressure and lengthy persuasion—was induced to take some gin. The result of this was that Len would be poured back on board.

The second day's racing had been concluded and *Nonchalant* lay at anchor fifty yards in front of the gaily bedecked and il-luminated Royal Kingston Yacht Club. I left the club and was put aboard about ten o'clock that evening where I joined some of the members of the afterguard who were sitting in the cockpit. I soon noticed that there was some restraint in the atmosphere and upon inquiry learned that Len had succumbed to temptation, had been put aboard by his tempters, and quietly stowed in the forecastle. The Corinthians at first mistook this delivery for our supplies for the following days, but shortly afterwards the inert parcel turned out to be Len, who soon was able to navigate and climb up the main hatch. When he had succeeded in getting his head and shoulders above the hatch, which faced the cockpit, he surveyed the illuminated shore and club-house with a very glassy stare and was heard to mutter that we were about to make a mooring, this in spite of the fact that we had been there for two days. The members of the afterguard tried to inform him of this with little avail. They finally succeeded in getting him down below and into his bunk. Just before I arrived, he had made his second appearance in the same place and again informed the afterguard that he insisted on making the mooring. Once more he was carried back to his bunk.

I had no sooner been regaled with this story than the head and shoulders of Len appeared, out of the main hatch. He seemed to be completely oblivious of everything; his befuddled brain was obsessed with the idea that we were coming into port, that he should go forward and supervise the mooring, as he always did. By this time it seemed that we would have a repe-tition of this as long as the effect of the gin lasted, and we all wanted to turn in. We got the steward, Len's brother Eric, up on deck, and told him to bring up some seizing. We laid Len in the bottom of the cockpit with his brother beside him. Then

I lashed their legs together with the seizing, so that we could be certain that Len would not end up where he thought the anchor should go. We all went below and had a good rest, and Len seemed to be in perfect spirits the next morning.

In 1933 I had a recurrence of an illness which had affected me first on my return from overseas. That first illness was only slight; at the time I was compared by my doctor to a "run-down storage battery". He told me that I needed some rest after a war that had taken its toll. A little of this cure produced the desired result and I soon was rid of the insomnia that constituted one aspect of the malady.

Fourteen years later, when the same symptoms recurred, I was not able to throw the illness off as readily. I was advised by my doctor to take a complete rest for at least a year. This, fortunately, I was able to do. I followed his advice and retired from all my business activities.

During this first period of enforced rest, my activities consisted of out-of-door sports. As soon as I began to feel the full benefit of the doctor's advice, I decided to see the America's Cup Races off Newport in 1934, and I was fortunate to be able to attend as one of the Canadian observers. I was on the coastguard boat which carried what was described as the "brain trust", which consisted of yachtsmen observers from various parts of the world. My addition to this group must have produced a decided drop in the average yachting knowledge on board. I did, however, get an excellent moving picture record of the magnificent spectator fleet and the series of races which followed.

In the fourth race of this series, I saw *Rainbow* come up to weather and try to pass *Endeavour*, and I started to photograph when I knew that the latter was bound to luff. I was able to secure a complete record of this highly controversial incident. From these photographs mathematical computations were made which seemed to prove conclusively that Sopwith would have been quite within his rights in continuing to luff. However, he bore away hard and lost his way in order to avoid the collision which would have followed and which likely would have resulted in loss of life. His action permitted *Rainbow* to go through to windward and win the race. It was most regrettable that this incident, on which no protest was permitted, should have become a deciding factor in the retention by *Rainbow* of the America's Cup.

Shortly after the race, the Royal Canadian Yacht Club was honoured by a visit from Field Marshal Viscount Allenby, G.C.B., G.C.M.G., and Admiral of the Fleet Sir Reginald Tyrwhitt, G.C.B., D.S.O. After luncheon we had an enjoyable sail with the Admiral of the Fleet at the helm of *Nonchalant*.

In the years between the last two of America's Cup Races, the last of which took place in 1937, *Nonchalant* and her crew continued the struggle in the First Division and maintained their efforts to capture some of the highly prized racing pennants so that on the proper occasions we could dress ship without having to rely almost entirely upon our strings of the international code. We had a merry and conscientious crew who seemed quite content to watch their skipper go through the long and painful process of being educated. Up forward Clarence McKee and the two Pangmans, assisted at times by Alan Wainwright, were soon setting and breaking out with speed and precision the various headsails and spinnakers as the occasion demanded; the afterguard, Newman Mallon, Jack Crean, and John Deacon, were as quickly sheeting down the canvas to its proper trim as it was cracked out forward, including the new quadrilateral jibs which *Nonchalant* carried after I had seen them used by Sopwith. In time the big main was quickly sheeted and winched to its proper trim or jibed when required in the freshest blow; the mizzen was properly doing its maximum share of work on any position off the wind. Others who sailed in *Nonchalant* were Roy Stewart, Gordon Herington, Bill Hearst, and Howard Griffin. *Nonchalant* was a beautiful sight hard on the wind, biting into the sea, sailing in a beam sea with ballooner and staysail drawing, or with her big parachute full as she was running before the wind.

At the beginning of each race, in the cockpit our reliable timekeepers and navigators, Joe Bishop, Dr. Frank Mills, Jerry l'Aventure and Ross Edwards, worked out the starting formula. Then came the thrill before the start, and the manoeuvring which, if carried out as we planned, enabled us to hit the line on the gun with full way and in good position. We had long since learned that a yacht race is never over until the finishing line is crossed, and the skippers with whom we were competing had gratuitously taught me a great many other things.

Nonchalant began to gather a collection of racing flags. In 1935 she was also flying the burgee of the Rear Commodore of the Royal Canadian Yacht Club from her mainmast. In that and the following year she won the Lorne and McGaw Cups. Twice she won the Boswell Cup for a race from Toronto, Oakville, Niagara, and return, a distance of some fifty-eight nautical miles. The record she made when she last won the Boswell Trophy still stands. We sailed this race, which started at 3.30 p.m., in something over eight hours. We were the first ever to finish the race and be at our mooring before midnight of the same day that the race was started. The name *Nonchalant* also appears four times on the Nanton Cup and the record that she made on one of these races still stands.

In one of these races we were in the fleet jockeying for position before the start. *Chimon* was in the race, skippered by the immaculate, goateed and experienced skipper, Aemelius Jarvis. The hard-driving Commodore had forgotten more about yacht racing than I was ever able to learn, and I had not yet been able to hit the line with the wily old Commodore under my lee. This day, *Nonchalant* under full way had her stem almost touching the starting line in weather position on the gun, with *Chimon* right under our lee for the first time. I was at the helm watching the luff of the sail, while Len was watching the face of the skipper of the *Chimon*. All of a sudden we heard Len shout, "Hey, the old man's whiskers are sticking straight out!" It was a good race, and always fun sailing against this grand old yachtsman.

In 1937 I again attended the America's Cup Races, this time in my capacity as Vice-Commodore of the Royal Canadian Yacht Club. I attended the complimentary dinner given for Mr. and Mrs. T. O. M. Sopwith at the British Empire Club in Providence, Rhode Island, to which I carried the greetings and good wishes of the R.C.Y.C. My family observed the races both from the coastguard vessel which again carried the "brain trust", and the

beautiful *Philante* which had been brought over by the Sopwiths.*
My young sons' main recollection of these races seems to be the
amount of food they were able to consume while guests on one of
the coastguard vessels which were used to keep the course clear.

In this series of races *Ranger* was so much faster than *Endeavour II* on every point of sailing that we were provided with
a great spectacle but not a yacht race that could be considered
exciting in any sense of the word. This was a great disappointment to all on board *Endeavour II* and to Charlie Nicholson, her
designer. There was, however, no gloom aboard, as they all
realized they had been beaten by a very much faster boat.

World-wide economic conditions have resulted in the virtual
disappearance of racing classes of the larger yachts. I wonder
when, if ever, we shall again witness the spectacle provided by the
last two America's Cup Races.

I skippered *Nonchalant* in the First Division until shortly
before the outbreak of the second World War. By that time we
had twice won the Lake Yacht Racing championship in our Division. This was an annual event and consisted of three days'
racing at one of the ports on Lake Ontario with the local yacht
club acting as host. The races were alternated each year between
Canadian and American yacht clubs. The efforts and persistence
of our crew also enabled us for two successive seasons to win the
highly prized club championship in the First Division of the
Royal Canadian Yacht Club.

During the years 1932-34 I was a member of the Committee
of Management of the Royal Canadian Yacht Club. I also had
the honour to serve as Rear-Commodore in 1935 and 1936, and
then as Vice-Commodore until 1947.

* Sir Thomas and Lady Sopwith.

PART FOUR

MUNITIONS FOR WORLD WAR II

CHAPTER VIII

THE GREEN TABLE

By 1935 I felt, and the doctors agreed, that the "storage battery" now showed a reading on the hydrometer which indicated that it was fully charged again. I developed a restlessness which was the outward expression of an inner urge to engage again in a constructive occupation. It was clear that at the age of forty-three I was not ready to retire.

I began exploring various possibilities in industry. This time my investigation was guided by my experience in business on both sides of the border, which enabled me to make a much more mature assessment of the requirements for and the possibilities of industry as it affected the economy of Canada.

I had visited many industrial plants both on this continent and in Europe. I had seen many products manufactured, and witnessed the various skills that were employed in their manufacture. From my experience, I had every reason to believe that Canadians were as capable and competent administrators as were to be found anywhere, and that Canadian craftsmen had the ability to produce every type of equipment that is produced anywhere else in the world. I have never been deterred from a course because "it has never been done before". My outlook has always been, "What is required in Canada, and how do we go about providing it?"

One of the first industries I investigated involved an operation on both sides of the border. I decided, however, that what I wanted was an enterprise directly tied to the basic industries of this country and therefore to the development of Canada.

My investigations ultimately resulted in the formation of the John Inglis Company Limited. A company with a similar name

had been established about 1860 to engage in the manufacture
of various types of steel products and machinery. Throughout
its long business history the company had an honoured reputation
in Canadian industry, and its products were widely and favourably known. The people of Toronto remember the old John
Inglis Company best as the builder of one of the ferries which
operate between the city and Toronto Island. During the depression years, the company like many others had suffered serious
financial reverses. At about the same time, its President, the son
of the founder, had died and the company was forced into a
receivership. I felt that the large plants of this company could
be utilized to re-establish the lines for which it had been so well
known, and, in addition, to produce a wide range of new lines
and products. I believed that these products could be manufactured in this country and that a Canadian market existed for
them.

The years preceding my re-entry into business were very un-
settling for me for reasons other than my health. The first time
I saw Hitler on a moving picture screen, raving to his audiences,
I turned to my wife with great concern and told her that I believed that here was a completely unbalanced fanatic. My feeling about him was strengthened by the news of the 1934 purges,
by which Hitler executed many of his associates without the
formality of a trial. The League of Nations, which had been
created after the first war by seven great powers, by 1935 had
already been defied by Italy's march into Abyssinia, and the Japanese aggression against China. Meanwhile the Treaty of Locarno
and the Treaty of Versailles were flouted with impunity when
Hitler marched his troops into the Rhineland in 1936. The
League soon degenerated into an impotent group no longer
capable of carrying out the purpose for which it had been created.
The shadows of coming events were everywhere visible. I remember looking at a Contax camera in the gift shop aboard the
Bremen, and being advised by the purser to buy it because, as he
said, "The Zeiss factory is now almost completely occupied making gun sights."

All actions, portents and indications pointed to one inevitable
end. It was more than disquieting to me, in view of my experi-

ences in World War I, to note how little action was being taken to counter the declarations and thrusts of Hitler. We are all too familiar with the almost complete inertia that existed on this continent during the years preceding the outbreak of World War II. I should prefer to quote an Englishman's assessment of the situation in England. A short time ago I read this in *Old Men Forget*, the autobiography of Viscount Norwich, who as Sir Alfred Duff Cooper was Secretary of State for War during this period.

In the summer of 1936 I was sure that war *was* approaching. I believed that there was only one way of preventing it, and that was to convince the Germans that if they fought they would be beaten. I did not then know that the German Generals were convinced at that time that they would be beaten, and remained so for two more years. . . . Chamberlain knew that he could not save money on the Navy or the Air Force, therefore the Army offered the only hope of economizing. A distinguished General, whom he had met fishing, had implanted in his mind the pernicious doctrine that if we contributed to the cause the greatest Navy in the world and a first-rate Air Force, our allies could hardly expect more. His aim, as his biographer Mr. Keith Feiling has told us, was an army of four divisions and one mechanised division, and he held that the duties of the Territorial Army should be confined to anti-aircraft defence. He also believed firmly "that war was neither imminent nor inevitable, that we could build on some civilian elements, such as the instability of German finance, which made it less likely."*

In 1932 Kurt Jooss conceived the choreography for the ballet called "The Green Table". This ballet was widely acclaimed in Europe and won the International award in Paris. My wife and I saw it later in Massey Hall in Toronto. In the prologue the curtain rose and disclosed a group of impeccably clad and be-medalled diplomats seated around a green, baize-covered table. They apparently were discussing some question of great moment. They argued, they cajoled, they entreated, they pleaded; there was anger; a pistol was fired; and there was WAR.

The curtain rose again and the dancers superbly depicted the significance and horrors of war. The different participants in

* *Old Men Forget*, by Duff Cooper (Rupert Hart-Davis).

the tragedy of war swept across the stage in scene after scene, and in each case the final victor was Death. Death finally took all the survivors.

The curtain fell on this scene and quickly rose for the epilogue which disclosed the same green table surrounded by the same diplomats, carrying on as before. This excellent ballet could not have been better timed or more prophetic; we left it feeling greatly depressed.

It was in this atmosphere, charged with ominous possibilities, that I started to lay plans for the rehabilitation and expansion of the John Inglis Company.

My plans were made and a five year budget was projected. I contemplated first bringing the sales of the existing lines back up to the maximum volume of the old company. Then I had made for me an analysis of the operations, products and production facilities of the plants, and a survey of Canadian requirements. These disclosed that two new major lines of products could be added.

The old company had produced propulsion equipment for ships, but this had been limited to the manufacture of the reciprocating type of steam engine. The most modern type of propulsion equipment, marine turbines, had not yet been built in Canada. I felt that the time had come when equipment of this type should be manufactured in this country, as well as the steam generating equipment and the major auxiliaries required by the modern ship.

It is interesting to look back to a conference held in my office some years ago with the Minister of National Defence, who had just made an inspection of our plant. He had expressed concern about undertaking in this country the task of producing these important propulsion units for the Canadian Navy. I recall answering his expressed concern thus: "They are being built elsewhere in the world, and can be built in Canada."

After the John Inglis Company started operating, I began negotiations which obtained for the company from leading British manufacturers licences to manufacture this type of machinery. I take pride in the fact that today over a hundred ships are at sea powered by the products of the Marine Division of the John

Inglis Company and that Canadian destroyers which participated in the Korean War were powered by these modern marine turbines which were built by us in Canada for the first time. As a result of pioneering successfully in this field, the company was later entrusted with the design and construction of the plant, and the production of the turbines required for the escort vessels which are being constructed under the latest Canadian naval programme.

The production of pulp and paper is one of Canada's most important industries. I discussed with members of the industry the opportunities offered in that field, and found that at that time there was in Canada only one manufacturer of the equipment needed. There seemed to be room for a second source of supply. After we had started to establish ourselves in the turbine field, we began the creation of a new Division and the company has since become one of the major Canadian producers of equipment for the manufacture of pulp and paper.

The plans that were laid years ago to make the company one of the major producers for the basic industries of Canada have almost exceeded my most hopeful anticipations. A great many other new commercial products were added from time to time. The company has grown to be an integral part of the fabric of our country's expanding industrial structure.

By 1936 the danger of war was being freely discussed, particularly among those of us who had survived the tragedy of World War I. We had witnessed the consequences of unpreparedness and the resultant cost in lives. I recalled the heavy shellings endured by our troops while our own guns stood silent for lack of ammunition. My twin sons were not yet in their teens, but I knew that if they were of age when the war came they would quickly fulfil their responsibilities to their country. If that were necessary, I hoped that they would do so under circumstances which would indicate a more intelligent and constructive preparation than we encountered at the beginning of World War I.

A glimmer of activity in this direction appeared as Britain

had just placed an order with another company for shells to be manufactured in Canada. Any sort of a backlog was most desirable at this time and would be of considerable assistance while my company was re-establishing its lines and preparing to add new ones. The old company had produced quantities of munitions in the first World War. I became interested in the production of munitions—and not only because of the commercial possibilities. I was ranging ahead and visualizing other requirements which I felt certain were fundamental and basic to the interests of national and Empire security.

During the ammunition crisis of the first war, Lloyd George dealt with the tragic shortage by decentralizing production and splitting England up into production districts. At that time there was virtually no dislocation of industry as a result of hostile bombing and this procedure resulted, towards the end of the war, in a flow of the required munitions. In view of the tremendous increase in air power and its potential as a destructive force, it seemed imperative that in the event of war the decentralization of the supply of munitions should be made much wider in scope than had been the case under Lloyd George's plan. I felt very strongly that proper secondary sources should be established in other parts of the Commonwealth and Empire, in sufficient time to enable the newly created facilities to provide munitions when required.

The major wars which history has recorded with disconcerting frequency have resulted from the belief of an individual or group that he, or they, could extend their power and territorial holdings. The attempt to express this obsession has always in the past brought untold sufferings to the people of both victor and vanquished, and under present-day conditions would produce results too tragic to contemplate. A fallacy frequently exploited, often as a matter of expedience, that wars are created or incited by munition makers, is a stupidity which has little basis in fact. Exploitation of any kind is not a monopoly of the conditions arising out of a state of war. It is a weakness which is found in individuals engaged in almost every sphere of human endeavour. I am certain it is now clearly visible that the entire industrial and economic structure of a nation is involved in providing not only weapons, but all the multitudinous and complex requirements of war. The responsible heads of enterprises, both industrial and economic, are sufficiently intelligent to realize that the long-range prosperity of Canada and the rest of the world depends upon the preservation of peace, and not on the costly stupidity and tragedy of war.

I have already recorded my early interest in guns; it had increased throughout the years. My wife often reminds me that when we first met I could think of no better method to indicate my affection for her than to permit her to fire a German Verey light pistol, which I had brought back with me from France. When we built our house, I had a pistol range included in the plans and I had the great pleasure of teaching our children to handle a rod and a gun at a very early age. I had acquired, too, through the years a collection of weapons which ranged from the fifteenth century match lock, through the wheel lock, the flint lock, up to the most modern firearms which I used mainly for bird hunting on this continent. I was, therefore, naturally interested in the new Bren machine gun which had just been adopted by Great Britain to replace the Lewis gun in the armed forces. I commenced extensive negotiations both in Canada and in London with the object of having the John Inglis Company undertake the first production of automatic weapons in this country.

My dealings in Canada with the Minister of National Defence, the late Honourable Ian Mackenzie, P.C., and his Deputy, the distinguished and gallant Major-General the Honourable Leo R. LaFlèche, P.C.(C), D.S.O., Légion d'Honneur, LL.D., who has since served Canada with great distinction in other countries as ambassador, showed that they were well aware of the urgency of the situation and the desirability of a programme of joint action with Great Britain, which could result in great economies. In this attitude they were joined and supported by many of their Cabinet colleagues. The Prime Minister, however, was extremely sensitive about any joint undertaking. His feeling was that any such joint undertaking might be construed as a commitment on the part of Canada.

I had an interview in London with Sir Thomas Inskip, Minister for the Coordination of Defence. At this I suggested a programme of combined action, and urged strongly an immediate programme of Commonwealth and Empire decentralization in order to ensure some degree of preparedness against the war which seemed now to be clearly imminent.

Sir Thomas had with him a general from the War Office who did not require to be sold on this idea, and who readily concurred in the desirability of the plan and its urgency. He seemed to be glad to hear a private citizen express himself so directly and emphatically on a subject which must have been very close to his heart, and which he had probably urged repeatedly. As a result of this interview, a conference was arranged with Engineer Vice-Admiral Sir Harold Brown, G.B.E., K.C.B., the able Director-General of Munitions Production for the War Office. He was interested in the idea and particularly in the economy that might be achieved through a combined venture. He told me that they were on the point of considering setting up a second source of supply in England.

During the course of these protracted negotiations which covered a period of nearly two years, we attended the coronation of the late King George VI in 1937. My wife returned to Canada after this event, while I was required to stay over until the Commonwealth Conference took place. I was given to understand that the question of decentralization of the supply of munitions and the joint British-Canadian effort would be included on the agenda of the Conference.

On the eve of the Conference, I was informed that Canada would not raise the matter in deference to the Prime Minister's opposition to any course that might be considered as a commitment prior to the event. So great was the anxiety of some of the Prime Minister's colleagues, and their realization of the urgency of the situation, that at their request the British delegation to the Conference placed the question of the decentralization of supply on the agenda, thus ensuring that it would be discussed.

After my wife left London, I stayed with the late Tom Waldon, then President of the Marshall Wells Company of Canada, who had also attended the coronation. I had met Tom Waldon very early in my business career and the association had ripened into a firm friendship. The head of a great distribution unit which served our four Western Provinces, he was known to Canadian industry from coast to coast, and to the representatives of foreign countries who were interested in merchandising their products in Canada. I always admired and respected the integrity, sound judgment and humour of this great Canadian citizen.

Tom Waldon was very concerned about the trend of events which seemed to be leading to another world disaster. During our discussions he recalled that the head of one of the largest cutlery firms in Germany for some years had paid him an annual visit in Winnipeg. On the occasion of his last visit, he had told Tom that he was one of ten German industrialists whose business activities took them at least annually to many foreign countries, and occasionally around the world. He and the others at the end of each trip reported directly to Hitler on the economic, commercial and political situations they found in other countries. Tom Waldon felt that it would be interesting to get the views of this man, who was a very intelligent and successful industrialist. While we discussed this, he picked up the receiver, called his German acquaintance, and invited him to England. He arrived from Germany the following day.

The German industrialist lived up to his description in every respect. He spoke perfect English, had been badly wounded in the first war, and abhorred the possibility of war in the future. We were told by him that Hitler had done wonders for Germany and had been largely responsible for the rehabilitation of its industry. He was convinced that Hitler had not the slightest intention of planning or provoking a war. He and the other German industrialists, he said, would be opposed to any such course; their main interest was to re-establish their industries in Germany and their products in their former export markets.

We had no reason to doubt his sincerity, although his statements of Hitler's intentions conflicted with our information and beliefs, and we were amazed to discover that he thought Hitler could do no wrong. The alarming aspect of this interview was the realization that if Hitler could so completely mislead, influence, and dominate a man as intelligent as the one we had just interviewed, he must have a following ready at any moment to attempt to execute any plans conceived in his erratic and fanatical mind.

It was arranged that I should have access to the Enfield plant outside of London, at that time the only source of supply in Great Britain, and there I made a study of the tooling plant and the skills required for the manufacture of the Bren gun. My study convinced me that there was no reason why the facilities and an organization could not be provided to produce the gun in Canada. I had already had considerable experience with the introduction and manufacture of equipment from designs made available to us from other countries, and it had long been apparent to me that blueprints alone were not sufficient to avoid the pitfalls that beset the first manufacture of a new product. There is a "know how" that can only be provided by men who have had a long and successful experience in the production of an article. These men must be located in the plant where the new production takes place, and they alone can provide and apply to production that valuable experience which cannot in any way be expressed or conveyed from the blueprint itself. With this type of experience in a plant we had been able to avoid, in other lines, the difficulties encountered by the pioneer manufacturer.

In the course of the long negotiations which took place in England, the War Office agreed to my request to provide a man with such experience. Mr. George Gillespie had been with Enfield for nearly forty years. He was on the Production Committee which had selected the Bren gun, and was in charge of the Planning Department of Enfield. He had been loaned by Great Britain to the United States in the first World War to assist in their production of small arms, and I felt I could not have a better man as Chief Engineer of the new Ordnance Division of the Canadian company if we proceeded with the manufacture of the gun.

The long negotiations were finally concluded in the early spring of 1938. We were entrusted with the task of designing and constructing the facilities to produce the Bren gun in Canada for the British and Canadian Governments. We were to introduce the art of making automatic weapons into this country.

I was by that time fully aware of and shocked at the state of complete unpreparedness and the almost entire lack of production of any new equipment for the army. In spite of all the portents of a war that was fully and freely discussed and that seemed to be imminent, little effective action was being taken to counter the situation.

The announcement of the award of the Bren contract was followed by criticism which developed into a political brawl that reflected very little credit upon the instigators of the attack. I look back with gratitude to my many friends from the ranks of both political parties who gave me wise counsel. They advised me under no circumstances to comment publicly upon the reckless statements that were being made, no matter how provocative or untrue these might be, but to concentrate on producing and delivering the guns. I followed this course, at times a most difficult one. The flow of production started when the first gun was officially accepted one month ahead of schedule.

CANADIANS ARE NOT bound or fettered by traditions or customs. Some customs should properly be observed and their usage continued; others should be abandoned which as a result of progress have outlived their usefulness, and serve only as a barrier which excludes what is new or useful. No individual or nation has ever had a complete monopoly of all the virtues, and we are indeed provincial in our outlook if we do not believe that individuals and nations alike have much to learn from each other.

The adaptability and ingenuity which had made such an important contribution to the distinguished record of Canadian soldiers in battle were evidenced again when Canadians were faced with important tasks in the new field of manufacturing.

Some of the vital requirements for the manufacture of guns are meticulous planning, tooling and tool proving prior to production. The loss of man power to the armed forces had, during the first World War, seriously interfered with the flow of munitions. By the 1930's weapons were so designed that up to seventy-five per cent of female, semi-skilled or unskilled labour could be employed in their manufacture in the event of an emergency.

During World War I ordnance components were still so designed that emphasis was laid on the performance of the weapon only, rather than ease of manufacture. There existed in the ordnance industry a reluctance to adopt some of the existing commercial practices of manufacture which would have simplified production without in any way sacrificing the efficiency of the weapon. This attitude introduced tooling problems which were not often encountered in commercial work and the tendency since that time—as I have very often stressed that it should be—has been to provide a better balance between design and ultimate production. More consideration must be given to the simplification of the manufacturing processes involved in the production of weapons. I am confident that this can be done without in any way impairing their efficiency, provided the production experts are on the team at the very beginning of the design of the new weapon and assist to design and create the prototype.

In 1938 we were called upon to undertake the manufacture of an automatic weapon which was then considered to require a series of the most complicated and difficult manufacturing processes. It might be of interest to mention briefly a few of the problems that were encountered when we began production in Canada.

As I have already indicated, we had a Commercial Division that was producing existing lines and to which we planned to add new lines which we believed were required for the development of the Canadian economy. We were fortunate to be able to get together the key personnel of the old company who had had years of experience with the lines formerly produced. In this Division our problems were the normal ones of administration and manufacture. Messrs. W. T. West, Jim Mackenzie, the late Fred Kalbfleish, and Harry Gowdy, were some of the executives, technicians and craftsmen who, with their staffs, helped to bring the commercial business to the important position which it occupies in Canada and in many world markets today. The wide experience of Mr. Charles Thompson who was supplied to us by Sir Harold Yarrow helped us to establish ourselves in the new marine turbine field. Later, during the war, the technicians of our various licensors assisted us to produce the lines in our Commercial Division which provided the vast array of propulsion equipment, the steam engines and marine turbines, for the naval shipbuilding programme, as well as many types of auxiliary equipment required.

The newly created Ordnance Division provided an entirely new and different problem, and the selection of key personnel to plan and execute the gigantic undertaking on schedule was of prime importance. I was joined by four men who had been associated with me directly or indirectly since I had been engaged in industry in Canada and who had a successful record in planning and executing mass production programmes which called for precision skills. The meticulous organization and planning ability of the late Mr. A. L. Ainsworth, O.B.E., Mr. W. R. McLachlan, both of whom became Vice-Presidents of the company, Mr. P. J. Baldwin, and Mr. A. L. Scott together with the able staff with which they surrounded themselves, formed the nucleus of the team responsible for the great contribution to the war effort made by our company during the war in the production of ordnance, a production which finally extended far beyond the scope of the manufacture of Bren guns.

Our inspection of the Royal Small Arms factories in England enabled us to determine the space, machine tools, fixtures, tools and gauges which were to be set up or provided for the Canadian manufacture, and the special skills and facilities which would be required to carry out the new and difficult project. They disclosed, too, that we must recognize the basic principles and many of the traditions in the manufacture of small arms as we had seen them in factories on the continent. We believed, however, that we should adopt the most up-to-date machine tools available anywhere in the world to provide the most efficient and economical method of manufacture in the new plant. As a result, while the machine tools for our operations were provided mainly from England, the United States and Canada, we also procured certain highly specialized machine tools from Switzerland and Germany.

The plans for the project were based upon discussions with

technicians who had had long experience in the field of arms manufacture. We had a wholesome respect for that experience, coupled with our own recognition and information of the technological progress in other parts of the world. We did not hesitate to adopt and employ new proven processes in order to carry out and expedite the programme.

The complexity of the undertaking is best illustrated when I reveal that the crates which we unpacked in Toronto disgorged nearly twenty-five thousand blueprints for the Bren gun. These were necessary to build the nearly twenty thousand fixtures, tools and gauges, and to provide the lay-out sheets for the twenty-six hundred manufacturing operations required to produce the one hundred and fifty individual components of the gun. One part alone of the Bren gun required the unusually long sequence of two hundred and fifty-two operations before it was completed. This in itself will indicate the preparation and the rigid accuracy of datum faces which were necessary to enable the continuous and essential accurate gauging; otherwise an accumulation of individual tolerances could produce the most disastrous results. It was one of the basic requirements of their manufacture that all the parts of the Bren guns should be interchangeable.

The plan of operation was a simple one: we selected a number of men who had had experience in Canada as similar as possible to the skills which would ultimately be required to produce the major components of the gun, and we sent these craftsmen to England to work in the Royal Small Arms factories. While these men were receiving their training in England and experience in the actual operations which they would be required to undertake on their return, we proceeded with the design and completion of the factory space required. We instructed our men in England to send us detailed information which they considered might be useful in preparing the facilities they would require upon their return, and any other information which they believed would expedite the tooling or production of the weapon itself. All the essential requirements recommended by them were incorporated in the construction of the buildings or their facilities, so that they found their units completely equipped when they returned to Canada.

As I have said, there were nearly twenty thousand fixtures, tools and gauges required for the production of one weapon. For the benefit of the layman whose interest lies in fields other than that of the manufacturing industry, the fixture is the holder that is made to hold a particular part or component in position on the machine on which it is to be cut. The tool is the cutter, in most cases specially shaped, which makes the particular cut required in the one operation. Many cutters of different shapes and sizes are often required for the processes necessary in the machining of one component. The gauges are the accurate instruments which are used to measure the parts or faces of the components while they are being machined, or after they have been machined, to ensure that they are kept within the limits of the critical tolerances required. These vary in their degree of fineness and depend upon the component of the gun; in some cases on the Bren gun, accuracy of machining was required within limits of one ten-thousandth of an inch.

We made a survey of the tool rooms in Canada and classified them as to their competence to handle and produce the huge number of fixtures, tools, and gauges within the critical tolerances required for this kind of manufacture, in sufficient time to enable us to meet our schedule. The survey showed that there were only a few tool rooms in Canada that had had the experience to cope with this kind of work. The vastness and urgency of our requirements made it necessary for us to give a great deal of help to these tool rooms, with the result that we ultimately had approximately forty Canadian tool rooms equipped and able to participate in the work. These were ready and available for the armament programmes and the various types of tool making which they were called upon to undertake for the heavy programmes later imposed by the necessities of war.

While we were developing these tool rooms, we received a great deal of help in the way of tools and gauges from British companies to tide us over until the Canadian firms were ready to supply our requirements. We ourselves, at one time, had selected and employed one hundred and eight British, American and Canadian tool shops used by us to manufacture the tooling in sufficient time to meet our urgent manufacturing schedules. It is not generally known that our company during this war produced the accurate tool-makers' precision gauge blocks which are the accepted standard of measurement and are still today relied upon by the master tool and gauge makers. In the sets of blocks which we produced, one of which was one inch thick at sixty-eight degrees Fahrenheit, an accuracy was maintained within four one-millionths of an inch.

It is quite possible to measure intricate parts which must be manufactured within the limits of extremely fine tolerances. One procedure used in the standards room, which is thermostatically controlled and constantly kept at the required temperature so that there are no inaccuracies due to expansion or contraction, is a very simple one. The tool or part which is machined to critical dimensions is magnified many times and its sharply defined image is projected and then measured upon the ground glass of a machine called an optical comparator. As a result of this magnification, it is possible to check extremely fine dimensions which would be very difficult to determine by any other method. It is unnecessary to add that Canadian administrators and workmen who were competent to organize and manufacture within the limits of such extreme accuracy were equally competent to undertake the manufacture of any other kind of equipment required for the industrial economy of Canada.

Another problem with which we were confronted was the fact that the original British steel specifications for the Bren guns were in terms of standards not familiar to Canadian or American steel mills. The quantities required for our original production did not warrant special heats, and the inspection requirements for these steels were not comparable to the requirements of North American production standards. Canadian adaptability again secured the required results, and steel mill practice in this country quickly succeeded in producing the required Canadian alloy steels to meet the rigid requirements for all the materials. Some of the heat treating problems were entirely new to Canadians, and these were successfully met by Canadian workmen. Considerable improvements were made, which resulted in a better performance from some of the components of the gun.

With the exception of the Ross rifle, no attempt had ever been made before to manufacture modern automatic weapons in Canada. The first venture of this kind originated with our company in March 1938, when we undertook to produce Bren guns and build them in batch production at the rate of some five hundred per month. When western Europe fell to the Germans, Canada became one of the important producers of guns and small arms. As a result of our successful experience with the Bren gun, we were required to undertake rapid and vast expansion of the Bren gun programme as well as the production of other weapons. The Browning aircraft machine gun, which was used as standard equipment on all British and Commonwealth aircraft, and which was pneumatically or electrically fired, was added to our programme. We were required to produce the Boys .55 calibre anti-tank rifle, which was used against light armoured vehicles and which was able to penetrate a three-quarter inch plate at five hundred yards. Later we received six handmade samples of a nine millimetre automatic pistol, originally designed by a Belgian ordnance company. These were produced by us in large quantities. In many cases the shipments of these weapons were flown to their destination. Our company was said to be the largest single producer of machine guns in the British Commonwealth, and the batch production of five hundred a month, called for in the initial plan, grew into the large daily mass production which during the course of the war produced something like five hundred thousand weapons. My prediction as to the importance of the strategic position of Canada as a source of supply in the event of war was fulfilled. Weapons from Canada were shipped or flown east and west to more than fifty destinations in various parts of the world.

To deal with an additional problem, we put into operation a cutting tool salvage plant for all the Canadian war industries. We were among those who led the way in the conservation of scarce metals and the redesign of many of the components which we were manufacturing. These activities reduced costs; they also resulted in important improvements in some of the weapons which we were mass producing. We were connected with the initial development in Canada of methods for the deposition of hard chrome, which led to increased life for tools used in the manufacture of the components. Our company also took much of the initiative in improving some phases of gun manufacture.

In the course of one of my wartime stays in England, General McNaughton informed me that he was not satisfied with the manually operated mounts of the 20-millimetre guns available for anti-aircraft protection, and asked me if we, in Canada, could develop a power-operated mount for it. I assured him that we could, and on my return to Canada I put the project into development immediately.

My lifetime experience as a bird shot had considerable influence in the development of this anti-aircraft mount. I could never understand why anyone attempted to engage aircraft, a fast-moving target similar to a flying bird, with only a single shot, or the relatively small pattern produced by shrapnel. I was convinced that planes could be successfully engaged only by putting up a group of shells which produced a pattern similar to that of a shotgun and which, other than barrage fire, could be obtained only by multiple guns with a high rate of fire per minute. We therefore designed a mount which could handle either one or four 20-millimetre guns. It would provide fire power greater than the existing light machine guns and could follow and engage rapidly and successfully the low-flying high speed enemy planes that were encountered towards the end of the war. It could be either drawn by or mounted on a truck, and could be brought into action with great rapidity.

We built a prototype of the new design and took it to London. General McNaughton was greatly impressed by the possibilities of the quadruple mount. Several of them were consequently made in Canada and shipped to England where, at the proving grounds at Shoeburyness in trials against all existing types, they so far proved their superiority that the mount was adopted that very day. They were immediately put into production and before the end of the war approximately 1,000 of them had been manufactured and sent to England for the anti-aircraft defences. I was later informed that they were used with success against the German V-1 weapons.

We also designed a belt-fed 20-millimetre gun for use on our mounts. It was not put into production, however, since it was not yet ready for mass production at the end of the war.

In addition to the guns produced, we provided large numbers of spare barrels for the weapons of the United Kingdom armies as well as for those of the United States. Shortly after Pearl Harbour, in response to the urgent demands for weapons that followed the attack, our Bren guns were loaded in quantities on bombers and flown to the Philippines. This fact was disclosed shortly afterwards by the Canadian Ambassador in Washington. We also received from the United States a prototype of one of their first recoilless rifles and undertook to complete the production design of the weapon for that country.

I doubt whether the full importance of the fact that this industry was established well before the outbreak of hostilities has ever been completely understood. We had by the start of the war established in Canada many of the new skills and had arranged the special material sources of supply. In addition, the tooling facilities in Canada, so vital to ordnance production, had been greatly expanded to meet our own particular requirements. We were then able to supply technicians to give assistance when called upon to other Canadian plants when they had to undertake armament production for the United Nations.

AT THE OUTBREAK of hostilities, Canada was ill prepared for the aerial warfare which was to play such an important role in World War II. In 1939 we had only a nucleus of trained personnel and a limited number of aircraft. By the end of 1939, however, the British Commonwealth Air Training Plan, operated and administered by the R.C.A.F., had swung into action. The first unit of the R.C.A.F. arrived in England in 1940; the exploits of Canadian airmen thereafter are recorded in history.

Not so well known are the exploits of the Canadian builders of aircraft. Among the organizations set up to construct the planes needed by our flyers was Victory Aircraft, a Crown company with factories at Malton, near Toronto. I was appointed a director and Vice-President of this company, and the record of its achievement is a matter of great pride to me. At the height of production, more than 9,500 people were employed by Victory Aircraft. These, working a forty-eight hour week in shifts around the clock, and provided with incentive pay, succeeded in turning out one Lancaster bomber every day till the end of the war—an impressive record.

When I was in England in connection with my duties as Director-General of the Army Technical Development Board, on one occasion I visited Headquarters of the No. 6 R.C.A.F. Group of Bomber Command which was located in Yorkshire. My purpose was to enquire from the men who were using them if they had any complaints about the performance of the Canadian-built bombers or suggestions for their improvement. In this way I was able to bring back to Canada first-hand reports on the effectiveness and performance of the Lancasters.

I have two other recollections of these visits which might be related here. One is of watching great fleets of allied bombers converging on the coast on their way to carry out their devastating attacks on German held Europe and later of being shown aerial photographs of the destructive results of these raids in enemy territory; the other is of being taken down into the location which housed the Anti-Aircraft Command Headquarters from which all the anti-aircraft defences of London were directed.

THE INCREASING INFLUENCE of Canada among the allied nations can be best illustrated by the part that Canada has played since the war in the standardization of weapons. That our country should have any role in the military affairs of nations would have been undreamed of in 1914. Her military and industrial achievements during World War II had earned for Canada a leading part in the discussions of the United Nations after the war.

In the late 1940's, the United Kingdom indicated that it was about to start production of a new auto-loading weapon, which would require a cartridge of a new calibre. I have always felt strongly on the subject of standardization: it seemed to me that the simplest procedure was for the governments of the allied countries to agree first on the standardization of weapons. In general this policy had been adopted. Thereafter, the Defence Ministers of the various countries could instruct their General Staffs to agree upon a definite specification of the ballistic and lethal requirements of a new round. When agreement on this had been reached, the Development Agencies of each country could manufacture the new round to the standardized specifications. Standardization on one weapon and one round for all of the United Nations seemed to me a fundamental necessity which, in view of the possible dislocation of the sources of supply in the event of hostilities, should have priority over any other consideration.

When the United Kingdom announced its plans for the new auto-loading weapon of a calibre lighter than that used by the other allies, the United States put forward its claim for a different weapon of a different calibre. Each nation urged the advantages of its own round, both of which had merit, backing its arguments with considerations of national pride and the sincere belief of the designers in the effectiveness of their designs. It became very difficult to make a fair and objective assessment and comparison of the two rounds, based purely on the inherent merit and effectiveness of the ammunition itself; and it appeared as though production of two weapons and two rounds would be undertaken and that the whole principle of the standardization of small arms would be abandoned.

The situation had deteriorated to the point where in April 1951 the Right Honourable Emmanuel Shinwell, Minister of Defence, announced the intention of the United Kingdom to commence working immediately on tooling up for the production of the British EM rifle. Had this course been persisted in, the British and United States forces would not have adopted a common rifle. Moreover, it would have reduced almost to the vanishing point the chance of arriving at a standard round of small arms ammunition. Worse still, it made the outlook bleak for any agreement on a standard. If three friendly nations, the United

States, the United Kingdom and Canada, could not agree on one of the simplest and yet most widely used and basic weapons what hope was there for the general cause of standardization?

Canada has always had a vital interest in standardization. In both World Wars Canada was a large producer of weapons and ammunition for other countries. If another war came she would no doubt have a similar, perhaps greater, role. Our own requirement for rifles has never been big enough by itself to provide for an economic rate of production, particularly in peacetime. Consequently, it was in the interest of this country, and of the whole cause of the forces fighting for freedom, that there should be an agreement on the rifle and its round and that the Americans and British should not be allowed to go their separate ways. Moreover, our own Canadian experts had grave doubts whether either the American or the British rifle had been developed to the point where they could be accepted as meeting the specifications for performance that had been agreed to by the three countries some years before.

Considerations such as these led the Honourable Brooke Claxton, D.C.M., K.C., Minister of National Defence, to intervene in an effort to get the countries to reconsider the position at a high level meeting. He sent strongly worded telegrams to Mr. Shinwell in the United Kingdom, and General George Marshall, Secretary of Defence in the United States. At Mr. Claxton's suggestion France was included, and the four countries agreed to meet in Washington at the beginning of August 1951, where each would be represented by a Minister and a senior Army Officer.

Canada, France and Britain were represented by their Ministers of Defence, Claxton, Shinwell and Moch, and the United States by the Honourable Frank Pace, Secretary of the Army. On the military side, the United Kingdom was represented by Lieutenant-General Sir J. F. Whitely, K.C.B., C.B.E., M.C., Vice-Chief of the Imperial General Staff, Canada by Lieutenant-General Guy Simonds, C.G., O.B.E., D.S.O., C.D., Chief of the General Staff, the United States by General J. Lawton Collins, Chief of Staff of the Army, and France by Vice-Admiral Louis Kahn, Secretary General of the Armed Forces. I was appointed Special Adviser to the Right Honourable C. D. Howe, P.C., Minister of Trade and Commerce and Minister of Defence Production. My appointment permitted me to attend the conference as technical adviser to the Minister of National Defence. It was with great pride that I heard the Honourable Frank Pace, Jr. open the conference with the statement that it had been called at the request of the Minister of National Defence of Canada. He added the hope that a solution might be arrived at which would be in the interests of the four nations represented, and the other nations of NATO as well.

The discussions and representations that followed were complete and constructive. The rival designers pressed their claims with energy and sometimes with unintentional humour. When the Wound Ballistics Report was presented, the British delegation indicated that they considered the wounding power of their round adequate up to and including a certain range: as a matter of fact, both rounds were completely lethal at the range referred to. The American report agreed that this round would be effective at this range "in producing wounds which sooner or later would require medical attention and with certain other reservations." Since at the range mentioned it was not a question whether the casualty would require medical attention, but whether he would require an undertaker, I could not resist turning to the Right Honourable Mr. Shinwell, and telling him that after hearing that statement I believed the British had lost their world position as masters of understatement.

In the end the conference unanimously agreed that any decision on the adoption of a new round of small arms ammunition would not affect the immediate situation and that the standard ammunition and weapons in use should be continued for some time. At the same time it was unanimously agreed that, as early as practicable, a new round of small arms ammunition should be adopted.

As a result of the conference the question of the standardization of weapons was brought back on the track and a standard round was agreed upon among the nations of the NATO Pact. Considerable credit for the accomplishment rightly belongs to the timely action taken by the Government of Canada, which was able to exercise an influence in this direction which would have been considered unheard of in my early days in the Canadian Army.

At this conference I was to have an indication of another pressing problem which confronts the NATO nations: the lack of continuity of an administration in the government of our French allies. At the end of the conference, I was bidding good-bye to M. Jules Moch, who was the possessor of a quiet sense of humour. He remarked to me with a somewhat sad twinkle in his eye that he might find on his return to France that he was no longer Minister of National Defence. As it happened, his prognostication turned out to be correct.

CHAPTER IX

THE ARMY TECHNICAL DEVELOPMENT BOARD

FOR MORE THAN five years before the outbreak of World War II, a strategic plan of attack was being formulated by the German General Staff, which included a well organized development programme designed to provide the equipment required to carry out successfully the field operations of the German Army. This development programme made full provision for additional requirements which might arise from the changing art of warfare. The Germans had concentrated their entire technical and research facilities in an organized manner on the weapons and equipment which would be required for the operations.

What a contrast was presented during this same period by the restrictions placed on our own armies. These prevented even a moderate programme for army equipment. During this time, most of the United Nations saw fit to provide only inconsequential amounts for the complete maintenance of their small armies, and the share of these sums devoted to the development of new equipment was so small and insignificant that very little was accomplished.

Thus, when war broke out in 1939, we were confronted by an enemy that had completed an equipment development programme on a scale that compared with the magnitude of the war he envisaged and was prepared to undertake. He had, too, the additional advantage that much of this equipment had been tried out in actual battle conditions by the German contingents sent to Franco's aid in the Spanish Civil War.

Once we were in the war, our first pressing problem was to procure such equipment as then existed, and to manufacture and distribute it to our expanding armies. The problem of organized

175

development had to be undertaken as best it could, concurrently with gearing the nation to full production. We were required to harness the national industrial resources for the production of weapons of war. This in itself threw an intolerable burden on the technical resources and facilities available at that time in our country.

It was not till the spring of 1942 that the creation of the Army Technical Development Board was announced by Colonel the Honourable J. L. Ralston, C.M.G., D.S.O., then Minister of National Defence. Its purpose was to deal with the development of army equipment in an organized manner, while the peak of industrial production was still to be reached.

The Directorate of the Board, as originally constituted, consisted of representatives from a number of organizations. The Ministry of National Defence was represented by the Master General of Ordnance who was Chairman of the Board, with the Deputy Master General of Ordnance as one of the Directors; the Ministry of Munitions and Supply was represented by the Coordinator of Production and the Director General of the Army Engineering Design Branch; the National Research Council was represented by the Acting President. Representatives of the General Staff and the Quarter Master General's Branch attended Board meetings and the development projects were made available to the Naval and Air Services. I was appointed to this Board and assumed the newly created post of Director General of the Army Technical Development Board.

I wished to be free to meet and to deal with officers in the Allied armed services without ever encountering the possibility of being out-ranked by any of them. For that reason I turned down the suggestion that I be commissioned into the army. Director General, as a civilian appointment, was a title of wide implications which left me free to come and go as I wished and confer on every level without difficulty. It was a much more effective title for my purposes than any military rank would have been.

The practical benefit of any development programme will be felt only when new and improved equipment is placed in the hands of troops. It had yet to be fully realized that a period ranging from many months to several years, depending upon the type of equipment involved, was required to carry a new idea through the stages of blueprint, prototype, field trials and the final "freezing" of a design before it could be released for production.

It was the function of the Board to assume full responsibility for, and to allot and carry out the projects for the development of new or improved equipment for the army. We were responsible, too, for the development of projects which we undertook as part of the co-ordinated plan of the United Nations. It was our task to co-ordinate all the necessary agencies in Canada and elsewhere, and we were required to drive through the developments with the greatest possible despatch.

Our first project was a study of enemy equipment then in use. This disclosed that the policy of the German General Staff had been to keep the variety of their weapons to the smallest possible number in order to provide operational strength. These had been designed for quantity production and were intended to provide the highest degree of fighting efficiency. An additional advantage of this type of production was that it simplified the training of troops.

Through the military attachés of the embassies of the allied countries, I arranged that examples of captured enemy equipment should be brought to Canada for our use. I had two ideas in mind. In this way we could familiarize Canadian troops with the equipment they would find used against them in battle. But I had also seen the War Museums in London and Washington and I had in mind that a similar organization might be established in Canada. The equipment brought in at this period was to form the nucleus of the collection of the National War Museum in Ottawa.

The development of German tanks provides an example of their farsighted planning. The Germans had used their tanks during the war in Spain to test the existing models and had then settled upon a basis of design. Four types were then created, all of which, we found, had the following main characteristics.

In the first place the tanks were roomy. This enabled the tank crew to carry out their duties with the greatest possible efficiency. They were designed to provide a good speed to carry out the tactical role assigned to them. We also found that they had a moderately stressed spring suspension of the chassis which provided a very large reserve over the requirement of the tank as it was initially designed. They had anticipated that as the war developed they would require additional armour thickness and increased fire power. The chassis and suspension as originally designed had sufficient reserves to take care of the additions in weight added from time to time as the war progressed, and consequently did not require a re-design of the chassis structure. Finally, the engines in the original design were provided with a large margin of reserve power to provide for the increased weight of armour and equipment which might be needed and which was added during the war.

These tanks were originally designed for mass production. After the Battle of France, the Germans added more armour to the designs for the existing tanks and, in some cases, heavier guns, and used them in the Libya operations in 1941. Before the end of the war still more armour and heavier guns were added, which improved them almost beyond recognition as a fighting weapon, but the tanks were still basically the same as those which had rolled through Poland in 1939. The enemy, we found, was not slow to put the lessons of each campaign into immediate and practical use.

Projects which the Army Technical Development Board undertook originated in the main from two sources. The armies in the field provided us with their requirements, which reached us through channels of communication which we organized; or we received new ideas from outside sources, which we submitted to the army to be appraised. If the army informed us that they were interested in the new idea, the Board proceeded with it as a development project.

The Army Directorates of the Department of National Defence were charged with the responsibility of carrying out each project that came within the range of its particular type of equipment. Each Army Directorate shouldered the heavy new burden of development and made a distinct contribution to the cause of the United Nations. At the same time the ground work was laid for the procedure and method for the development of army equipment in Canada.

An early and important task was to co-ordinate our liaison with the other members of the United Nations to ensure that there was no overlapping of development. A seat was arranged on the corresponding Technical Committees in Washington for the heads of our various directorates. Australia and New Zealand were kept informed of Canadian development through the Canadian Army Staff in Washington, and in London our liaison was conducted through Canadian Military Headquarters, through whom we arranged to have Canadian representatives on the various Technical Committees in England. In London we also exchanged technical information with other members of the United Nations.

In the light of later events it is interesting to record here that Russia, of all the United Nations, while willing to accept information from us, was unwilling to supply us with information on the development of anything but clothing. The Russian representative was quite blunt in his reason for this; in his opinion the representatives of the other United Nations talked too much. After repeated efforts to secure the cooperation of Russia, we were in the end forced to cut that ally off from sources of information on all developments except those in clothing.

Through this comprehensive liaison we obtained the information which enabled us to consider any weapon or development of any member of the United Nations as a possibility for our own armies. We were also able to analyze and assess the value of any prospective development after we had considered it in the light of all the information available through the technical liaison which we had established. Through the Board, the Army Directorates, the National Research Council and their Development Agencies, we organized and harnessed the entire engineering, industrial, research, and technical facilities of Canada from coast to coast to cooperate in the great task of providing our troops with new weapons and in reducing the disparity in equipment that existed at the outbreak of the war between ourselves and our enemy.

For obvious reasons I cannot here discuss the complete list of projects undertaken by the Development Board. They were comprehensive, ranging across the entire field of army equipment. At one time we had in hand more than two hundred projects covering such matters as weapons, anti-mine devices, vehicles, clothing, medical supplies and engineering equipment.

In many of the most vital projects, several countries were asked to work on sections of them at the same time. Nearly a year before D-Day, when I was in London, several different plans were disclosed to me for the provision of harbours to enable troops and supplies to be landed in France after beachheads had been secured. The project, ultimately known as Mulberry, was, obviously, shrouded in secrecy.

One of the plans called for a great rubber contrivance which could be inflated and floated across the Channel. Such a device would be a sitting duck for attacks by aircraft; consequently we were asked to try to devise a type of rubber which would seal itself if perforated by a small shell. We allotted phases of this project to different manufacturers in the United States and Canada who had not the slightest idea of the purpose of the material which they were asked to develop to our specifications. The material was produced and tried out successfully at gun ranges near Toronto. However, as history has now recorded, in the end another plan was put into effect by which cement laden ships were sunk off-shore to provide a breakwater and concrete docks, made in England, were floated across the Channel.

Another project that was undertaken in Canada was transmitted to us by the Prime Minister of Canada from Winston Churchill. It was more in the nature of an Air Force and Navy project and was discussed with me by Dr. Jack Mackenzie, the able and distinguished President of the National Research Council of Canada. Losses among the merchantmen making up the convoys that crossed the Atlantic from this continent to the United Kingdom ran high and in the first years of the war there were not enough escort vessels to supply adequate protection. Patrolling aircraft over the Atlantic would have been a great help, but the range of these was limited. It was believed that if a series of landing fields could be anchored in a chain at intervals across the

WARTIME VISITORS: THE RT. HON. W. L. MACKENZIE KING
Among the statesmen who visited our factories was the Prime Minister of Canada.
With him here are the two vice-presidents of the company, Lee Ainsworth, O.B.E.,
on his right, and W. R. McLachlan. At right rear of the Prime Minister is
Art Scott.

WARTIME VISITORS: COLONEL RALSTON
Colonel the Rt. Hon. J. L. Ralston, P.C., C.M.G., D.S.O., Minister of National
Defence, is followed by my old friend Colonel John Lash, O.B.E., K.C., and
Mr. E. P. Taylor, C.M.G., executive assistant to the Minister of Munitions and
Supplies.

Atlantic, the difficulty of range could be obviated. The obvious solution would have been aircraft carriers, but even had there been enough of them, they would have been much too easy a target for submarines. Some ingenious mind conceived the idea of landing fields constructed from ice, each with its own refrigeration system built in. It was considered that these floating fields could absorb considerable punishment from torpedoes and still perform their function.

Experiments were conducted on the waters of Lake Louise to determine the destructive effects of high explosives on this type of hull. As a result of the tests, and other considerations, the idea was abandoned. It illustrates the kind of original and imaginative plan that was likely to commend itself to Sir Winston Churchill's mind.

Canada's engineers will recall the special projects they were called on to perform by the Board. One of these will illustrate their originality and ingenuity. Before the landings in Normandy, all of the groups charged with the task of planning for D-Day were much preoccupied with the question of mines. It was known that the Germans had evolved many new and ingenious types of mines and that these were used in profusion as part of their coastal defences. The Development Board, among other organizations, was asked to work on anti-mine devices which would aid in cutting down the casualties to be anticipated from these mines. To this end I mobilized the entire engineering profession of Canada. Teams of men travelled across the country, briefing the engineering associations on the problem, giving them all the information we had, showing them motion pictures and examples of disarmed German mines which had come into our possession. The engineers went to work immediately and within two weeks I had their ideas on the subject. It was interesting, and a source of great pride to me that the Canadian engineers, without previous knowledge of anti-mine devices, developed elsewhere, came up with every single device that had yet been submitted for that purpose, as well as other original ideas.

My own duties with the Army Technical Development Board were intensely interesting, although strenuous. We were constantly working against time. In the first place, there was the allotment of projects and the need for driving them to completion. There were also the constant visits to the establishments and agencies which existed from coast to coast on this continent, and in Great Britain, where, in an atmosphere of urgency, secrecy and pressure, projects of every conceivable nature covering every branch of the service were to be found in every stage of development or trial. I became a commuter between Ottawa and Washington, and from this continent to England by bomber. In the earlier days of the war, we crossed the ocean lying across the fuselage head to foot on the floor of an unheated bomber. It was a trip sufficiently trying for a young man. Some of us, not so young, found these winter crossings in the unheated bombers very hard. There were occasions when at the end of such a flight, a passenger would have to be transferred to hospital suffering from exposure. The younger members of the crew developed a little pleasantry on this score: "When we land, shake the passengers three times. If they don't move, bury them."

I found most interesting the contacts made in this kind of work with the War Office in London and the War Department in Washington, as well as the interchange of ideas relating to new equipment. The American viewpoint was very brief and to the point: their policy consisted of "providing the proper and necessary weapons and in sufficient time to be used in this war." In contrast was the lament of a very old and senior British Army officer, who told me sorrowfully that the Navy and Air Force had priority and that as far as equipment for the Army was concerned, he felt that they were "one war behind".

I remember one occasion when I was discussing a new American auto-loading rifle, just after its initial release. There were then minor problems which affected its accuracy. They were soon solved, but the rifle had not yet been adopted by the United States Marine Corps. An officer of this Corps told me, "You see, we Marines are kind of old-fashioned; we like to hit what we are shooting at."

Several months before D-Day I was present at a conference in the United States. It was also attended by members of the Staffs who had been flown in from the different theatres of war. A replica of the various types of enemy defences which Intelligence reports showed would be encountered on the French coast in the course of the landings had been constructed in front of, on, and behind a nearby beach. Each day during the conference we were taken to sea in a landing craft escorted by destroyers, and every conceivable type of weapon, some specifically developed for D-Day, was launched against the shore defences.

At one of these trials, which was conducted at sea, our escort of two destroyers suddenly left us, speeded up, and started to circle us. It was obvious that something was afoot. Later we learned that their detecting equipment had picked up a signal which seemed to indicate the presence, in the neighbourhood, of a submarine. However, nothing further came of it, and it was later presumed that the intruder had been a whale.

After each experiment we met again in conference rooms behind locked doors guarded by U.S. Army personnel and determined whether the concentration of fire had been sufficient to accomplish the proper destructive effect, whether a greater concentration was needed, or whether some modification of the weapon employed would be necessary.

It was known, for example, that the coasts were heavily wired and that if infantry were to be put ashore, something must be done to render this wire ineffective. The original plan included the use of small ships loaded with up to twenty-five tons of explosives to be floated over the wire and there blown up by their crews. The experiments showed that this method was not reliable and that the wire was not always destroyed. As a result a change in tactics was made. On D-Day itself the first assault waves went in at low tide when the wire was clearly visible and the engineers were able to clear a path to the shore.

The wide experience of those present at the trials, who had already planned and carried out landings in other theatres of the war, made it possible to assess the suitability and potential of the weapons and methods which were demonstrated at these trials.

A short time before D-Day, I took off once more for London. I wished to be as close as I could to the actual theatre of events when the great day came. Part of the day I spent with Major-General J. F. Evetts, C.B., C.B.E., M.C., Assistant Chief of the

Imperial General Staff, listening to reports as they came in, watching the progress of the landings. Forty-eight hours after the landings, it became clear that the first stage, at least, of the attack on Hitler's Fortress Europe had been carried through with brilliant success. The thorough preparation, the patient experiments, the research and the planning had not been in vain.

IT WAS ODD to be back in London in war time. It is impossible to make a comparison of the conditions in London in the first war with the suffering and endurance of the people of the city in the second World War. Several times when I was in London I heard the lone, undulating wail of a siren, joined by others in rapid succession, all mounting in intensity, and finally sounding from all directions. These were followed by the hurried movement to the air raid shelters and into the tube stations, as we knew that the bombers were on their way. I have always suffered from claustrophobia; in World War I, if any one particular fear had precedence over another, it was the fear of being buried alive. As a result, wearing my old World War I tin hat, and equipped with gas mask and field glasses, I witnessed the bombing raids from the roof of the Ritz Hotel in the company of the fire watchers stationed there.

We would first pick up the flash of shrapnel bursting in the sky as the anti-aircraft batteries began to engage the bombers approaching London. Later the noise of gunfire could be heard in the distance and finally the crescendo of the guns of London and the loud hisses of the rocket guns as the Command responsible for the anti-aircraft defence of London engaged the raiders. A series of explosions heard above the gunfire, mounting in intensity, indicated the approach of the sticks of bombs dropped by the raiders.

The bombing of Britain, in which nearly 300,000 people were killed and injured, over one half of these in London, was in itself sufficiently grim and tested the endurance of its people as they carried on their tasks. Nearly a year before the event we knew that they would be subjected to still greater tests, as the information in our possession indicated that some form of rocket or guided missile attack would be launched against England. The sites on the coast from which these rockets were to be launched had been under attack by the Air Force for many months before the first V-1 was fired against England.

One night I was on the roof with the fire watchers as the sirens sounded. I picked up in my glasses what seemed to be a single low-flying plane pinned in the beams of the searchlights, approaching us under continuous anti-aircraft fire. In spite of the fire which was concentrated upon it, it did not take evasive action. As it passed to the south of us less than four hundred yards away, it became clearly discernible. Seconds later there was a tremendous explosion. I felt with certainty that the new missile which we had been dreading and anticipating for months had been launched against the city. The keen-eyed fire watchers on the roof of the Ritz that evening were by this time thoroughly familiar with all the different forms of deviltry that London had been subjected to. They were quick to detect that this was something new. As the V-bomb exploded, the watcher beside me turned to me and said, "Say, that was a fishy one."

The guided missiles first arrived singly, then in coveys, and the intermittent day and night bombardment with these highly destructive missiles added further to the trials and the mounting casualties of the people of London.

Later, the city was attacked by the V-2, another form of rocket at least as destructive as the V-1 but less harrowing on the nerves. The V-1 could be seen and heard approaching. Then, when its engine cut off, we could follow its dive to earth or into buildings. There followed a terrific explosion and the column of smoke and debris rose hundreds of feet into the air. The V-2, however, travelled with a speed faster than sound, and its arrival was announced by its destructive explosion.

It was small consolation to see the almost endless flights of our own planes crossing London in the evening as they converged on their rendezvous before proceeding on their way to deliver the destructive attacks which helped to bring the war to its conclusion.

It is a fair statement that only by the grace of God and the accident of geography we on this continent have not been required to endure the horror and tragedies that would accompany the destruction of our cities. We know that destructive forces can now be unleashed which would make the devastation and horror of World War II pale into relative insignificance. Peace in the broadest sense is one of the greatest blessings that can be bestowed on mankind. We know that we must work hard and consistently to obtain and maintain any of the things we value most in life. Peace, therefore, will not just happen: we must play our part and do our share to make it happen and to maintain it. We must also do our best to ensure that those who follow us are equally alert to their obligation. Let us hope that those of our leaders who now have had the experience and grasped the full significance and all the implications of what will happen if we lose the peace will not be followed by those to whom the lessons of history are of academic interest only.

PART FIVE

SOME INTERESTS

CHAPTER X

FISHING ROUND THE WORLD

ON MY FIRST TRIP to Florida in the middle twenties I had my initial experience of deep-sea fishing. At that time we fished for sailfish and landed a few "trash fish", or such fish as do not properly fall within the category of game fish as this term is defined by those who seriously follow the sport of deep-sea fishing. Deep-sea fishing was then a relatively new development in the art of angling.

Records exist of tarpon and tuna being caught on a rod prior to the turn of the century, but deep-sea fishing can be said to have begun as a sport with the formation of the Tuna Club of Catalina some fifty years ago. Here devotees fished off the Pacific coast with rod and reel for both swordfish and tuna.

In spite of the large commercial catches and the domestic consumption of the broadbill swordfish, very little is known about its habits and breeding places, although it is known that in the Pacific it feeds on flying fish. Swordfish have been taken on rod and reel for nearly thirty years on the Atlantic seaboard, where mackerel bait or squid are used when trolling for them. Christopher Columbus, after his first voyage across the Atlantic, brought back to Spain the sword of one of these fish which had been used as a weapon by a native he encountered on the shores of the New World. It reposes, with other mementos of the discoverer of America, above the gates of an old church in the city of Siena, where Columbus received part of his schooling.

Sport fishing for tuna soon reached the Atlantic coast, where the International Tuna Cup Match is held annually in the waters off Wedgeport, Nova Scotia. The teams that enter this competition and compete for the trophy are made up of deep-sea fishing enthusiasts from all parts of the world. Here specimens of the blue fin tuna weighing up to nearly 1200 pounds have been harpooned commercially, but the record of 977 pounds taken on rod and reel stands as the world record up to the present time. Tuna provide a great test of endurance. I have found that it takes a great deal of brute strength to pump these powerful fish up as they make their runs and sound deep down into the sea.

The marlin are surface feeders and like the sailfish are members of the spearfish family. Records exist which show that marlin were taken off the Pacific coast nearly fifty years ago, and later off Block Island on the Atlantic seaboard. Other records indicate that sailfish were taken in the Gulf Stream off Miami about ten years later.

Interest soon mounted in deep-sea fishing. It is a sport which requires a great deal of patience, as the game fish must be hunted and the areas in which they have established their feeding grounds located. Many days may elapse before one of the highly prized game fish is sighted. Experience has shown that "cut bait" is best in trolling for these fish. While I have seen different methods of preparing cut bait in various parts of the world, the principle is always the same. The large, forged hook on the end of a long, braided metal leader is either set into the fish used for bait with the barb projecting from the side or belly, or else it is sewn on to the side of the bait, whose mouth has been sewn shut so that it will not spin, but will seem to swim or skip along the surface of the water when it is being trolled astern of the boat.

Most boats, in areas where deep-sea fishing is well organized, are fitted with outriggers. The line from the rod runs up to the clamp on the outrigger and the bait is trolled astern well out of the wake of the boat's propellor. The advantage of the outrigger is twofold, as I have seen these fish strike in as well as out of the boat's wake. In the first place, the line which runs astern from the outrigger can be adjusted so that the bait is trolled in the best possible position and to the best advantage in any kind of a sea. Again, when the strike pulls the line off the outrigger, the interval of time required to take the slack out of the line is often sufficient to allow the marlin to swallow the bait, or to permit the fisherman to use the "drop-back method", which has been found necessary to hook these spearfish.

The marlin swallows its food whole and on account of the bony structure of its mouth and jaw, it is difficult to hook it other than in the stomach or gills. That is one reason why it is often possible to bring these powerful fish to boat in a shorter period of time than it takes to kill a salmon less than one-tenth of its weight. I have seen different intervals elapse between the time the fish had taken the bait and the setting of the hook when using the drop-back method. In some localities in which I have fished I have seen the hook set as soon as the slack to the outrigger had left the line. In other waters the fisherman was advised to permit several hundred feet of line to run off the reel with the drag completely off and avoiding backlash only, before an attempt was made to set the hook.

In the middle thirties an attempt was made to standardize and categorize deep-sea tackle, so that those interested in establishing records were required to do so within the limitation set for the weight or type of rod, the number of threads and test-strength of the line, and in some cases the type of hook or bait employed. At the beginning very little knowledge was available on methods that should be used to take the different kinds of game fish, but by the time equipment had become reasonably well standardized, a good deal of experience had been accumulated by amateur sportsmen as well as the professional boat captains who had pioneered in this type of fishing. Today, while something is known of the habits of the various species, a great deal remains to be learned about many of the phenomena connected with the habits and migrations of game fish.

One of the main attractions of all types of fishing is environment. The day can begin in a spreading glow of sunrise which illuminates the beauties of the lake, or of the rivers flowing along beautifully wooded valleys or rushing through rugged rocky gorges. The waters of the oceans disclose coastlines of beauty or grandeur; the skies forecast the sea in its varied moods, as the birds wheel overhead. The day may end in a magnificent, flaming sunset. For me these things have always belonged to fishing.

We first fished on both the east and west coasts of Florida and

among the Florida Keys. It was off Palm Beach that we hooked
our first sailfish. Our fishing guide, the son of Captain Herman
P. Gray, one of the great deep-sea fishermen of his day, looked
disappointed as we boated this brilliantly-hued but exceedingly
small fish. He must have believed that I was expecting to bring
in a much larger fish, which was not the case, as I have never been
interested in attempting to set a record in any of my hunting or
fishing activities. My guide, however, possessed high qualifications for the Diplomatic Corps. After casting a somewhat
dubious look at the fish, he told me that he knew of fishermen
who had "fished for years trying to get a small one like that."

We fished out of Pirates Cove and in many of the waters of
the Keys. In these waters we hooked and boated our first tarpon,
and made the acquaintance of the powerful runs and leaps characteristic of this bony-mouthed silver king. It was in the same
waters that we watched the sharks which had come in from the
deeper waters, singly or in pairs, hunting for their meal in the
crystal-clear, shallow waters. We followed them with hand and
gun harpoon as they zig-zagged slowly in front of the boat while
we attempted to take our shot or get moving pictures. Here, too,
we saw a large sawfish with its long, flat, tooth-edged blade projecting from its upper jaw, resting in the shallow waters awaiting
the school of mullets upon which these fish feed. Later I saw
him moving through such a school, with his saw slashing from
side to side killing or disabling the mullet, his course defined
by a milky path as he churned his way through the shallow
waters. Some years later, half way around the world, I saw the
thrasher shark, which is found off the coast of New Zealand.
This huge fish depends upon a similar procedure to obtain its
food: it also swims through schools of fish and thrashes about
with its powerful, long, slender, weighted tail, killing or stunning its prey before it returns to feed.

In the Florida Keys we saw the leopard-spotted ray swimming
slowly ahead of us under the surface of the water, its large wings
moving with the grace of a slow-flying bird. On other occasions
we saw him on the bottom with his bony jaws crushing the crustaceans upon which he lived.

The sharp strike of the mackerel, the sharp-toothed barracuda, or the kingfish, with the runs that followed, contrasted with the pumping required to raise the open-mouthed grouper, or the giant sea bass, which had to be worked up from the bottom following his continuous attempts to sound.

In hunting the elusive bonefish we had first to find where he came in at floodtide. The bonefish is one of the speediest fish that swims in the sea, and is as alert and timid as a trout. We staked our boat in position and quietly awaited the approach of the school at floodtide, hoping to see the transparent dorsal fins or tail as they moved along towards us in the shallow water, seeking and feeding upon the crustaceans on the bottom. I hoped that one would take my shrimp-baited hook which had been cast out well ahead of the boat. My line ran through the small, round lead sinker which lay on the bottom and I watched, hoping to see the slack suddenly tighten, the signal that I was waiting for to set the hook. Then would follow the long, fast runs which have placed this fish in the ranks of the sporting game fish of the world. My wife, however, should be relating this story. She caught the first bonefish, an event which to this day has thrown considerable doubt upon my status as a fisherman.

The equipment I used in my early days of fishing was selected from Abercrombie and Fitch, one of the great havens of sportsmen on this continent. It ranged from the light bone fishing rods to the medium-weight deep-sea rods equipped with reels from 1-0 up to 10-0, the latter for the marlin fishing which I hoped to try some time in the future. I also acquired a 16-0 reel with which the late Zane Grey had fished in New Zealand. I had a light and heavy harness and a cushioned seat which contained a rod socket, invaluable in later years when I was fishing in localities in other parts of the world where it was not possible to obtain properly equipped fishing boats. Without this socketed seat it would have been almost impossible to handle the deep-sea equipment required to take the fish encountered in those waters. I have always carried fly rods on all my fishing trips, and many fishermen will agree that bluefish, mackerel and snapper taken on extremely light tackle provide interesting fishing and some of the real delicacies for the table.

We had one trip with Captain Herman P. Gray, who had

taken two Presidents of the United States on deep-sea fishing
expeditions. We chartered his comfortable, well-equipped *Orca*,
at first intending to spend some time fishing off Bimini. Captain
Gray, however, had long had a hankering to try new waters
and suggested that we fish off the edge of the huge under-water
shoal which extends to the northwest of the most northerly of
the Bahama Islands. This island is the southern outcrop of a
huge semi-circular shoal roughly the shape of half a plate. The
southern edge or diameter of the semi-circle projects above the
water and forms the Grand Bahama Island. From both its ends
the shallow bottom of the sea, covered with only two fathoms of
water, extends to form a great shoal, the outside perimeter of
which sweeps some seventy miles to the northwest of the island's
shoreline.

We left West Palm Beach before midnight and watched the
shore lights disappear in the distance as the broad-beamed, fifty
foot *Orca* entered the turbulent seas of the Gulf Stream. An
easterly course had been laid and at dawn we made our landfall
off Settlement Point at the most westerly end of the island. We
then steered a course approximately northeast, running through
the different areas of water with their startling and varied hues
of colour, and late that afternoon reached the cays that lie on the
outside perimeter of the Little Bahama Bank. From here we
could see and hear the surf of the blue ocean to the north as it
crashed upon the coral reefs; beyond the reefs the floor of the
sea fell to three hundred fathoms.

Each day we carefully threaded our way through the reefs
into the open sea to fish, and returned in the evening to lie in the
shelter of the cays. A few natives lived there in thatched huts
under the most primitive conditions. Their main source of
food was mackerel and the huge snail which is found in the large
conch shells, out of which they made an excellent stew. Their
occupation was "turtling" and "spongeing". They dived for the
large sea-turtles lurking in the coral reefs and collected and dried
sponges which they found in the barracuda-infested waters.
Twice a year the sponge fleet arrived, bringing supplies for
their meagre requirements, and purchased the sponges which

they had accumulated. One of these visits coincided with our stay in the cays.

The natives were not familiar with fish found in the deeper waters of the sea, as they never left the shoal water of the reef, but from time to time on the edge of the shoal they had seen fish in the ocean which we thought were probably marlin. They had also seen what from their description we recognized as bonefish coming in at floodtide to feed. They guided us to these localities, where we had excellent bonefish catches which we used for bait.

Each day we slowly picked our way over the edge of the shoal with some of the natives aboard acting as pilots, and then, heading out to sea towards the three hundred fathom line, we began our daily search for the marlin that Captain Gray believed should be found in these waters. On each occasion we ran into schools of tuna, some of them breaking out of the water and landing with a resounding splash in the sea as they bored up from below in their effort to strike the baits that we were trolling. Each evening we returned, bringing in a number of large fish which we distributed among the natives, who gleefully and immediately salted them down for future consumption.

For over a week we hunted the elusive marlin without success. On the day before we left, Captain Gray, who had been steering with a wheel that extended through the cabin roof, suddenly shouted, "Marlin!", and the boat started to turn and head in the direction in which he had seen them surface. Shortly after, we saw the dorsal fin of a marlin break water as the fish followed the bait I was trolling and continued to do so for some ten seconds or more. My wife, who was sitting on the roof of the cabin with a moving picture camera, was too excited to take photographs of the first marlin we had seen. The big fish suddenly struck the bait, the line came off the outrigger, and before it had a chance to tighten, one of the Captain's men, who was standing beside me, in his excitement seized my rod and attempted to strike the fish which, apparently disturbed by this premature manoeuvre, simply let go of the bait.

A few minutes later, while we were circling in the same area, there was a terrific swirl and a smash at the bait which was being trolled by the other rod; the line came off the outrigger and a well-hooked fish immediately started his run. He took with him about three hundred yards of a parted line which had not been properly wetted. Another loaded reel was put on the same rod; shortly afterwards another marlin struck violently without warning, and commenced his run. This time Captain Gray asked his man to undo his harness, stepped into it himself, got into the seat and began to play the fish; I heard him mutter that he was "going to get that — fish if it's the last thing I do." Before and since, this skilled deep-sea fisherman has added many laurels to his fishing records, but he was not able to boat that marlin, which finally disappeared with a great deal of the veteran's line. This was my first experience with marlin and it stood me in good stead; on the next occasion in other waters, we were fortunate enough to hook and boat three marlin in two days.

We returned to the mainland next day. Our trip saw the beginning of deep-sea fishing in this area, which has since become a well-known rendezvous where deep-sea fishermen hunt and fish for marlin.

IN THE YEARS that preceded and followed World War II, my wife and I spent part of the winter months on some of the islands of the Caribbean Sea or in Mexico. The warm sunshine, the long white beaches with their inviting surf, the exotic flowers and vegetation of the tropics, and the beauty of the plains, hills and mountains over which we travelled were joys sufficient in themselves. I am afraid, however, that on these journeys I always succumbed to the lure of the sea and enjoyed hunting and fishing in the new waters, often without much success.

In the early thirties, my wife and I motored from Mexico to Acapulco over the old road which twisted and curved its tortuous way through the hills. The narrow road over the mountains in places seemed to hang on the edge of a precipice. There were occasional right-angled turns near which a few rough crosses had been erected. Our driver casually informed us that certain drivers and their passengers had been "unfortunate" at these places. We

WARTIME VISITORS: SIR JOHN DILL
We were also visited by Field Marshal Sir John Dill, G.C.B., K.C.B., C.B.,
C.M.G., D.S.O., Head of the British Joint Staff Mission to Washington.

QUADRUPLE GUN MOUNT

General McNaughton informed me that he was not satisfied with the manually operated mount of the 20-millimetre gun available for anti-aircraft protection and asked if we in Canada could develop a power operated mount. On my return to Canada, I put the project into development immediately.

understood this better when we passed several loaded buses that came rollicking towards us with passengers hanging on to or seated on the swaying roof.

Acapulco was founded in the early sixteenth century as a harbour for the galleons which sailed from the Far East. On our first visit we found that this busy city, situated at the foot of the heights which overlook the blue waters of the Pacific, had little accommodation for visitors. The new road and air transportation have since made this one of the great Mexican resorts; it is now well known to travellers and fishermen the world over. I fished there in the early days with very primitive equipment. Its waters were noted for their sizable sailfish.

My most vivid recollection of fishing off Acapulco in the rolling Pacific is of a very large, ugly, powerful and persistent hammerhead shark which gave me a long and exhausting tussle. I finally cut him loose after I had brought him sufficiently close to the boat to enable me to take moving pictures.

Our travels also took us to Cuba. On our first visit we had been fishing in the Florida Keys, and it was not until we had boarded the boat and were well out to sea in the Straits of Florida that I became aware of the notice which prohibited the entry of firearms into Cuba. I had with me, included among my fishing equipment, a .45 calibre automatic pistol and a 7.9 mm. carbine which I used for killing shark, as well as a light Norwegian harpoon gun and the harpoons, line and barrel that formed part of its equipment. In view of the notice, I was somewhat apprehensive as we passed the sixteenth century Morro Castle at the entrance to Havana harbour. After we docked my apprehension was confirmed, for a convention of customs officials descended upon my assortment of firearms, and seemed to believe that in me a one-man revolution had arrived in Cuba. I explained to them the purpose of the equipment and they were particularly interested in examining the set trigger on the Mauser carbine. They finally decided that even if my intentions were as sanguinary as they would appear, it was unlikely that I would harpoon anyone, so they contented themselves with taking into custody the automatic and the carbine during my stay in Cuba.

We had arrived just a few days before the new and imposing

State Building in Havana was to be formally opened by the President of Cuba, and I inquired if the seats which had been arranged for us were sufficiently close to the President to enable us to get a good view of the proceedings. We were informed that as conditions at the moment were somewhat unsettled in Cuba, a position in close proximity to the President and his party would not be viewed with any great degree of satisfaction by the companies which held our life insurance policies.

Marlin and broadbill swordfish had been taken off the north shore of Cuba for a good many years by commercial fishermen. I learned that these fishermen moved with the Gulf Stream and used baited hand lines as they drifted along in the current. The boat end of the hand line was attached by a slipknot to a limber stick stuck over the side of the boat and when the fishermen saw this pulled down, they knew that the bait had been taken. This is not unlike the drifting method of fishing with rod and line sometimes employed in New Zealand waters when the fish are not taking well on the surface. There a small inflated rubber balloon is tied to the fishing line, and the bait allowed to sink as the engine is cut and the fishing boat drifts with the current. The line between the floating buoy and the rod is kept near the surface by the rubber balloon which bobs on the water some fifty yards from the side of the boat.

The activities of the commercial fishermen informed us that the season for marlin was between the months of March and July. We also learned that the mako shark, which, on account of its fighting qualities, is considered one of the sporting game fish of New Zealand, was to be found in these waters and that sizable peto or wahoo were caught in the winter months.

My deep-sea fishing in Cuba, however, consisted of two ventures in the days long before boats were available for this type of fishing. On the first occasion I went out in a large skiff with the heavy harpoon equipment on board. As we were leaving the harbour, the blade of the propeller suddenly came through the hull of the skiff. At this point we decided that we had better get ashore, which we succeeded in doing after strenuous bailing. On the second venture, we went out in a very large boat which was completely safe and adequate for the shark we encountered at the entrance of the harbour. Under these circumstances, we did not pursue the hunt of the marlin any further. By the early thirties properly equipped fishing boats were available and very good sport fishing has since been enjoyed in these waters.

Possibly one of the most interesting fish fables concerning Cuban waters was related to me by General Fulgencio Batista, the present President of Cuba, when some years ago he visited my home in Toronto. To get the point of the story, one has to understand the structure of that speedy fish, the porpoise. Anyone who has observed the head of this mammal has been surprised to find that it is not provided with the gaping jaws of other fish of similar size. Instead the head narrows down to two elongated jaws which look more like bills, and which are provided with small teeth which permit him to feed on very small fish only. The President told me that the well established belief about the porpoise being the sailor's friend was all a myth. The story had its origin when a sailor falling overboard near the shores of Cuba landed in the midst of a school of hungry porpoise. These porpoise, with their long, small mouths, rushed at the sailor and in their desperate but futile effort to devour him, only succeeded in pushing him ashore.

During our travels about Cuba, we had with us as a guide a journalist who spoke excellent English. I have rarely met an individual, however, who was so completely devoid of any sense of humour. As we travelled along the roads on one of our first trips on the island, we passed an oat field. We asked him what kind of grain it was. He was unable to recall the English word and without a flicker of an eyelid he said that it was "horse meat".

I had for some years been interested in antiques. We visited several of the antique places in Havana without our guide, who was interested in our purchases. I could not resist the temptation to pull his leg when I related the histories of some of the objects which we purchased as these were told to us by the dealer. I had bought a very finely engraved suit of armour which the dealer claimed originated in the seventeenth century. I described this to our guide as best I could, and untruthfully added that the dealer had said that it had been worn by Julius Caesar. There was no comment from my guide, but on the following day he told me that he had been thinking over what I had told him about the history of the suit of armour, and he had come to the conclusion that if the dealer had said the suit had been worn by Julius Caesar, the dealer undoubtedly was "a — liar". In this my guide was not too far from the truth; this suit of armour was one of the few pieces that I have purchased which on inspection by the Curator of the Royal Ontario Museum was pronounced a fake.

Another fishing trip took us to Jamaica, which still retains its aboriginal name although it was christened Santiago when Columbus discovered and landed on the island in 1494. We had heard that the seas off its shores would provide interesting hunting for spearfish. Some had been taken off Kingston, but their haunts had not yet been established off the north shore.

We motored from Kingston over the hills across the island to Montego Bay, where we hoped to enjoy the beaches and waters of the Caribbean, search for marlin in the waters off the north shore and hunt the alligators that lurked in the mangrove swamps along the southwestern shore. We travelled along the north shore through St. Anne's Bay, where Columbus was stranded for a year in 1503 and is said to have awed the natives by predicting an eclipse. At Port Antonio we spent a few days, but were unable to locate the marlin that we believed should feed in these waters and which in the years that followed were often taken there.

At Port Antonio I heard that large kingfish had been taken in the waters off Lucea, thirty miles west of Montego Bay. When I arrived there, I found waiting for me a dugout canoe equipped with an outboard motor. We left the large harbour, reached the open sea and followed the shore in a westerly direction, trolling in a fairly heavy roll. I had brought my fishing seat, which again stood me in good stead. I was fishing with a light tarpon rod, 4.50 reel loaded with thirteen-thread line, and trolling a Japanese feather on the end of my light braided wire leader. The guide told me that we were in the waters where I could expect some action from the kingfish. Almost immediately I received a hard, vicious strike, and several hundred feet of wetted line were torn off the reel on which I had fortunately set a very light drag. The bait had been hit hard by some kind of surface feeder who proceeded to put on as speedy a rough and tumble performance as I have encountered in my many years of deep-sea fishing. After a series of runs along the surface, and deep sounds, and after considerable time had elapsed, we finally boated the cause of this trouble. I had hooked a member of the mackerel family, the sharp-nosed, streamlined, swift-swimming wahoo. This tropical game fish was called the "Queen Fish" in the Caribbean. In Hawaiian waters he was called the "ono", meaning sweet, though I do not know anything that could cause this prefix to be included in his description when he was alive. He is one of the hardest bait hitters I know. The voracious lead-striped speedster apparently will strike almost any kind of bait and consider later whether or not it suits his fancy. Some consider that the wahoo provides the link between the sailfish and the marlin, but this is in the realm of conjecture only, along with many other mysteries yet to be solved relating to the history and habits of the great sport fish of the seas.

We continued our fishing and boated three wahoos. The wind had freshened considerably and our dugout canoe did not provide sufficient tonnage to cope in either comfort or safety with the rough seas which were rapidly building up. I was wet, tired and happy when we turned into the shelter of the lee provided by the headland as we entered Lucea Harbour.

I had heard that tarpon were to be found in the Cabaretta River, which flows into the sea on the other side of the island just west of Savanna la Mar. In the mangrove swamps along the south shore alligators were plentiful, though they were not found at all on the opposite side of the island.

I found tarpon in the river on several occasions, but they would not take in the early spring and contented themselves with rolling in the river, paying not the slightest attention to my changing baits.

I frequently travelled along the road that swings to the west from Montego Bay, up Mount Pleasant Hill, and across the island through the impressive-sounding landmarks—Haughton Grove, Chichester, Ferris Paradise and Savanna la Mar—to meet the guide at the rendezvous where he had made arrangements for alligator shoots. On these hunts our party would move to the shore and enter a dugout canoe. My attire was a sun-hat, a pair of shorts and rubber-soled shoes. We proceeded west along the shore in a sea which sometimes became quite choppy from the on-shore winds which usually sprang up in the afternoon, and made us spend much time bailing our canoe. In the sunny clime and the shallow warm waters the swamped canoe was not at all un-comfortable and even added to the pleasure of the sport. A party of natives followed on shore, keeping slightly astern of the canoe; one of its members carried my gun, a 7.9 millimetre with set trigger and 'scope, and field glasses.

We beached the canoe before approaching the mouth of any small tributary running into the sea from the mangrove swamps and then carefully approached the mouth of the stream to see if there were any alligator basking along the shore. Sometimes we got a shot in this way; but if no reptiles were to be seen at the mouth of the river, the natives would silently disappear up-stream moving with the agility of monkeys along the stilt roots and branches of the mangrove trees. In the darkened grove, they perched in the branches watching the turbid waters. At the mouth of the river I awaited their signal, a low whistle to indicate that one of them had sighted an alligator. When I heard this, I also clambered along the roots and branches of the mangroves until I reached the tree in which the native was seated. He pointed out what was often the only indication, the forehead, or the eye or eyes of the alligator lying in the water, almost com-pletely concealed under fallen leaves or in the shadows of the grove. The report of the shot would reverberate through the swamp and we would see the reflection of the white belly of the reptile as it slowly turned and sank to the bottom. The alligator was then recovered by means of long poles with parts of the branches projecting from the ends.

On one occasion when I heard the whistle upstream and reached the native, I had considerable difficulty in distinguishing the only part of the alligator which was visible, his one eye. After I had fired, he turned and sank to the bottom. At this moment I heard another whistle at the mouth of the river. I laboriously clambered downstream through the grove to the mouth of the

stream. I looked upstream from behind cover and saw thirty
yards away a small alligator whose head appeared on top of the
water about ten feet from the shore. He turned over when I
fired and slowly sank to the bottom. The natives who had scattered along the shore and the river congregated at the foot of
a tree which was overhanging the water and whose outermost
branches were just above the point where the alligator had disappeared. Several natives immediately shinned up the tree with
their long sticks and one, more daring than the others, moved out
to the light, outermost branch overhanging the water which
broke off and precipitated him on top of the dead alligator, and
near any other live alligators which might be in the vicinity.
In the interval between the time that he struck the water and
reached the shore, he not only learned to swim but broke all
world speed records as well.

The alligators we shot along this shore and in the swamps
near the New Savanna River averaged between six and eight
feet in length. Each year they were responsible for the maiming
or death of a number of natives in the vicinity. They had frequently attacked young children and goats, which they dragged
under water and then to their holes along the river.

For several years I had heard of one particularly vicious specimen which had killed several victims. Although it was considered to be a record size for the island and constantly hunted, it
was still at large in the open swamp just west of Savanna la Mar.
One season I had been fishing for tarpon in the Cabaretta River
with no success. After my morning's fishing, I had gone to Blue-
fields for lunch, when suddenly some natives burst in, and in
great excitement told me that they had "holed in" the "big fella"
that they had been hunting for the last few years. I jumped in the
car and soon reached the marsh. There I found a large group
of natives assembled at the scene. One of them had discovered
the alligator swimming to and entering a hole along the bank
of the creek which ran through the marsh. With the assistance
of several other natives he had driven a double row of three inch
stakes across the entrance to the hole. They had then woven a
long rope out of bark and made a slip knot at the end. The
noose had been placed in the water which showed in the open

portion of the hole, and which extended some five feet back from the river. This was the entrance to the tunnel, or lair, of the alligator. It extended back under the quagmire which formed the shore.

I was told to stand at the edge of the hole with my rifle ready. Four of the natives with long, pointed poles took a position in a row a few feet apart and started to probe into the quagmire, working back inshore from the hole. Wherever the poles broke through the quagmire they knew they were following the course of the tunnel. If they touched the alligator he would likely swim out of his tunnel; his jaws would get into the noose of the slip knot, which would be drawn tight by the native, and I was simultaneously to fire the usually fatal shots into the eye and brain.

After the probing had progressed some twenty feet inshore, one of the natives struck the back of the alligator, who was not at all amused by the procedure and indicated his annoyance by squaring his legs on the bottom of his tunnel and heaving his powerful body up and down against its top. The marshy ground on which we stood received a good shaking. My guide and his crew were concerned by this demonstration of power and shouted to me, "Hey, Mister, he's a big fella: when he comes out, shoot him and shoot him good."

Another prod started the reptile on his course. Soon, preceded by a heavy surge of water, the largest alligator head and snout I had ever seen suddenly emerged from the hole, at whose edge I was standing. The native with the slip knot suddenly remembered an important business engagement elsewhere and departed. A large head and shoulders smashed violently against the stakes, while a long, wide-open pair of hissing jaws emerged ready to take my leg or any other part of my anatomy as a small hors d'oeuvre.

My first shot passed through the jaws about three inches in front of the eye, but he was fortunately stunned by the blast of my rifle, which was fired at pointblank range. A second shot struck him in the eye, and the quiver which ran along his body indicated the fatal brain shot. He turned out to be the record for that year; though considerably smaller than the alligators which I later saw in India, he was one of the largest killed in

Jamaica. He was twelve feet long and weighed just under five hundred pounds. The killer was carried with great glee into the nearby village, the home of one of his victims.

THROUGH THE YEARS I had often heard and read accounts of the fishing in the islands of New Zealand. Tom Hyslop, the High Commissioner of New Zealand to Canada, with whom I had fished, still further whetted an appetite that required little encouragement. We decided to visit these islands.

We flew to Auckland and from there started our journey to fish the inland waters of the North Island, well known for their rainbow trout. We motored south and stopped on our way at the Waitomo Caves, caverns formed as the Waitomo River follows its winding course under a hill. It is difficult to describe the pale blue, phosphorescent glow which faintly illuminated these caverns as the boat in which we were sitting was pulled silently along the water by a cable which had been run through the cave. This eerie fairyland is produced by the glow of millions of minute creatures which are suspended from the roof and sides of the caverns. The myriads of small flies which are hatched on the banks and edges of the underground river, attracted by the faintly illuminated ceiling of the cavern, fly up and are caught on this sticky strand which the glow-worm then hoists up until he is able to reach and devour his prey. The slightest sound will cause the insects to extinguish the unusual display and they will then remain in darkness for several hours before they again venture to produce the glow.

Huka Lodge is a fishing resort known to fly fishermen the world over. Ideally located on the fast-flowing Waikato River, famous for its rainbow trout, it is best known for the excellence of its food, its comfort, and its hot thermal bath, set among the colourful flowers. These, together with its fisherman-owner Allan Pye, almost make the large rainbow trout, which I took from the waters in front of the Lodge as well as the other pools along the Waikato, seem incidental even to a fisherman.

One of the strangest and most interesting sights that we encountered was "the skirmishing line" of fly fishermen which stretched across the strong rip of the Waitahanui River where it flowed into Taupo Lake. Twenty-five fishermen in waders stood in the lake shoulder to shoulder in a row, waist-deep in the powerful rip fifty yards from the mouth of the river, casting a wet fly into the waters of the lake where the rainbow were congregating and feeding, or preparing to proceed up the river. I joined several other fishermen on shore waiting to step in and fill a gap as members of the line who had taken their quota waded back to the shore. After a fisherman had hooked a fish, he would step back behind the line, hold his rod high over his head, and work his way to the extreme right flank of the row while the other fisherman behind whom he was passing would cease casting and partially strip or reel in their lines until he had cleared all of them. The fisherman would then play his fish in the normal manner and work his way towards the shore. The difficulty of fishing under such conditions and some of the comments can be imagined. On occasion I saw at least four fishermen step back and start moving along towards the end of the line at the same time. However, it was new and exciting, for, when the trout were taking, it provided one continuous round of action with never a dull moment.

We did not pursue our fishing too vigorously as there were so many interesting things to see on the island, with its rolling hills and pastures, where the climate is such that cattle and sheep feed and roam the year round without requiring any shelter. We took the usual trips through the thermal areas and watched the various geysers at the times they were scheduled to play. In and about Rotorua we visited the Maori village, guided by the well known and personable Rangi. We thoroughly enjoyed the poi dance, which resembles the movements of the dances of the Hawaiian Islands, but in dancing the Maoris very dexterously spin the pois. These are balls which they manipulate at the end of a thong and with which they strike their swaying bodies, and so add to the rhythm and beat of their chanting. It would be most unfortunate if this delightful dance, in which the younger Maoris seem to take so little interest, should be lost to posterity.

Before we left Huka Lodge, we found that arrangements had

been made for us to fish in two different stretches of water off
the North Island, well known to deep-sea fishermen. We first
proceeded to Tauranga where we boarded a fully found forty-five
foot cruiser in charge of a well known deep-sea fisherman, Captain Hunter, who was ready to take us to Mayor Island, which
lies about twenty-five miles to sea almost due north of Tauranga.

Accommodation available on the island was somewhat primitive and my wife decided to stay at Tauranga. We started out
in the *Moana* and set our course for Mayor Island which we
reached after several hours at sea. First we fished for the kahwai,
with which we stocked our fish box and which we prepared
for bait when we trolled for marlin. We cruised to the east side
of the island and found the cove in which the anglers fishing
in the waters off this island had congregated. We were told
that this cove provided the harbour and shelter for the fleet as it
came in after the day's fishing. In the afternoon we joined the
fleet, which was trolling off the coastline where the blue and
black marlin feed from February to April. We saw several of
these fish played and boated by some of the fishing cruisers in
our vicinity.

I did not get a marlin strike that afternoon and swung my
bait away from several large sharks when I saw their fins cutting
the water on either beam or astern, and near the course along
which we were trolling. Before dinner the fleet converged on the
cove, some of the boats flying their marlin flag or flags, according
to their success during the day. We joined an enthusiastic group
of deep-sea fishermen at dinner on shore, watched the fish
weighed in, and then went aboard so that we would be ready
for an early start on the following morning.

On the two days that followed we had, and witnessed, interesting fishing. On the *Moana* we boated three blue striped marlin which we gave to the commercial fishermen who used their
flesh as bait for the extensive snapper fishing, which furnishes
one of the most delicious staples of New Zealand.

The fleet available for sport fishing off Mayor Island was particularly well equipped and many boats, including our own
cruiser, had a ship-to-shore telephone as part of the installations.
A central clearing station was located at Tauranga and it was

interesting in the evening to hear the members of the different
fishing cruisers talking to each other or to Tauranga, and relating
the results of the day's fishing. I was able to communicate with
my wife and keep her informed of our daily activities on and
off the shoreline of the island.

Around this island about three hundred marlin were boated
each season during the run. Of these about ninety per cent were
blue striped marlin which run anywhere from two hundred to
five hundred pounds; the remainder were large black marlin,
nearly double the weight. In addition, of course, a great many
mako sharks were boated; these are quite rightly considered a
sport fish in New Zealand. I have seen this powerful, hard
fighting fish, whose gills seem to be the only characteristic that
identifies him as belonging to the shark family, put up a terrific
and spectacular battle before being boated by a tired fisherman.
Thrasher shark are also found in these waters and in view of
their size and weight require strenuous handling before they can
be boated.

From Tauranga we motored north to the long, narrow pen-
insula that juts into the Pacific from the uppermost coast of the
North Island, and travelled to Waitangi, around which is centred the early history of New Zealand. It was there, on the
lawn in front of the house which is now included in the national
reserve, that the treaty was signed which composed the troublous
and warring situation between the British and the Maoris. Here
we had our first view of the Bay of Islands, where the author,
Zane Grey, first established his fishing camp, and here we spent
several days in the company of fishermen from other parts of
the world. We fished each day in the vicinity of Cape Brett, a
picturesque coastline studded with caves. At noon we anchored
in a lee near one of these and lunched aboard our fishing cruiser
while we watched the water wash in and out, or through, these
erosions of the seas created through the ages.

My latest recollection of fishing in the Pacific is of the Fiji
Islands, where we spent several very pleasant days at Korolevi.
Here I saw natives fishing in the same way their ancestors must
have done throughout the ages. They were still obtaining their

food by spearing the small fish found in the shallow waters near the shore.

In the museum at Suva the curator showed me a photograph of a very savage-looking Fijian who, he told me, had died some years ago. This man had been known as one of the most savage cannibals on the island, but the curator assured me, as the result of the work of missionaries, "he died a very cultured gentleman".

CHAPTER XI

COLLECTOR

ELSEWHERE IN THESE PAGES I have written of my interest in fishing, hunting and sailing. Out of my interest in guns, as I have mentioned, grew my collection of weapons. It is, then, not surprising that from my activities as a manufacturer I have developed over the years an interest in, and an insatiable curiosity about, the means by which objects were manufactured, from ancient times down to the present. This in turn led to my becoming a collector of some of these objects. It was a happy coincidence that my wife, in her travels before we met, had acquired a similar interest in the arts and crafts.

It should be made quite clear from the start that I lay no claims to being an expert in this field; to become one would require a lifetime of study. Throughout the world there are experts whose judgments are based on long experience, and whose conclusions are formed from a profound and thorough knowledge of their subject. In my activities as a collector I have leaned heavily upon the experience of such men and upon the study of books written by the authorities in their fields.

In the spring of 1919, the Mayor of Brussels, Burgomaster Max, who did everything in his power to make the stay of Canadians in Brussels a pleasant and memorable one, learned of our visits to the museums and art galleries of Brussels and suggested a visit which he thought would be interesting and instructive to us. He made arrangements for us to see Gaasbeek Castle, originally a thirteenth century fortress, which was being left to the state by its owner, the Marquise Arconati Visconti. Situated in the centre of a ninety acre estate, it had survived the vicissitudes of the centuries in spite of the fact that it had been besieged, pillaged, and partially devastated. It was in an excellent state of preservation and had been continually restored and rebuilt, and it retained a complete collection of the art of the Middle Ages, which had been added to by the owners throughout the years. We were shown through the castle by the old Marquise herself. Even the huge kitchen had been kept in spotless condition and both it and the dungeon contained some of their original equipment. There was also a huge library containing many early documents, some of which related to the barony of Gaasbeek and the Visconti family. I was interested and fascinated by the luxurious furnishings, the fine tapestries, the early furniture and plate. The fine examples of carved boxwood and ivory especially appealed to me.

This visit woke in me a latent interest in the arts. From that time on I made it a point in every country and at every opportunity to be "exposed" to the many fine objects which have been created by man throughout the ages. Possibly because the technical skills always appealed to me, my early interest focused on the examination and study of the arts of the later Chinese periods. We found great pleasure in the superb and meticulous craftsmanship of China during the reigns of the Emperors K'ang Hsi and Ch'ien Lung which spanned the latter half of the seventeenth century and all of the eighteenth century. The former Emperor founded an academy for the applied arts in Pekin and greatly encouraged the production of objects of art of the materials worked at that time, which included metal, lacquer, jade, enamel, wood and ivory. Ch'ien Lung continued and encouraged these interests and during his reign we find the minute and skilful carvings of the time in the red Pekin lacquer, and the wealth of ornamental detail and wonderful exhibition of technique which characterized the Chinese art of the eighteenth century.

In the early twenties I brought back with me from New York a Ch'ien Lung vase carved from an ivory tusk. The main carving around the centre of the vase depicted a thanksgiving procession, a custom of the time which was an expression of the people's gratitude for the harvest they had reaped from the sea. The carving also depicted a game of football and the children's game of "blind man's buff", both of which were popular pursuits of the day. The panel carved into the neck of the vase showed the Chinese playing with pin-wheels and flying kites, the latter one of the ancient sports of China and Tibet. Later we acquired other examples of ivory craftsmanship.

When I studied the many applications of ivory I soon found that I was taken back to the very earliest periods of civilization, to those ages where some of the early records in our possession are the graphic ones which had been executed in horn, bone, and ivory. Many of these records had survived and escaped destruction because of their low intrinsic value. This is particularly true in certain centuries of the post-Christian era where the stories unfolded by the ivories of the period fill in the gaps and provide much of the information concerning living conditions.

The elephant was found not only in Asia and Africa, but aeons ago in the temperate and northern parts of Europe and America; we can readily understand then why this material, which could be easily fashioned, worked and inscribed, was used by man in different ways from prehistoric times. It was logical that my investigations into all the uses of ivory should take me quickly into a study of the history and the art of the entire world throughout the ages.

On those early business trips to New York, I frequently examined a very finely designed and carved amber ornament of the Ch'ien Lung period. It was amber of a very deep rich colour and, when the light shone through it, one could see embedded in it the wings of tiny insects. Millions of years ago, when the forests were submerged by the seas, the resin of the pines became fossilized and on account of its viscous nature carried within itself a partial record of the insect life of the time. It is on the ocean beds and the beaches that this substance we call amber, which has been in use since legendary times, is found. The ancient Greeks believed it was the solidified tears of the mother and sisters of Phaeton, that reckless youth who drove the chariot of his father, the sun god Apollo, nearly destroying the earth. To save the earth, Jupiter slew him with thunderbolts. I later acquired this ornament, which has given us all much pleasure through the years. It is so placed in our home that in the daytime the sun streams through it; at night the same effect is produced with a small light bulb, well shielded, behind it.

FOR MANY YEARS my wife and I have admired the beautiful creations in jade which were fashioned by craftsmen long before the Christian era. This rock, whose hues range through the colours almost from white to black, has from the earliest times been associated by the Chinese with perfection and the many virtues that they esteemed.

Jade is characterized by a toughness of structure which makes it very difficult to carve and a hardness which approximates that of feldspar or quartz. The stone possesses the highly desired green shades which range from the opaque through the semitranslucent from which some of the finest art objects have been fashioned, to the beautifully translucent lively and limpid applegreen or imperial green colours from which are formed the gems so highly prized by the women of the Orient.

In earliest times the cutting of jade was done by toothless saws, the top side of which supported a wicker basket filled with rocks or other forms of ballast; this additional weight aided the two workmen who operated the saw in a fashion similar to that of a crosscut saw. Sticky cutting abrasives were applied to the saw, which enabled the cut to be made. The abrasives were produced on a crude form of mill which consisted of a rock or boulder more or less flat on top and half round underneath. The boulder was rocked back and forth on another flat rock by a man standing on the flat surface. An attendant shoved the materials to be used as abrasive between the flat platform and the rocking boulder. In this manner the first crushing operation was performed. The abrasive, partially crushed, was swept off the flat rock and ground to a greater fineness by a pestle and mortar. After being mixed with some sticky substance, in some cases fat, it was applied to the saw and provided its cutting edge.

The drilling operation was equally primitive. The equipment consisted of a round piece of metal or shaped flint of the diameter required to which an abrasive was continually applied. Tubular drills, however, were known to have been used from the earliest times and were fashioned to hold the abrasives in niches on their cutting sides. In this way the craftsmen were able to cut out cores which were finally chipped out. The exquisite craftsmanship of the carvings speaks for itself and the final grinding and burnishing operations were completed on primitive wheels faced with abrasives and used somewhat like our buffing or grinding wheels of today.

Most of the drilling and polishing operations of the earliest days were carried out by handpower, and later by means of the foot treadle. It is the great development and use of the different types of power which have enabled modern man to transform these primitive operations into the modern techniques.

Instead of the old toothless saw of the pre-Christian era, a modern circular saw, with its inserted alloyed cutting teeth, can cut ordinary steel billets to a depth of ten inches per minute. Instead of the one-man power foot-rocked mill, three hundred horse-power today enables the modern crusher to break up one thousand tons of ore per hour between its five-foot jaws into lumps ten inches in diameter. These lumps are then placed in the modern rod mill, which powered with six hundred horse-power now grinds them at the rate of one hundred tons per hour and converts them into the finest powder.

The modern four inch diameter drill can sink itself in steel at the rate of two inches per minute. I have seen the modern counterpart of the hollow drill, the diamond rock drill, driving through average tough rock at the rate of ten feet per hour operating at depths of over one mile.

The great modern artist and craftsman, Carl Fabergé, was partial to the use of jade, particularly the green Siberian nephrite, although occasionally jadeite and a yellowish-green form of serpentine which resembled jade were used in his exquisite creations.

The Revocation of the Edict of Nantes in 1685 caused many

thousands of Huguenot artisans to flee from France. The ancestors of Carl Fabergé fled from Picardy at this period and toward the middle of the nineteenth century the family was operating in St. Petersburg. Carl Fabergé, who was born about this time, later visited many parts of Europe. His designs showed French influence but at all times were the product of his own distinctive styling. He gained an international fame which was given recognition when he exhibited in Paris in 1900.

This magnificent artist not only fashioned his own pieces, but used his wealth of knowledge of the use of jewels, the crafting of metals and production of beautiful enamels to direct his master craftsmen, whose initials on the many objects of art produced by his firm are now well known and recognized. The Easter eggs which formed the Imperial gifts between members of the Romanoff family, the exquisitely fashioned functional objects devised of the most luxurious and artistically styled combinations of precious metals, stones and enamels, the carved animals and the life-like flowers fashioned by his highly skilled experts rank among the finest examples of the jeweller's art.

The majority of the treasures produced by Carl Fabergé which have come out of Russia have found their way into the museums and private collections of the world. A few examples of this master craftsman's works are among my most treasured possessions.

How some of the Romanoff treasures, among them the works of Carl Fabergé, reached this continent makes an interesting story. I have already related how the Russian ambassador in London in 1917 gave a shocking description of his own people. A few months later the great Bolshevik revolution took place.

In 1921 there was a great famine in Russia and the government returned to what they called a "new economic policy"—ostensibly a system of free trade—which was supposed to permit something like private enterprise to form part of its internal economic structure. This scheme, under strict government control, was designed to encourage foreign capital to come into the country, and permitted some private initiative. The products manufactured under this closely controlled and limited system of private industry could be paid for in the currency of the country or some equivalent.

The American Relief Administration helped to combat the famine conditions and Dr. Hammer of the United States visited Russia with this organization. Following discussions which he later had with government officials, a Concessions Committee of the Soviet Union was formed and the first Concession Agreement was signed in 1921 by Lenin and Bogdanov, Chairman of the Supreme Council of Peoples' Commissars. Bogdanov later became the President of Amtorg Trading Corporation, the trading monopoly of the Soviet Union in the United States.

Dr. Hammer and his brother were successful in obtaining a concession to manufacture indelible pencils in Russia, a profitable venture since pencils at that time were so scarce and in such demand that their price, in terms of our money, was over fifty cents. The Hammer brothers employed technicians from Germany and England and developed an industry employing a large staff. In time they were successful in reducing the retail price of pencils to a reasonable level.

During their ten years' residence in Russia, the Hammers collected many art treasures. The Czar Nicholas II owned six palaces, each containing five hundred rooms. He had his own Imperial Porcelain Factory at Petrograd, whose products were destined exclusively for the use of the Imperial family. The extent of the art treasures which became available to the Soviets after the Revolution was enormous, and some of these were sold to meet the requirements of the government. Many of the Imperial art treasures were purchased by Dr. Hammer and his brother. They had cannily provided in the agreement under which their concession was granted to them that they should be permitted to take out of Russia the art treasures they had collected during the ten years they resided there. The government adhered to the terms of the agreement and at the termination of the concession Dr. Hammer brought his acquisitions to the United States. There, in galleries opened by the Hammer brothers in New York and Palm Beach, some years later I viewed the fabulous treasures of the Romanoffs, among them some of Carl

Fabergé's creations, and heard from one of the brothers the story I have just related. It is an odd turn of fate that linked the high cost of indelible pencils in Russia with my acquisition of a few examples of the matchless craftsmanship of Carl Fabergé.

ONE OF MY EARLY acquisitions was a small Chinese lacquer bowl, on the outside of which was inscribed a poem minutely and exquisitely carved, the red Chinese characters against a green background. The bottom of the bowl carried the carved inscription of the reign of Ch'ien Lung, and on the bowl the poem ended with the carved seals of the Emperor. We have since acquired a cabinet in which the Emperor used to keep the silk scrolls on which his poems were written.

I became interested in finding out why carving in lacquer is one of the most characteristic Chinese arts. I found that the materials used in China were the main reasons which differentiated the lacquer products of that country from those produced in many other parts of the world. In most countries the basic material used is the gummy deposit of an insect. This is best known as shellac and has been familiar to craftsmen in Europe for centuries.

Chinese lacquer, however, is made from a white or grey viscous fluid which is tapped from trees. It is put through a process of straining to remove excess water. After this, it is stained the colours required and it is then ready to be applied. The basic form of the lacquer object to be created was usually an exceedingly thin piece of wood, the surface of which had been thoroughly prepared by being covered with a fine layer of cloth, paper or silk before the first coat of lacquer was applied. Coat after coat of lacquer was then laid on and each coat was allowed to harden and was polished before the succeeding thickness was added. This procedure was carried out until the successive applications had provided a body of lacquer of sufficient thickness to enable the craftsman to execute the carved designs which he had planned. The edges of these designs in many cases included the key, diaper or swastika patterns.

The multi-coloured carved lacquer, which has sometimes been brought up to a thickness of nearly half an inch before being carved, was produced in a similar way only the different colours were applied one on top of the other and the carving was then executed from the surface into the layers below. The various colours were wrought in the order and at the depths required by the artist's conception of the final plan.

In these multi-coloured pieces can be found the various shades of green, plum, buff, brown or black, in addition to the satisfying cinnabar red. The lacquers were polished and buffed to produce a high finish which is not unlike that to be formed on some of the finer forms of pottery.

During this time my wife was making a collection of pottery and porcelain birds, animals, and tiny figures. We read about these things together and finally collected a few examples of the remarkable pottery produced by the Wood family of Burslem. The beautifully modelled statuettes, groups, birds and animals, with their soft and pastel coloured glazes, are considered to be the finest examples of the work of the English potter. Some years ago I met Mr. Frank Partridge, the English connoisseur and collector who has assembled one of the most complete collections of Ralph Wood pottery in existence. He told me that these figures with their beautiful glazes are not excelled by any known examples of pottery elsewhere. This is a judgment in which I concur.

My interests as a collector have never been focused on one field. As most collectors know, an interest in one field soon leads to another. Throughout the years, however, no matter what other items claimed my attention as a collector, I maintained a steady interest in early Chinese bronze. As a manufacturer, I was greatly taken with the beauty of many of the ancient bronzes, as well as with the fine detail and finish which characterized these early castings which were produced when there were none of the facilities which have since been so highly developed. To me it was interesting to learn that man may have cast his first molten metal in a natural hollow stone. This gave him an ingot for working, but its shape was the shape of the natural hollow. It is logical to assume that his next step was to shape the hollow to a form closer to his ultimate need which would require less working.

He soon developed and used the two-piece mould, shaped probably again from stone, which produced still more accurate castings. From these the finished product could be more easily completed.

Many of the hollow vessels and statues which have come down to us from earliest periods were produced by the use of cores, which are still employed and have the widest application today. The old method has been called the "lost wax process". The craftsman, after visualizing his creation, would construct a fireproof core, usually made of sand held together with a resinous binder. This became the hollow part of the statue or vessel. He would then model over this core in wax the article which he wished to produce in bronze. Over the wax model an outer mould was formed and the completed mould was then heated; this permitted the wax to run out. The molten metal was then poured and was held and cooled between the outer mould and the core. Then the outer mould was broken off, the core chipped out, and the bronze casting remained. Many of the earlier bronzes cast in one piece in this way included the handles and knobs; later pieces had separate castings made and the various appendages riveted on.

It is not my purpose to compare these primitive methods with the modern practice that I have seen in use in foundries on this continent and Europe which produce the intricate castings required for the endless variety of products manufactured today. It is interesting, however, to note that the principle of the hollow stone is still in use, though it has been extended to the point where highly intricate castings over one hundred tons in weight have been produced in the elaborately prepared and cored pits dug into the floors of foundries. Two-piece moulds are still in use, but in conjunction with high-speed mechanized foundry equipment and combined with modern and scientific sand-handling machinery. The principle of the lost wax process is still employed to produce small precision components which are accurate within limits never considered possible when the method was initiated. Cores, large and small, are today mass produced and baked in ovens which scientifically and automatically provide the proper temperature control. These modern cores are produced at a rate and of a consistency and uniformity undreamed of by the ancients. During a study of the use and application of this metal, I first became interested in a pair of relatively late bronzes, eighteenth century Foo dogs, one of the characteristic figures long connected with Chinese mythology. Each lion sits on a detachable base and each unit is about eighteen inches in height. They represented to me a type of the most artistic bronze creations of that period. They were strongly modelled, represented great vitality and showed a high degree of perfection in the art of casting. The various parts of the castings had been chased with all the patience and skill which the finest silversmiths applied to the plate for which England became so famous in the early eighteenth century.

These conventional forms, known everywhere as the "Lion Dog", were believed to have been introduced into China from India during the Han dynasty (206 B.C.-220 A.D.). Many temples in China are guarded by two of these Lion Dogs carved in stone. In Bangkok, at the Wat-po and Wat-arung, towering, grotesque guardians are stationed at the entrances to these temples and serve the same purpose. The great mythological figures, which we have seen, also guard the entrances at the foot of the wide, pillared structure, topped with its many pagodas, which one mounts to reach the level upon which is set the magnificent temple of gold in Rangoon.

I have always believed that one should acquire some knowledge of the multitude of different subjects that are encountered in a lifetime and should develop to the full those interests which most engross him. I am convinced that a diversity of interests is not only satisfactory in itself but leads to a fuller enjoyment of life.

ABOUT THE TIME that I was attending lectures in political science as an undergraduate at the University of Toronto, the efforts of Dr. C. T. Currelly to found an archaeological museum in that institution began to bear fruit. In 1912 the first Board of Governors of the Royal Ontario Museum was appointed by the provincial government of the day and on March 17th, 1914, a few months before I went overseas with the Canadian First Contingent, the first wing of the Museum was officially opened.

It was perhaps inevitable that my interest in the arts and crafts, expanding with a general interest in archaeology, should lead to my becoming a Director of the Royal Ontario Museum.

I do not know if the people of Canada realize what a marvellous asset they have in that Museum. In the forty years that have passed since the opening of the original wing, it has grown and developed till, today, it is of international stature. It is one of the leading museums of the world, and has probably the largest and certainly the best collection of Chinese art objects of any museum, comparing favourably with those of such long-established organizations as the Metropolitan Museum in New York, the Chicago Art Institute, the Freer Gallery in Washington, and the Victoria and Albert and British Museums. Its Museum of Zoology and Mineralogy is the finest of its kind in Canada, while that of Zoology and Palaeontology is internationally outstanding.

It has been a matter of great pride with me that my hobby as a collector and as an amateur in archaeology brought about an association with an institution of such repute as the Royal Ontario Museum.

EARLIER IN THESE PAGES I have told of my love for music which I inherited, unaccompanied by any of his talent, from my father. As a boy I played the violin, without distinction, in the New Hamburg Orchestra; later, at collegiate and university I amused myself playing the mandolin.

It was this fondness for music that led to my appointment in 1932 as a Director of the Board of the Toronto Symphony Orchestra. This group was first organized in 1906 by Mr. Frank Squire Welsman and Dr. Edward Fisher as the Toronto Conservatory Symphony Orchestra; two years later it became the Toronto Symphony Orchestra, which continued its operations till 1918, when they were suspended owing to the difficulty of financing in wartime.

Luigi von Kunits, an able and cultured Viennese musician, undertook to revive the Symphony in 1922. At that time only afternoon, or twilight, concerts could be held since most of the musicians played also in the orchestras which in those far-off days accompanied the showing of silent films.

On the death of von Kunits, who had done much to establish the reputation of Toronto as a good "String Town", Ernest Campbell MacMillan was the unanimous choice of the directors as conductor of the Symphony. A musical prodigy who had made his debut at ten as a concert organist in Massey Hall, Principal of the Conservatory of Music, and Dean of the Faculty of Music at the University of Toronto, Dr. MacMillan, later knighted for his services to music in Canada, added more and better musicians to the orchestra, increased the number of performances, and when the advent of talking pictures made the players available for evening performances, brought the orchestra to the high place that it occupies today as one of the top ten on this continent.

I was Director of the Symphony Board from 1932, became Honorary Secretary from 1936, and President in 1937 and 1938, remaining on the Board until I resigned at the outbreak of the war. At that time the Orchestra gave twenty-five concerts in a season. Nowadays it gives approximately eighty. It has also gone on tour in the United States and Canada and has been heard over the national networks of the Canadian Broadcasting Corporation. It was during my term as President that we negotiated the arrangement for the first C.B.C. broadcast. I was most gratified this year to read of the standing ovation accorded the Toronto Symphony Orchestra and the Mendelssohn Choir when they performed Handel's "Messiah" in Carnegie Hall in New York.

I enjoyed enormously my association with the Toronto Symphony Orchestra, with the energetic members of the Board and the Women's Committee, who collaborated in our successful efforts to put the Orchestra on a sound budgetary and financial basis. It was also a great pleasure for me to work with Sir Ernest MacMillan and the members of the Orchestra.

It was always of the greatest interest to me to meet the guest conductors and the guest soloists. One of these, Dr. Kindler, conductor of the Washington Symphony Orchestra, told me a story about an internationally known conductor which has always delighted me.

He was conducting a rehearsal of the New York Philharmonic Orchestra at a time when his knowledge of American English was limited. In the course of one difficult passage he was distressed to hear a member of the brass section blow a series of flat notes. The conductor halted the musicians, scowled at the offender, and started back at the beginning of the passage. Again the distressing sounds were made. For the second time the conductor halted the orchestra; he turned to the offender and said, "You're fired!" The musician got up from his seat, put his instrument under his arm, and walked towards the wings. Arriving there, he turned, glared at the conductor, and said, "Nuts to you." The conductor waved his hand grandly. "It is too late now to apologize," he said.

On one of the visits of the Governor-General, Lord Tweedsmuir, to Toronto, His Excellency sat with me in the President's Box. After the performance, some of the committee members remarked that we had certainly been engrossed with the music, as we had been engaged throughout the programme in almost constant conversation. Without in any way detracting from the Governor-General's interest in the music of the Symphony, I should, perhaps, here reveal that that night I had discovered that His Excellency was also an ardent salmon fisherman.

During the seasons 1945-46 and 1949-50 I was on the Executive Committee of the Toronto Art Gallery and to the present time I remain on the Advisory Board. The Toronto Art Gallery is probably the liveliest in Canada, and certainly one of the best, and under its Director, Martin Baldwin, is rapidly gaining for itself an international reputation. However, my own contributions to the advancement of the Gallery were limited, as I was deeply occupied with the problems of converting the output of our factories to a peace time programme.

This, then, is an account of some of the activities that have engaged my leisure hours for more than forty years. They have been doubly precious to me since I have held them in common with my wife. They made our travels more enjoyable, adding other interests to the normal ones of the sightseer and tourist; they have directed much of my reading and have made it interesting and intelligible and have added enormously to one individual's enjoyment of life.

If I have seemed to dwell longer than is seemly in an autobiography on the history and life of such organizations as the Toronto Symphony Orchestra, the Art Gallery, and the Royal Ontario Museum, it was purposely done.

We hear much these days of the emergence of Canada as a great nation. A great nation requires of its people an interest in cultural pursuits, and Canada has made more than a promising start towards acquiring a native culture. The preoccupation of the people and the government with the arts and letters in Canada was demonstrated by the recent Royal Commission which, under the distinguished chairmanship of the Right Honourable Vincent Massey, enquired into the cultural health of the nation. The Commission found it flourishing and presented as evidence of that fact the influence on our national life of organizations such as the Royal Ontario Museum, the National Museum at Ottawa, the various symphony orchestras and art galleries in the major centres throughout the country, the Canadian Broadcast-the Corporation, the Drama Festival, the Opera Company of the Royal Conservatory of Music, the National Ballet Company, and a host of others. To these, since 1953, has been added the Stratford Shakespearean Festival which, in two short seasons, has already established itself as an integral part of our cultural life and has demonstrated the talents of our Canadian actors. Such interests add to the stature of the citizens of the nation and through them to the culture of the nation.

PART SIX

RECONVERSION

CHAPTER XII

PLANNING

THE WARTIME YEARS were very busy ones for me; they were equally strenuous. My wartime duties with the Army Technical Development Board brought me into contact with a large number of interesting people. I had the opportunity of meeting the civil and military leaders of many of our allies, including men who were helping to guide the efforts of the United States and Canada.

One of the interesting people I met during that time was a Canadian. Frederick Walker Baldwin, better known as Casey Baldwin, was a grandson of the Hon. Robert Baldwin, the great Reformer of Canadian history. Casey became a partner of Alexander Graham Bell, and from 1908 was manager and director of the Graham Bell laboratories at Baddeck in Nova Scotia. Here, in the fall of 1907, the Aerial Experiment Association was conceived and formed. Financed by Mrs. Bell, its members, besides Alexander Graham Bell and Casey Baldwin, were Glen Curtis, Lt. T. E. Selfridge of the American army, and John McCurdy, all great names in the history of aviation. Early in 1908 this group moved to Hammondsport, N.Y. where Curtis had a motorcycle engine plant and here, on 12th March, *Redwing*, the first plane constructed by the group, was flown off the ice of Lake Kuka with Casey Baldwin at the controls. This flight, undertaken just five years after the Wright brothers' success, covered a distance of 319 feet, and Casey Baldwin became the first Canadian to fly an aeroplane. *Redwing* made one other flight, a distance of 120 feet, but, on landing, one wing struck the ice and buckled, damaging the machine badly. Selfridge had been responsible for the general plan of *Redwing*. It could be steered, left or right, but its lateral stability was crude, being accomplished by wing warping as the Wright brothers had done. The plan of the Association was to correct in succeeding designs the faults made evident by their experiments. To overcome *Red-wing*'s lack of lateral control the aileron was invented, a tremendously important development, which became the most valuable of the Association's patents. *Whitewing*, the next plane built, was also the first machine to have a tricycle landing gear with a single wheel in front. She was flown successfully from the racetrack at Hammondsport on May 18th, 1908. When the Association disbanded the following year, Casey Baldwin and John McCurdy continued their flying experiments in association with Alexander Graham Bell. They built two machines, the *Baddeck No. 1* and the *Baddeck No. 2*, a two-seater.

The Navy had requested the Army Technical Development Board to work out a problem for them and we selected Casey Baldwin to develop one phase of the project. I had the pleasure of taking him to my fishing camp for a few hours' trout fishing while we discussed the project, which was particularly interesting. It concerned the design of a light plywood motor-boat, supported on hydrofoils, which were winglike structures under the hull that allowed the boat to lift itself out of the water and develop great speed. It was intended for the invasion of Normandy. With smoke-making equipment fitted to them, these boats were to head rapidly into the shore, then turn and run parallel to the shore line, laying a smoke screen in their wake. A secondary task for the boats was to act something like a torpedo. They were to be loaded with high explosives and aimed directly at the object they were to destroy. I attended trials which were held in the Pacific, but the project was not completed in time to be used in the invasion, though experiments on the boats continued. I have since noticed that the Royal Canadian Navy has demonstrated and adopted a type of boat which is an adaptation of their original request to us. They have named it the K.C.B.

With me at my fishing camp when I entertained Casey Baldwin was my old friend and associate, Jack Lash. Colonel J. F. Lash, O.B.E., K.C., one of Canada's leading corporation counsel, was Casey Baldwin's brother-in-law. I had known him since the days of the first World War, and later he became my legal counsel and a member of the Board of Directors of our company. He was a fine sportsman and a true gentleman. I miss his companionship and warm sense of humour.

I have before me the guest book of visitors to our plants. The date on the first page is August 21, 1941, and the signature there, the single word "George", is that of the Duke of Kent, the King's brother, who was killed in a plane crash the following year. The Earl of Athlone, then the Governor-General of Canada, visited the plant in 1944, accompanied by the Princess Alice. Among the statesmen of the Allied Nations who inspected our factories were the Rt. Hon. Mackenzie King, Prime Minister of Canada, and members of his cabinet, the Rt. Hon. Vincent Massey, Lord Halifax, Wendell L. Willkie, E. Lewis, Director-General of Munitions Production for Australia, Colonel Batista of Cuba, and the Brazilian and Mexican Ambassadors and the Consul-General of Peru, the Czechoslovak Minister, the Minister of Chile. There were touring parties of Members of Parliament from Canada and England, of Trade Commissioners and Labour representatives from the sister Dominions. We were also visited by General A. G. L. McNaughton, Field-Marshal Sir John Dill, Major-General Williams, Controller of the Ordnance Services of the War Office in London, and Major-General J. F. Evetts, Assistant Chief of the Imperial General Staff*, and other military missions, while the artists brought to Toronto in support of the various Victory Loan drives were represented, among others, by Judith Anderson, Gracie Fields, Adolph Menjou and Irving Berlin. We were naturally gratified by the interest shown in our work and our people by our many visitors.

Another interesting visitor was the Princess, now Queen, Juliana of the Netherlands. She was gracious, charming and alert, and was most interested in our plant and products. During the course of my conversation with her, she informed me that when she escaped from Holland she was accompanied by a bodyguard whose members were armed with the new Bergman sub-

---

* General the Honourable A. G. L. McNaughton, P.C., C.H., C.B., C.M.G.; Field-Marshal Sir John Dill, C.B., C.M.G., D.S.O.; Major-General T. R. Williams, C.M.G., D.S.O.; Major-General J. F. Evetts, C.B., C.B.E., M.C.

machine gun which was standard equipment in the German army, and that her guards at Ottawa still had these. The Princess acceded to my request for a loan of one of these. When it arrived, I tested it on my own range and then had other tests run and comparisons made with our own and other weapons. The gun was of great use to us.

On one occasion I was informed that we were to have as a visitor to the plant the Voice of Donald Duck. Shortly afterwards, I found myself being introduced to a charming and attractive young lady whom by no stretch of the imagination could I identify with the mouthpiece of Mr. Walt Disney's famous creation. She turned out to be Miss Jean Dickenson, a Canadian singer who had earned herself great distinction in United States radio circles where she was known as the Nightingale of the Airways. She was amused when I told her later of the confusion which had existed in my mind when I first met her.

Early in 1942 a great number of canvassers were visiting various factories on behalf of local charities. I decided that it would be much more efficient and cause much less disruption of our plant activities, if one group canvassed for all charities. I therefore became chairman of a committee which sponsored a fund known as the "Employees Welfare Service Fund of Greater Toronto". This fund, of which I was the first President in 1942, collected an amount equal to fifteen minutes' wages per week from each hourly-paid member, and one half of one per cent of the salary of all salaried members. Each member was immune from further canvass of funds for social welfare services. The fund was administered by a committee of employees in each member company and collected in its first year $206,000, which was then distributed to local social service work. It is still in operation and has grown to the point where the collections in 1953 have more than quadrupled the original amount.

By the end of 1942, there was in our company a large "family" of some seventeen thousand people who were engaged in the multifarious activities of the Commercial and Ordnance Divisions.

Many of these had developed highly specialized new skills, and I felt very strongly that they should not be dispersed, nor the skills lost, after the cessation of hostilities, but that both should be usefully employed in our post-war activities. I was convinced that plans could and must be laid at that time so that when the end of the war came, we should be ready to direct the knowledge and skill of our work force into commercial ventures. I felt that such time as was left me from my many other duties could most usefully be spent, as far as the Company was concerned, in seeing that these plans were made, that they were thorough, and that they were ready to be implemented when required.

At that time a National Post-War Planning Committee had been set up under the chairmanship of Dr. F. Cyril James, Principal of McGill University. One of the first statements produced by this Committee read as follows:

Fundamentally, then, it still remains true in the post-war period that government should not undertake those tasks which can be handled by private enterprise. . . . But I wish to emphasize the fact that it places squarely on the shoulders of all individual Canadians a direct responsibility to play their own part with wisdom and energy in the planning of Canada's future. The philosophy implies that each Canadian industry, indeed each Canadian enterprise, will consciously consider, to the best of its ability, the task of readapting its policies and facilities to peace-time utilization, as soon as the opportunity arises. It demands careful study by individuals of new sources of raw materials, new technical processes and the creation of new products, so that the large and growing consumer demand of the Canadian population may be adequately and promptly supplied.

I was forcibly struck by this philosophy, which placed upon each section of Canadian industry the full responsibility for its own reconversion plans. We were to plan for ourselves, and not wait for someone to do it for us. This coincided with my own beliefs. I accordingly called the first meeting of our own Post-War Planning Committee, consisting of the top executives in our organization. I have the agenda of that first meeting before me as I write. It carries the designation "For Action".

Our first consideration was to consolidate our existing products. We had already added to our products the line of the well-known

Worthington Pump and Machinery Corporation of Harrison, New Jersey, and this line, which had played a large part in the naval building programme by supplying pumps and other auxiliary equipment for ships, was one which had many potentialities in the post-war development of Canada. We realized that there would be need for this type of equipment in many of the construction, power, mining, chemical, ore, and gas developments, and projects that were bound to be carried out in Canada after the war. We were the first Canadian company to introduce the art of building steam turbines and, in so doing, we had helped give the Royal Canadian Navy its first Canadian-built destroyers. The steam turbine was a product that would be important in Canada's future. We held Canadian rights from the American firm, A. O. Smith Company, for their process of fusing glass to steel to form large tanks and vessels. These would be needed in future processing plants. Finally, we had our normal range of boilers and other products that we felt should be developed and consolidated to meet the time when the demand for them arose.

Our second consideration was the addition of new lines. In this we were guided by three factors: we had to take into account our existing plant and equipment; we had to use the types of skills we had developed in our work-force; and we needed products that would satisfy a future market demand. We set up a screening board, as part of our Committee, to receive and screen suggestions for new lines in terms of these requirements.

The third main consideration of the Committee was that of markets. We knew that we would have to complete and maintain a national sales organization to enable us to carry out our policy in the domestic market, and we made plans to do so; but we also turned our thoughts to foreign markets. During the war, our company had learned skills that might be useful in other countries. Our services and products, we felt, should be considered in this light. At the first meeting, the second part of our agenda dealt with studies and plans that would enable us to formulate a policy of foreign operations.

Besides deciding on our products and markets, we planned other phases of our operations. We considered the steps that would have to be taken to develop our own engineering staff to cope with new products, and to obtain licensing agreements where it was felt we needed more specialized technical help than we had available within our organization. We also planned in the financial field and set up what we termed our Post War Shrinkage Budget.

Reports of this Committee were available to me bi-weekly, or whenever my duties at Victory Aircraft or the Development Board took me to Toronto.

As we drew up our plans and developed our policy, several things became apparent. We had one set of equipment and a group of people well suited for heavy engineering; in this type of engineering the products tend to be custom made and large, and a high degree of skill lies with the individual worker. We had another group well versed in the art of gun-making, which involved large quantities of like items, well-tooled and meticulously planned, where, in some cases, a large degree of skill was required of the individual worker, but an even greater degree of skill was required of the planners, tool designers, and tool-making personnel. This division of skills indicated to us the need for two types of operations, after the war, one carrying on the heavy engineering part of the operation, the other utilizing our gun-making skills and practice in new lines. This second group formed what later became our Consumer Products Division.

Another fact that became obvious as we laid our plans was the need for something to fill in the transitional period. We should require a great deal of time, perhaps a year or more, to complete the tooling and plant facilities for the products and lines we were developing for the new Consumer Products Division before they could go into production, and we felt that it was vital to find some means of keeping our personnel together during this period so that they would be available when the time came for the manufacture of the new lines. We therefore set up what we called "the Bits and Pieces Programme". This called for our taking, immediately upon the cessation of hostilities, any sub-contract work or order for bits and pieces that could be put into production with a minimum of tooling delay, and so give immediate employment to our valuable work force. In this way, we would have time to prepare properly and put into production our new permanent product lines.

The work of the Planning Committee, and the fact that it was started well before the end of the war, enabled us to effect the transition from the production of military and war material to normal commercial output with the utmost speed, and the minimum loss of our most important asset, our trained personnel.

In 1945 THE WORLD suddenly found itself at peace after six years of war. The time was at hand when we were to put into effect plans we had made three years earlier. We were about to determine the soundness of these plans.

The heavy engineering operation, known as the General Engineering Division, was able to start almost immediately on its planned course of producing machinery and equipment for the basic industries of Canada. The licensing agreements and product lines that we had decided on in our early planning were soon put to good use. We counted on an increase in the Canadian economy, and our hopes were realized.

We found a demand for our skills as turbine builders, and produced turbine-driven generator sets for U.N.R.R.A. These were self-contained units which were to be mounted on railway cars and taken to devastated cities and towns to provide emergency electrical power. Turbines for French cargo ships followed, and these were succeeded by propulsion equipment for Canadian oil tankers which were required to bring Canada's new-found oil through the Great Lakes to the marketing areas of Central Canada. We were proud to complete, in recent months, turbines of the most advanced design for the Royal Canadian Navy's new escort vessel programme. Our pioneering of steam turbines had borne fruit.

Some of our other pioneer lines did equally well. The agreement made several years before with A. O. Smith Company, to give us a process of lining steel tanks with glass, found a ready market. Practically all the breweries in Canada have replaced their fermenter tanks with glass-lined vessels from the Inglis shops. These tanks are horizontal, about thirteen feet in diameter by about twenty-five long, and have provided the plate shop with work for a number of years. In thinking of the endless number of these tanks that we have made, I can only wonder if water is still considered a suitable beverage for Canadians.

We also developed the skill of spot-welding stainless steel sheets to a normal steel backing to provide a clad sheet with the corrosive resistance of stainless steel, but at a fraction of the cost of a solid sheet of stainless steel of the same thickness. This sheet was widely used in building processing tanks and digesters for the pulp and paper and other industries. The cladding was done with a machine that we designed and built to do the job. It was the first of its kind in Canada.

The pulp and paper industry produces one out of eight dollars of Canadian income and supplies more than half the pages of the world's newspapers. We felt that after six years of war there would be a need for new equipment in our paper mills, and that this, coupled with an expansion of the industry, would create a demand for paper-making machinery. We had accordingly acquired licences from a leading American company and after the war we were able to maintain a steady flow of work turning out new paper-making machines and providing spares for existing units.

Another new major product group we had after the war was equipment for generating power from water. We had already built several large water turbines, and as our country continues its growth, and consequently its power demands, I can see a continuing need for this type of equipment.

In addition to our new lines, the older ones were also active. Worthington pumps and compressors were used in many phases of industrial growth, as were the boilers, pressure vessels and other pieces of equipment and machinery that we were producing. These went to all parts of Canada, so that our products became known from coast to coast. The General Engineering Division is now in a sound competitive position in Canadian industry, and is adding to and developing the lines needed to fulfil its purpose of equipping the basic industries of Canada.

The transition from wartime to peacetime activities for our gun-making personnel was more complicated. There is little difference between a turbine for a naval vessel and one for a cargo ship; they are still turbines. Guns, however, are guns, and military weapons have little use in a peacetime economy. A general engineering shop equipped with the normal range of machinery can produce various types of equipment on that machinery with the minimum of new tools and fixtures. The products we had in mind for our new Consumer Products Division were of a nature susceptible to mass production, and until the plant could be set up, and the tooling provided, some time was to elapse. Our Bits and Pieces programme filled this gap.

We took contracts, during this programme, for any items that could be put into production in the shortest time. Aluminum pots and pans were polished and assembled by hands that had polished and assembled gun parts a short time before. Knives and cigarette lighters were produced, as were guns, only the latter, instead of being the lethal weapons that our people had turned out during the war, were children's toys. Finally we built trailers that provided temporary relief to the housing shortage for some, and week-end or holiday pleasure for others. These products, though not our permanent ones, kept our personnel together until we were ready with our main lines.

Gun-making involves precision machining of small parts in large quantities; so does the manufacture of fishing reels. Add to this the interest in fishing in Canada, and the abundance of fine lakes and rivers in which to practise it, and there is a ready-made product that offered scope to our company. We obtained a licence from the Shakespeare Company in the United States and soon were in production. We made rods, reels and lines, as well as baits, and tackle boxes, rounding out a complete line of fishing equipment.

The Fabrique Nationale Company in Belgium had designed the pistol we had made for the allied armies during the war. We used our connections with this company and those we had established by the sale of fishing tackle to sporting goods dealers, to import Browning sporting guns that had been made in Belgium, and resell them in Canada.

We selected another precision product with good market potentialities. This was a small fuel pump for use on domestic oil burners. The increase in the need for housing, coupled with the rising popularity and availability of oil as a fuel, forecast the use of a large volume of these, while the manufacture of the pump itself required many of the skills our people had acquired. We obtained a licence from the Sunstrand Company in Rockford, Illinois, and have built up a business that provides fuel pumps for most of the oil burners now being installed in houses throughout Canada.

Our agreement with the A. O. Smith Company gave us the right to build and sell domestic glass-lined water heaters in Canada. There were no other heaters of this kind on the Canadian market, and the corrosive-resistant qualities of our product met with consumer acceptance, so that the output of the heaters has been increasing steadily since the war. A similar product from the manufacturing point of view was the cylinder used to store liquid propane gas. These were manufactured and sold by us in large quantities.

The last new product line we had selected for the Consumer Product Division was wringer washing machines. We had completed an agreement with the Whirlpool Corporation, the largest producers of home laundry equipment in the world, and we were able to manufacture their line in Canada. Our start was with wringer washing machines, and we soon built up a volume of business in a market which had been denied domestic appliances for more than six years. As that market eased, we held our place, and we realized that our products had caught on. To wringer washers we added automatics and today the company has a leading position in this field in Canada.

The rapidity with which we were able to effect the conversion from wartime activities to those of a peacetime economy is a great tribute to the entire personnel of the company. This successful change-over in the main involved the following ingredients: planning, which enabled us to take our time in selecting products and gave us an orderly means of carrying out our reconversion; the splendid co-operation of our Board of Directors who backed up effectively the plans of the management; the success of our sales people in setting up quickly the necessary outlets and channels of distribution for our new and diversified lines. They successfully broke into a number of new fields and put the name Inglis on the map with products ranging from paper machines to fishing reels. Then came the skill and effort of our craftsmen, by means of which our plans were implemented. And, finally, there was the great help and encouragement given us by our bankers. The problem of financing the tooling and inventories required by these new lines was greatly eased by their vision and help. In this connection, I can never be sufficiently grateful for the constructive co-operation and advice of Mr. Harvey Skey, Manager of the Toronto branch of the Bank of Montreal, and of Mr. A. G. Gardiner, M.C., the President of the same organization.

As we were laying out our plans for reconversion, I felt that there was something still missing in our operations. We had our Consumer Products Division, which was more or less self-contained, and our General Engineering Division which supplied the basic mechanical equipment required by many of the industries of Canada. We built machines requiring power, but could not supply the power to run them, or we built machines that could produce mechanical power, but could not convert that energy into the more readily distributed form of electricity. The item that was lacking was the electrical equipment connected with the products we were then making. If we could supply that equipment, we would have a well-integrated operation.

The gap was filled in 1946 by the purchase by our company of a controlling interest in the English Electric Company of Canada Limited. This company, which was largely Canadian-owned, was located in St. Catharines, some seventy miles from Toronto. It produced motors, generators, switchgear and transformers in all industrial sizes, and operated under licence from the English Electric Company of England. This firm, under the energetic direction of Sir George Nelson, is one of the leading manufacturers in Great Britain and operates nearly fifty plants located in the United Kingdom, Canada, Australia, South Africa and India. They control Marconi's Wireless Telegraphy Company, D. Napier & Son Limited, as well as their own English

Electric companies, and their products range from domestic appliances through major installations of electrical, hydroelectric and mechanical equipment to diesel locomotives, aircraft engines, and the famous Canberra aircraft.

The British firm gave us close technical liaison, and with this help we were able to integrate the company into our new operations. The English Electric Company of Canada became a wholly owned subsidiary in 1948. I then felt that our Company was in a favourable position to compete in the engineering field both in Canada and abroad.

Before and after the end of the war, I had had several warnings that the state of my health was deteriorating. In 1950, therefore, I sold the bulk of my interest in the John Inglis Company to the English Electric Company of England. I felt that their great research and technical background would enable the Canadian operation to develop fully along the paths we had laid out, and that their success in other countries would make that development sure.

CHAPTER XIII

SAILING AGAIN

In 1944, after serving twelve years on the committee of management and as flag officer, I was honoured by being elected Commodore of the Royal Canadian Yacht Club. The task was of particular interest to me at that time, as it offered the opportunity of welcoming back the many members of the Club who had distinguished themselves by rendering a service to their country. It also permitted me to give such assistance as I could in the problems faced by the Club at the end of the war.

The *Nonchalant* had been hauled out, in 1939, and had sat patiently waiting out the war years. In the late spring of 1945, shortly after V.E. Day, she again slithered down the marine ways, her timbers dried by five years of hibernation. A month later, her mast stepped, her standing rigging taut, her running rigging reaved, and her planking tight from a much-needed soaking, she once again became alive and sensitive to the touch on the helm and the urgings of the wind.

She was sailed sparingly during the summer, both due to the pressure of business and the lack of capable hands, since both my sons were still in the army. The summer of 1946, however, was a more active one. A crew was assembled, and light racing canvas was hoisted and lowered until familiarity with these sails was attained by its members. We participated in some of the club races. There were a good many changes; we no longer would battle with our old foes, the *Yolanda*, which had been skippered ably by the late Norman Gooderham, and the *Gardenia*, which had always been an elusive opponent under the wily helmsmanship of Eddie Wedd.

Our youthful post-war crew, always enthusiastic and energetic, was somewhat lacking in experience during the first sailing season, and provided some incidents which, amusing in retrospect, at the time produced a string of invectives from the skipper. Just before the start of one of our first races we had hoisted our large Genoa jib, tied up in stops which could be broken out by a ripcord if the situation required it. As we approached the starting line, with roughly one minute left before the starting gun was fired, it became apparent that we were going to be late by a few seconds. The order was given to break out the Genoa, which was executed almost immediately. A shocked silence ensued for a few seconds when it was realized by all on board that the Genoa was upside down. Our competitors were hilarious.

The same summer, in the middle of August, we left Toronto harbour early on a Saturday morning and headed roughly E. by N. down the north shore of Lake Ontario for a week's cruise in the Bay of Quinte, that delightful stretch of inland waterways that extends eighty miles at the east end of Lake Ontario. The crew consisted of my wife and two sons, the paid hand (who had been suffering from an illness associated with the gin bottle) and our cook, who had reluctantly agreed to accompany us at the last minute when other plans had gone astray.

The Saturday morning and part of the afternoon passed uneventfully. We had broad reached steadily down the lake under a freshening breeze from the west and by four o'clock in the afternoon we were registering nine and a half knots under our working canvas of jib, main and mizzen. Until that time it had been a brilliantly clear day, with the sun sparkling on the whitecaps which were slowly being pushed up by the winds behind us.

Shortly after four, a black, menacing formation masked the sun and it became apparent that a line squall, only too familiar to sailors on the Great Lakes, was approaching quickly from well astern. We held our course and deliberated the course of action to be taken. By this time the wind had freshened perceptibly and our speed had increased to just under ten knots. We were roughly sixteen miles from Presqu'île Bay, where we intended to anchor the first night. We decided, wrongly as it turned out, to hold our course and continue to carry our canvas, as we were making such good time that we would reach our anchorage before dark.

The squall seemed to pass to leeward of us and we relaxed, as we appeared, for the moment at least, to be out of danger. Minutes later, however, a second black mass, flecked by white patches indicating wind, appeared dead astern. Orders were given to batten down all hatches and drop the mainsail. Hatch covers were hastily brought on deck and were quickly lashed in place. As this task was nearing completion the wind slackened perceptibly; a glance astern confirmed the uneasy suspicion that we were in for it. As far as the eye could see was a white wall, overtaking us rapidly. The force of the wind in the oncoming squall was cleaving off the tops of the waves and driving the finely divided spray before it, blocking out all visibility. In a matter of seconds we were enveloped, and, as the course was altered to bring the ship on a reach, we were nearly laid on our beam's end by the heavy gusts of wind. In the minute or two of pandemonium which ensued, my wife was unceremoniously pushed to safety down the main hatch by her two sons. She, however, refused to stay below. An attempt was then made by them and the cook to lower the mainsail; the paid hand had been afflicted by another attack of his mysterious illness seconds before the storm had struck, and had disappeared below.

The cook, despite his most gallant attempt to help lower the main, had managed to weave the main halliard into a robbel through both his legs. By this time he had lost all interest in participating as a member of the ship's crew, and was mainly concerned with self-preservation and a longing for the cessation of the pitching, yawing motion as we struggled through the now heavy seas.

The mainsail was slatting thunderously along the leach as we attempted to fisherman reef through the violent gusts. The battens cut through the batten pockets and seconds later the main was flayed and slashed into many pieces, which were carried off to leeward by the invisible force of the storm.

The main intensity of the storm passed as quickly as it came. We had lost our first main in twenty years of sailing. The cook had nearly lost his teeth in one of his many trips to the lee rail.

Our spare main was shipped down to the Bay of Quinte, and

was duly bent on our naked main spar. We continued a pleasant and otherwise rather uneventful cruise.

During the years 1947, 1948 and 1949 we participated in most of the major cruising races on Lake Ontario. Our low handicap rating made it virtually impossible to save our time on short course races; on longer cruising races, under heavy wind conditions, we had a reasonable chance of placing in competition with yachts of lower ratings.

We raced three years running in the Freeman Cup, a well-known classic on Lake Ontario, which usually covers a course of approximately 130 miles. Although we never managed to pick up the hardware in this race after the war, it was always a very enjoyable event. *Nonchalant* led the fleet home on two occasions, but failed to pick up sufficient lead to place on corrected time.

We had a very thrilling start on one occasion against *Alondra*, a sixty-five foot ketch from Boston. It was blowing a steady twenty-five miles from the west, the first leg of the journey carrying us on a dead run from Toronto to a marker off Rochester harbour, ninety-one miles away. We took a long running start with our spinnaker ready to crack out as soon as we hit the line. Seconds before the gun was fired, after having jockeyed our way through a fleet of roughly fifty yachts, we found the *Alondra* directly to leeward with just sufficient room to sneak through between ourselves and the leeward marker. We both arrived on the line as the starting gun was fired; seconds later the great parachute spinnaker was cracked out. For an instant it billowed out to leeward, missing the spreader stay of the *Alondra* by inches as she bore up to windward not more than ten feet from our leeward rail. Providence averted a near mishap, for the spinnaker, on filling, drifted forward and clear of the leeward yacht.

It was an exciting first leg. We gradually drew well in front of the whole fleet as the breeze freshened. By mid-afternoon our spinnaker pole, a solid spar six inches in diameter, was bent in an arc under the pressure of the spinnaker. We expected the pole or the trimming tackle to part at any moment, but continued under full sail until we rounded the Rochester marker well ahead of the fleet. Our luck for the day ended then, for no sooner had we laid our course for Cobourg, forty miles off, on the other side of the lake, than our main halliard parted. The mainsail plummeted to the deck and our speed slackened, as we were now carrying only jib and mizzen. Half an hour later, despite rising seas and descending darkness, we managed to masthead the mainsail, using the spinnaker halliard and the anchor winch to crank the sail aloft. We sailed on to finish the race, but had lost our chance to place when the mishap occurred. Such was the fortune of racing.

While I was in India in 1948, I visited the Royal Bombay Yacht Club, where I noticed a beautifully illuminated parchment adorning one of the walls of the club, which I reprint in full:

KNOW ALL MEN BY THESE PRESENTS that whereas certain lewd persons of the baser sort have bruited it abroad that the Honourable Knight Commodore, Sir Henry McMahon, G.C.V.O., K.C.I.E., C.S.I., hath the habitude of using oaths, imprecations and violent objurgations to such as serve as mariners aboard his craft, now we, having served faithfully and lovingly under the said Honourable Knight Commodore in our several degrees as mate, jib-trimmer and sail-maker throughout diverse perilous ventures wherein we have ofttimes suffered sore stress both by the hand of God and the devilish villainy of shipwrights, do hereby testify and confirm under this our proper hand and seal that the aforesaid Knight Commodore, albeit of a nature firm in command and insistent on service rightly rendered, hath at all times and in every season comported himself as a right courteous and gentle shipmaster withal, of sober address and chaste diction, so that never shall you hear any naughty word fall from him but only "prithee jibe tenderly" or "an it please you, dwell not overlong with the jib sheets" or "peradventure, as you love me, be featly with the weather runner" or "eke, dear hearts, stay not until the day of salvation in the scuppers" and such like sweet and comforting exhortations passing all belief and experience of those acquainted with the common practice of Master Mariners. Wherefor may all such as have spread abroad the aforesaid blasphemous fable and damnable invention against the said Honourable Knight Commodore, his fair name and credit, be eternally shamed and confounded. And hereunto we have each severally set our hands on this, the fifth day of August in the Year of Grace one thousand nine hundred and thirteen.

G. Farel, Mate
Malcom H. Hailey, Jib-trimmer
Nan G. Farel, Sail-maker

I chuckled so heartily on reading this statement that the Commodore of the club presented me with a copy. On arriving back in Canada I had another copy made, which now hangs in the Royal Canadian Yacht Club. Often thereafter certain skippers of the club, when under great stress, were known to address their crews by the term "Dear Hearts", but with an emphasis that soon gave this term a significance that was more ominous than anything the crew might have been called before.

In August, 1948, the first Rochester Race for the Snyder Trophy was held, with yachts from all over the Great Lakes participating.

This race was inaugurated by a group of members from the Rochester Yacht Club who wished to provide a race on Lake Ontario which would exceed the distance of Lake Michigan's famous Mackinac Race. The course was triangular, the first leg carrying eighty-one miles N.E. by E. to Stoney Island at the eastern end of the lake. The second leg was a 163 mile stretch along the north shore in a westerly direction to Toronto; the last ninety-one mile leg returned to Rochester. The course was a total of 335 miles, slightly longer than the Mackinac, and had the advantage of being triangular, thus offering different points of sailing, which would be a real test of both ships and crews.

We mulled over the idea of entering this event in the early spring. It did not take long to reach our decision. We sailed for Rochester midway through August, carrying an experienced crew and feeling confident that the ship would withstand the heaviest weather likely to be experienced on the lake. We had carefully checked our running and standing rigging from stem to stern, reaved new sheets and halliards where necessary, and carefully stowed all equipment that might be required, from storm trisail to wire cutters.

On our arrival in Rochester we lightened ship by pumping our gas tanks nearly dry, leaving only a few gallons in case of emergency, and lowering the level of our water tanks. Shortly before the race our engine was sealed, a race regulation to make sure no unofficial use was made of auxiliaries during the race. On a Sunday night with a listless breeze we made our way slowly out of Rochester Harbour, through the gap at the mouth of the

Genesee River, and out into Lake Ontario. The lake was as smooth as glass, broken only by an occasional puff as it rippled its way across the surface. Fifteen minutes before the start we were towed to the right side of the starting line, as were many others, since we had virtually no steerage way. The preparatory gun was fired at ten minutes to seven. Five minutes later the warning gun was fired. Seconds later we were rail down as the rest of the fleet heeled to sudden puffs of wind which appeared from nowhere. It was phenomenal the way the wind rose minutes before the start; a mighty bellows had been squeezed somewhere on a slight command, or perhaps our wishful thinking had been heard.

The gun cracked and eighteen yachts plowed across the starting line. Before the start I had attired myself in long woollies, heavy wool hunting pants, thick wool socks, flannel shirt and two heavy pullovers. I received many rude remarks from the crew, who suggested that perhaps I had no confidence in the navigators and was anticipating a trip through the Bering Strait. However, I was accustomed to the caprice of the weather, and prepared accordingly for a late August night on Lake Ontario. A few hours later I noticed the scantily clad crew make frequent trips below, hastily to pull on warm pants and heavy parkas. No comments were forthcoming, only sheepish grins.

The wind steadied shortly after the start and gradually increased as we headed on a northerly course out into the lake. A large number of the fleet had stayed inshore, hoping to pick up a fairing off the shore as the night wore on. However, we elected to follow a plumbline course for Stoney Island, feeling that should the wind shift more northerly, we should be in a windward position and not be forced to tack. This proved to be a wise decision.

As the sun set in a bright orange sky, we could make out the grey shapes of several others astern who were approximating the same course. A half mile to windward, and abreast, was the large ketch *Oriole IV*, a ninety-eight-footer which had been owned by the late George H. Gooderham. She was footing fast in the fading light and was as anxious for heavy wind conditions as we were. We anticipated a close boat-for-boat race with her, feeling our advantage lay on windward legs, while she possessed more speed off the wind under fresh conditions. By eleven o'clock we were sailing alone, unable to pick up the position of any of our opposition.

The wind picked up to half to three-quarter gale force and hauled steadily around to the north. We replaced our large reaching balloon sail with our Genoa jib as we close hauled to the shifting wind. Our log was registering ten knots as we sliced through rising steep short seas. The crew were in good spirits, despite the drenchings they received from handling the headsails when she drove her bow through a white roller. We were rail down and every so often a torrent of water came surging aft along the deck. The crew by this time had moved well aft on the windward side. As an added precaution, lifelines were strung forward; a man overboard in heavy seas at night is a sailor's nightmare.

As we approached Stoney it was necessary to decide whether to round from the north or the south. The shift in the wind settled the matter; it soon became apparent that, should we take the southerly route, it would necessitate tacking up through the strait between the island and mainland. We held our course hard on the wind until our dead reckoned position indicated we could come about on the other tack and lay the northerly tip of the islands. Just before we reached this position the lights of a large lake freighter loomed up on our port bow. Her course lay directly across ours and, according to the rule of the road, should have altered, as sailing vessels have right-of-way over ships driven by power. We flashed our identification and received the answer, "You are sailing into danger." This, quite properly, might have been interpreted, "Go to hell!" We eased our helm to round the stern of the freighter, and by so doing lost valuable moments. It was probably fortunate for the captain that our voices could not be heard above the roar of the wind.

Shortly afterwards we came about on the port tack. Our navigator on watch informed us that we were approximately eight miles from the lighthouse on Stoney Island, which we should be able to pick up after holding our course for about twenty minutes. Half an hour later we were still unable to pick

up the light. By this time there appeared to be some confusion as
to whether we were still in Lake Ontario or had by chance strayed
up the Hudson Canal waterway. The navigators, both of whom
were ex-naval officers, had a hurried consultation. Numerous
charts were unrolled in succession, and I am not sure that one of
the Bering Strait was not among them. By this time we could
make out the dark shape of land all around, and as this end of
the lake was spotted with treacherous shoals, we virtually hove
to until an accurate position could be fixed. Some twenty minutes
later the experts came on deck and I was informed that, as they
had expected all along, we were in the eastern end of Lake Ontario. Shortly thereafter we picked up the Stoney Island lighthouse.

Adjacent to Stoney Island was Galoo Island, a narrow channel
less than a quarter of a mile wide separating the two. By staying
dead centre in the channel there was sufficient depth of water
to sail between the two. We decided to gamble, thereby saving
two miles, and fortunately managed to grope our way between
the two islands.

We left the two islands astern just as the grey dawn started
to break. It was three-quarters of an hour later before it was
light enough to pick up the position of the rest of the fleet.
Binoculars were quickly brought on deck; a careful scanning
produced nothing. Just when we were about to give up, one
of the crew spotted a large white hull with two masts, which
appeared to be the same size, anchored under the lee of Stoney
Island. It could not be identified as one of the yachts entered in
the race and it remained a mystery until some six hours later.

The wind maintained its strength and we were reaching
effortlessly down the lake, carrying in addition to our jib, main
and mizzen, our balloon sail and mizzen staysail. The wind
proved too much for the mizzen staysail, which split across the
head. It was quickly lowered and needle and thread put to work
to make it usable if and when it should be required again. The
spinnaker met a similar fate later in the morning when it was
hoisted to replace the balloon sail as the wind came astern. It
was a twenty-foot rip this time, which required several hours of

stitching by four or five of the crew before it was ready for use. We hoisted a smaller spinnaker in the interval.

By early afternoon the wind had slackened perceptibly and was gradually shifting ahead. Eventually we were tacking, with what little wind there was right on our nose. Fearing that we had sailed into doldrums off the Scotch Bonnets we expected to see other yachts popping over the horizon at any moment.

Just at this time we picked up the first broadcast describing the race. We were jubilant when the commentator announced that the Canadian ketch *Nonchalant* from Toronto was leading the fleet, and dismayed to hear that *Oriole IV* had lost twenty feet of her mainmast in the heavy seas the night before. We realized that it must have been she that we had seen anchored under the lee of Stoney Island. The thirty-five to forty-five mile an hour winds had taken a heavy toll in addition to *Oriole IV. Fo'castle* from Rochester had also lost her spar. Five other yachts had shredded their mainsails or suffered some other damage which forced them to retire.

By seven o'clock the wind freshened and once again we were on the move. Gradually the wind eased aft until we were laying our course to Toronto. By nine o'clock we were again rail down, the foam boiling under our lee.

At one o'clock we rounded the island in front of Toronto, passing into Toronto Harbour through the western gap. There we were greeted by the Royal Canadian Yacht Club launch, packed with sailing enthusiasts from the club. Vociferous greetings were exchanged as we slid through the harbour, the launch struggling to keep up with us. We cleared Toronto Harbour through the eastern gap and set our course on the last leg.

A steady thirty mile an hour wind held all the next morning, and with Genoa set we reached across to Rochester in nine hours ten minutes, breaking our previous record for the ninety-one mile run by twenty minutes.

On approaching the finish line we could see no sign of the judges' boat, which was caught completely off guard by our quick arrival from Toronto. They just managed to arrive on the finishing line to fire the gun. It was a tired but happy crew that lowered the canvas as we moved slowly under power into Rochester Harbour.

We completed the course in forty-one hours and forty-two minutes, our log reading just under 400 miles for the total distance, a record which, it is claimed by many, will stand for years.

Victory was not ours, however. *Avilion*, skippered by Fred Temple from Toledo, Ohio, sailed an excellent race to take the laurels and we had to be content to take second place on corrected time despite the fact that we finished ten and a half hours ahead of the nearest rival. Such are the vicissitudes of yacht racing. We did, however, win a trophy for finishing first, and another for placing second on corrected time.

Over the past twenty years there has been a most noticeable trend in sailing. There are few places in the world today where the harbours lie crammed with the large yachts that sailed the waters two decades ago. In such places as New Zealand and Australia I was impressed by the hundreds of small sailing craft of all descriptions swarming over the harbours. In Canada, England and the United States the same trend is in evidence. There are few yachts requiring large paid crews today. However, this exciting, keenly competitive sport is increasing in popularity every year with the introduction of small one-design classes. The Dragon class at the Royal Canadian Yacht Club, which was non-existent in 1951, has been built up to a competitive racing fleet of twelve in three years. A boost was given to the popularity of the Dragons by the visit in 1954 to the Royal Canadian Yacht Club of the Duke of Edinburgh's *Bluebottle* which was raced in Montreal and Toronto against stiff competition from Canadian Dragons. The Duke of Edinburgh's Cup was captured this year in Montreal by a Royal Canadian Yacht Club crew skippered by Spence Hanna.

Also gaining in popularity are yachts of the metre class. Lake Ontario now has one of the best 6-metre fleets in existence. In 1954 the George Cup, awarded for United States-Canadian competition in 6-metre craft, returned to Canada after an absence of two years. Later in the season, the North American 6-metre championship was won for the Royal Canadian Yacht Club by *Buzzy II*, skippered by Bill Gooderham. In the 8-metre class,

Venture II, flying the R.C.Y.C. colours, skippered by Dave Howard and owned by Norman Walsh, defeated *Iskareen* in a breathtaking series of races at Rochester and brought the Canada's Cup back to this country after a fifty-one year residence in the United States. The outstanding success of this season must be a great source of satisfaction to the members of the Club, its committee of management, the flag officers, and that fine yachtsman and sportsman, Tom Wade, who after long years of service to the Club has been again honoured by his second term of office as its Commodore.

International competition has flourished since the war years, particularly in the metre class and international ratings. One need only glance at the list of entries for such famous classics as the Bermuda and Honolulu races to see the international flavour of these events, as yearly the list of foreign entries increases.

I no longer participate actively in sailing events, but I am still keenly interested in the sport which provided me such immeasurable enjoyment for so many years.

CHAPTER XIV

THE EXPORT PROGRAMME

THE THIRD PART of our plans for post-war conversion concerned our expansion into the field of foreign markets. After the war's end we started to put these plans into operation. One of our first foreign enquiries came from a Chinese gentleman named Lu. We negotiated with Mr. Lu for a contract to build turbines for ships that he was to operate on the Yangtze River.

I met Mr. Lu in New York to discuss his proposals, and was impressed by the fine appearance of this dignified and courteous Chinese. He was in his hotel suite, and had with him two Chinese engineers, one of whom was a Cornell graduate. The latter acted as interpreter for Mr. Lu spoke little English.

The interpreter traced the life story of Lu, who was apparently a large operator in China, with whom shipping was only one of many activities. He outlined Mr. Lu's humble beginnings, his early life of poverty, and how, due to his energy and enterprise, his fortunes and his influence had grown. He told how, when Mr. Lu's power was fairly widespread, the Yangtze River was infested with bandits. Mr. Lu, however, wanted to operate on this river, so, the interpreter blandly put it, when Mr. Lu moved in the bandits moved out. We did not conclude a deal with Mr. Lu.

We were also interested in the possibilities in Mexico, for we felt that there was a demand in that country for some of our skills and experience.

During the war, members of the Mexican Embassy visited our plant. They were interested in what we had accomplished in Canada. One day I was taking the Mexican Ambassador, and a man named Tollidero through the plant. Mr. Tollidero, the tough boss of the unions in Central America, was visibly impressed when he saw the array of firearms we were producing. When we reached the ranges where we tested our weapons I asked them if they would like to shoot. They both were anxious to try, and each took his turn with one of our Browning automatic pistols. Both hit the target and then asked me to try my skill; I agreed, and took my turn. That day my shooting eye was in and I turned in an unusually good score. Mr. Tollidero, on seeing my target, turned to me and said, "Major, in my country you would be a very respected citizen!"

After the war, with a group of Canadian businessmen, I visited Mexico, at the invitation of the President, and met and dealt with members of the Cabinet. I had an interview with the President, General Avila Camacho, to whom I presented a pistol. The President fondly toyed with his new weapon and we exchanged polite pleasantries through an interpreter. I viewed the facilities in Mexico, and made a survey of their requirements, and then met the Finance Minister with whom we dealt.

As a result of this trip, we received a concrete proposal from Mexico to set up and equip a first-class tool-making shop there. I felt that any industry setting up in Mexico would provide its own toolroom, and that one of their first requirements should be for a general plate shop, developing from that into a more general engineering type of plant. They, however, wanted a toolroom. At this time we were negotiating with a group in India, and as I did not believe that we had sufficient technical personnel to handle both situations, I decided to carry through the Indian proposal and drop the one in Mexico. It seemed to me at that time that India had greater potentialities for us than Mexico.

These trips to Mexico were fascinating for me for we saw a great deal of the country, and were entertained in the best possible fashion. It was somewhat trying at times, however, for I found it difficult to adjust to the Mexican tendency to disregard the clock as a thing of importance. This fact earned for me the title, among my Mexican friends, of "Major Right-now".

Our group visited Vera Cruz, where we were scheduled to be entertained by the Governor of Vera Cruz, who is now President Adolpho Ruiz Cortinez of Mexico. On arriving in the town,

General Escobar, our host, was somewhat perturbed when he realized that he had neglected to find out when and where the Governor was to entertain us. We asked him what we were to do, and he said to follow him, the Governor would find us.

He led us to a beautiful restaurant, near the edge of the sea, and we sat out under the stars in the warm tropical evening, eating a delicious meal on the patio. The sea provided a backdrop for a most excellent marimba orchestra, and the air, the food, and the wine made the time pass very quickly. It was quite late and we had all but forgotten our would-be host when the General announced, "Here comes the Governor now, and he is looking very sad." He brightened considerably on seeing us, and joined us for the rest of a delightful evening.

We fished for tarpon at Vera Cruz with some success. We visited the Governor, Mr. Cortinez, at his palace at Jalopa and stopped off at the ranch of Miguel Aleman who was to succeed Camacho as President. I have retained the most pleasant memories of the warm courtesy extended to me by the President, and by the two distinguished Mexicans who succeeded him.

I returned to Mexico as a guest of the Government for the Presidential inauguration of Miguel Aleman. The guests were all assembled well before the time scheduled for the inauguration. The retiring President, Avila Camacho, and his retinue took their places on the platform at 11.00 a.m. and we waited, expecting at each moment the arrival of Aleman. General Escobar had been assigned to look after me. I noticed he wore a small silver button in his lapel. I asked its significance, and he told me that special friends of the new President were responsible for his personal safety, and that each wore a silver button identifying him as a member of this elite guard. Time passed, and the President did not arrive; he was five, ten, twenty and then nearly thirty minutes late, without any word or sign of his coming. I turned to Escobar and told him I was afraid he had lost his button. He smiled and said, "He will be here." The President-elect arrived at last and the ceremonies were started. The following evening there was a wonderful inaugural ball attended by diplomatic notables, and Lana Turner. It was a successful day.

IN 1947 INDIA WAS TAKING its first steps as an independent nation.
I was interested in India for many reasons. It seemed to me that
she must embark almost immediately on an industrialization
programme and if that were to be the case the country would
offer a fertile field for the exploitation of that phase of our post-
war programme which called for expansion into the export market. Also, I already had friends in India.

I first met K. C. Mahindra during the war, when as head of
the Indian Mission to the United States and Canada he visited our
plant in Toronto. He was a man of great charm, exceptionally
able and possessed of a fine sense of humour. We became friends,
and our discussions, together with those I had with others of his
country, convinced me that Canadians could play a part in helping the people of India to develop their country.

Accordingly, even before India had been granted Dominion
status, I concluded, in 1946, arrangements with Indian industrialists which enabled us to participate in the proposed industrial
expansion of India. These resulted in two major projects. The
first was put into effect in 1947 when Inglis personnel were
selected to act as consultants for the complete design, construction
and equipping of a plant in Calcutta. This plant is now producing textile machinery for the existing textile mills and is
expected to equip those that are yet to be erected.

We also executed a contract to design and manufacture a
paper-making plant which would produce fine paper from bamboo pulp. The machinery was designed and manufactured in
Canada, transported to India, and erected there under our super-
vision. We sent Canadian personnel to train Indians to operate
the machines and to put the mill in operation. Our men have
now returned, leaving the Indian group in complete charge of the
new factory.

It was a project undertaken jointly by government and private
capital, although the mill is now in private hands, and it was
the first such installation by a Canadian company. The design,
manufacture and installation of this equipment offer a good
example of how our country, by supplying and imparting technical knowledge and experience, gained in our own plants, to
personnel in India, can help in the development of that country.

While the contract for this project was being negotiated, I made several visits to India, in order to study general conditions there. I made the first trip there in 1949, via Egypt, where I spent some time in Cairo negotiating with the Egyptian government to see if we could make some business arrangements there. I went first to the Commerce Ministry, since I was interested in possible pulp and paper developments, and I was requested to visit the Defence Minister, who had some proposals for us concerning gun plants in Egypt. Those proposals were of such scope that I considered them unrealistic for a country with so little engineering and production background. There was no further discussion, as I had no interest in any project other than the production of equipment for commercial use.

I stayed in Egypt only a few days; in that time I could not form an appraisal of the country. I was nevertheless struck by the obvious luxury in which a few people lived in contrast with the extreme poverty of the majority. Peasants were tilling meagre fields with implements that differed little from those used in Biblical times. Such a situation must inevitably create unrest, and the later overthrow of the monarchy was no surprise to me.

I took many photographs in Egypt, despite warnings that non-Egyptians with cameras were not popular. My wife and I were being driven through a street in Cairo, and I was photographing some buildings, when suddenly a policeman jumped on the car and said that I was under arrest. He had us driven to the police station where he took me inside, leaving my wife sitting rather uneasily in the car. It did not make her any less uneasy when she recalled that only a short while before an angry mob of Egyptians had stoned an American tourist to death for taking pictures.

Inside the police station I was questioned first by a sergeant, then by a captain. While the latter questioned me, a man whom I took to be a colonel in the police sat and listened, saying nothing. I told them that I knew of no restriction on photography and that I could not leave Egypt without at least a few pictures of that country's beautiful mosques. Then for the first time the man I took to be the colonel spoke. He said, "I will help you get your pictures." He turned out to be the head of the Cairo police force and he provided me with a police escort so that I got my pictures in safety, and with the blessings of the law.

On our first trip to Egypt we were met and entertained by Mr. Boyer, the Canadian Trade Commissioner in Egypt. He looked after us, and helped us in every way possible and I was more than proud that our country was represented abroad by men of his calibre. We were in Cairo again in 1952, but owing to the unrest in the city we were not permitted to leave the airport. Two days later I was shocked to learn that Mr. Boyer had been killed in the riots in Cairo during which the Cairo Jockey Club was burned to the ground. He was killed in the club at which he had entertained us on our first visit.

From Egypt we went on to Pakistan, and then India. We arrived by air at Bombay which is a modern, cosmopolitan city of some two million people, situated on a natural harbour and possessing miles of boulevards flanked by modern apartment houses running along the water's edge. There is great commercial activity in Bombay and here I spent several days in discussion with our Indian associates. In my journeys about the city I saw no rope tricks, and the only snake I saw was an ancient and sleepy cobra that danced up out of a basket to the tunes of an ancient and sleepy snake charmer who sat begging on the street, looking most incongruous and anachronistic against the background of the modern city. It is, I suppose, completely understandable that some reports from India should feature the exotic and the sensational rather than the factual and realistic, and that the visitor's preconceived notions of this fascinating country should be coloured by these accounts.

I had the opportunity of travelling over a part of India to see the way of life in the cities and the country, and I met people from all grades of society while I was there. John Kearney, who was then Canada's High Commissioner to India, arranged many meetings for me, as did my Indian friends. In Delhi I met several members of the Indian cabinet and had the privilege of an interview with Pandit Jawaharlal Nehru, the Prime Minister. This meeting was arranged by Mr. Malik, the Indian High Commissioner to Canada, a charming Sikh and a great golfer, whom I had met in Toronto. In talking to Nehru, I had imme-

diately a feeling of the great sincerity of the man. Here was a
patriot who had no thought of politics, except as a means for
the betterment of the condition of the people of India. His
every action was directed to tasks of great magnitude, always
with the idea of raising the standards of living in his country.
He was opposed to Communism, and had instigated severe legis-
lation against it. He came from a wealthy family which had
abandoned all the comforts and luxuries of life for the cause they
all believed in. He struck me as an idealist who may yet be
faced with some phases of the grim realities of life which sur-
round his country. He was socialistic in his outlook. This is
not difficult to understand when one considers his personal sacri-
fices and the conditions in some of the Princely States with their
examples of a few men of great wealth presiding over the lives
and fate of millions of men and women living in extreme poverty.

At that time there was little evidence of Communism in
western India, on the Bombay side, although there were some
signs of it in the eastern part near Calcutta. We flew to Calcutta
in a plane which included among its passengers Lady Mountbatten. When we arrived at the airport we saw great numbers
of troops stationed in all sections of the field. Close at hand a
plane was burning. We thought the troops were there as a guard
of honour for Lady Mountbatten. Later we learned that only a
short time before Communist raiders had shot some guards,
burned the aircraft, and killed several English executives in a nearby plant by throwing them in the furnace.

Three years later I saw what might have been the first signs
of Communism in Bombay. There was a strike of the Bombay
hotels that was possibly Communist inspired, although the Indian
people there claimed it was not.

In India we attended, among other things, the garden party
at the palace of the first Indian Governor-General and the Bombay races. These are two of the most colourful events I have
witnessed in all my travels.

The Bombay races presented an unforgettable scene. Sixty or
seventy thousand people were in attendance, and there was some
exciting racing. We admired the diversity of costumes worn by
the beautiful Indian women who, in their magnificent saris, pro-

vided every colour in the spectrum ranging from white through the daintiest pastel shades to the most vivid hues. The costumes of the men, most of whom were in native dress, were also interesting and colourful. The colourings were all the more striking in the bright and clear sunshine of the Indian winter.

All this colour, and more, was in evidence at the garden party at the Governor-General's palace in New Delhi with its imposing approach and magnificent gardens. We passed through the palace into the garden where the Governor-General, clad in his white lalchi costume, was receiving his guests. Lady Mountbatten, who was his house-guest, received with him. It was a magnificent spectacle. The members of a lancer regiment, in bright red uniforms with lances and coloured pennants, were stationed at intervals at the rear of the palace and down the path leading to the receiving line. Here in the formal garden with its beautiful flowers and many fountains, members of the Diplomatic Corps, some in native costume, mingled with the other guests. The Indian women in their gorgeous saris contributed further colour to this scene. At the end of the garden were the tea tables presided over by the turbaned servants of the household, in bright red uniforms.

In all, I made four trips to India, and my discussions there with the Prime Minister, Nehru, and some of his Cabinet Ministers, as well as my association with Indian industrialists, taught me a great deal about the country. It is, of course, trite to say that India is a land of great contrasts; yet that is the visitor's foremost impression of the country. It is a land of efficient airlines, and a literacy rate of only ten per cent; of modern cities and jungle villages; of brilliant doctors and a low life-expectancy. These are some of the things which provide the challenge that is being met by the government.

India is a country with a population of 327,000,000 people. It is old in history and culture, rich in resources, and stands on the threshold of a great industrial development. The possibilities of this sprawling giant of a land are beyond the farthest reaches of the imagination and Canada can play a great part in its development.

It is obvious that this government is in the hands of a sincere group of men, conscious of their responsibilities and determined that India shall and must take her proper place among the nations of the world. There are problems to be solved that will take many years, and doubtless many mistakes will be made, but the goal is clear, and is being brought closer day by day. Two major problems have been overcome in a time thought impossible to outside observers. The religious differences between Moslem and Hindu have been composed to the point where many Moslems, who fled India during the upheavals that followed partition, have now returned home. Secondly, the integration of the Princely States has been accomplished in a manner and time that was not thought possible half a dozen years ago. The problems of illiteracy, of low standards of living, of resources yet to be developed, remain, but a promising start has been made on their solution.

The development of resources and industrial expansion are now under way. This, the government hopes, will lead to the improved living standards they desire. The government, in seeking to develop the country, has nationalized railways, arms, and atomic energy production. They may also, at the end of ten years, take over steel, coal, the manufacture of aircraft and ships, telephone, telegraph, wireless and mineral oils.

Between the East and the West there are certain fundamental differences which must never be lost sight of in any dealings that Canada may engage in with countries of the East.

Some centuries ago the relationship between East and West became that of subject peoples to colonizing powers. In my travels I grew accustomed to hearing of the ills and woes that befell various countries colonized by the West and it would appear that their present ills, of whatever nature, should be laid at the door of the colonizing power.

The truth is that those countries were inhabited by human beings who possessed all the virtues and weaknesses that beset the entire human race. This resulted in the exploitation of the masses by their own nationals long before Westerners reached their shores. It is equally true that the colonizing powers, in

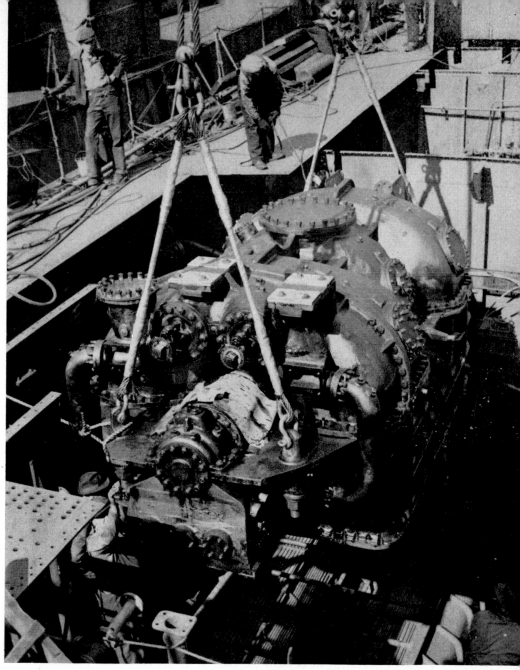

Royal Canadian Navy

THE FIRST MARINE TURBINE BUILT IN CANADA
Canadian destroyers which participated in the Korean War were powered by these modern marine turbines built in Canada for the first time by our company. The first turbine built is shown here, being lowered into a Tribal Class destroyer.

THE END OF THE FIRST ROCHESTER RACE

Nonchalant, shown at top, had completed the course in 41 hours, 42 minutes, her log reading just under 400 miles, a record which, it is claimed by many, will stand for years.

many cases, did not carry out the full responsibilities imposed upon them by the advantages they enjoyed; but as I have suggested elsewhere, there is little evidence that the native rulers did as well for their people. In any event, the question is now academic. Many of the Eastern countries have gained their independence and their destinies are now in the hands of their own governments.

There is a great disparity in human affairs in the two segments of the world. Here, on the North American continent, we continue to pile up tremendous surpluses of food and stocks of grain while in the East hundreds of millions of people are undernourished. They suffer malnutrition, lack of medical attention, and, indeed, of most of the facilities which we consider essential to our health and well-being. Illiteracy is a serious problem in the East and the average life expectancy runs as low as thirty years. Only a quarter of the world's population lives in the favoured areas.

The gap between East and West is so wide that it will require years of careful planning and patient waiting to bridge it. In the West for centuries we have been accustomed to representative and responsible government; authoritarianism in one form or another has been the most customary government in the East. There is no point of contact between our standards of living. Here our preoccupation is with the latest design of automatic washing machine, or the newest model car; in the East, too often, every effort must be concentrated on the single task of staying alive. Under these circumstances it is idle for our statesmen to talk only of the advantages of an abstract ideal called democracy over another political philosophy known as Communism to peoples few of whom could define either term.

The civilization and the cultures of these peoples are much older than our own; their sense of time and their philosophy of life are completely different. Where we might want something done and think six months too long to do it in, they might have until recently considered as satisfactory progress a step forward in a hundred years. For the Westerner to attempt to speed up the course of events is not the most sensible procedure. One recalls *The Naulahka*, Kipling's tale of the American who "tried to hustle the East" and the author's wry commentary on it:

> *Now it is not good for the Christian health to*
> *hustle the Aryan brown*
> *For the Christian riles and the Aryan smiles,*
> *and it weareth the Christian down.*

Before we can deal effectively with the East we must learn to understand its peoples, and we shall never accomplish that by sitting at home and reading about them. During my combat service in the first World War we always considered to be a good general the one who went to see for himself, who visited the front line and familiarized himself with conditions there. He was then able to interpret more intelligently the reports which he received from his commanders in the forward areas. If we are to understand the peoples of the East more and more of our leaders in government, in business, in industry, and in the arts must go to the countries of the East, to see them for themselves, to meet and to talk with their opposite numbers. In this they might well take a leaf from the book of that gentleman and states-man, our own Prime Minister, the Right Honourable Louis St. Laurent, whose recent journey to the countries of the East and conferences with governmental leaders there have done so much to strengthen our relations with them. The reports from his embassies will now carry more significance. Incidentally, perhaps the greatest service that Mr. Malenkov might render to his country, to the people whom he governs and the cause of peace, would be to leave the fastness of the Kremlin and travel about the world, meeting and talking with the peoples of other lands. Understanding and co-operation must always move along a two-way lane.

It is my belief that the principal contribution that Canada can make to the cause of better understanding between East and West is to do everything in her power to help the peoples of the countries there help themselves to a better standard of living. I have already told how our company, immediately after the war, designed and manufactured a paper-making plant for industrial interests in India, supervised the erection of it there, and sent

Canadians to India to train Indians to operate the machines and the mill. India also sent technicians to be trained in our plants. An extension of this policy on a greater scale is what is required for better East-West relationships. Fortunately, this policy has been accepted by our leaders and the machinery set up to implement it. The Colombo Plan of the Commonwealth of Nations, designed to help the peoples of under-developed countries make the utmost use of their rich natural resources, is a long step towards dispelling ignorance and poverty wherever these might be found and towards the much-to-be-desired betterment of East-West relationships.

CHAPTER XV

HUNTING IN INDIA

DURING MY STAY in India, in 1949, I had the good fortune to see something of life in one of the Princely States. By that year most of the States had acceded either to Pakistan or to India. Cooch-Behar was the last State to be taken over by the Central Government of India. At the time of my visit, arrangements had not yet been completed for the accession and the Maharaja invited our friend, K. C. Mahindra, to spend a few days at his palace. K.C. arranged for my wife and me to accompany him on the visit. I was all the more interested since a tiger hunt from elephants was afoot.

Cooch-Behar lies in the plain of the Ganges, about 300 air miles north-by-east of Calcutta, and only fifty or sixty miles south of the foothills of the Himalayas. We flew there from Calcutta and joined the house party which included Maharajas from other States, and their Maharanees.

The principal topic of discussion among the guests, naturally, was the drama of the accession of the Princely States in which they were all actors. They recognized that they were witnessing the end of an age, that they, their States, and their way of life were anachronisms in the modern era, and that they were powerless to stop the transition even if they wished to do so. Their desire was that the change-over be made slowly, for they felt that the Princely States might still serve a useful purpose as a bulwark against Communism. The Central Government, however, urged by Patel, the Deputy Prime Minister, demanded speed in the change-over, arguing that far from being a bulwark against Communism, the feudalism that marked the governments of the majority of the States might be an inducement to it. The Government had other arguments. In all there were 562 of these Princely States which occupied two-fifths of the area of India and were inhabited by a quarter of its population. They varied in size from very large—15 million inhabitants in the largest— to very small—the population of the smallest was twenty-seven. Autonomous in varying degrees except for the conduct of foreign affairs, they had their own police, coinage, postal system, laws and standing armies. The Central Government felt that India, as a nation, could not exist while such a large proportion of the land and the people still lived under feudal régimes. They were afraid, also, that if haste was not made, certain of the States with Moslem rulers might accede to Pakistan, and that other Maha-rajas might attempt to strengthen and maintain their positions. As the States declared their independence, then, the Central Gov-ernment acted with speed to incorporate them into India. Though there were many problems of geography, religion and politics to be solved, the bold stroke succeeded and the drama was played out to its last act more quickly and with less difficulty than had been anticipated.

The rulers of the Princely States were well treated in the final settlement. These men were of a character as varied as the States they ruled. Some were good and progressive men who worked for the welfare of their people; others were indifferent, absentee rulers, interested in racing, polo, and hunting; a few had little to commend them. As part of the terms of the settlement the Maharajas were allowed to retain a portion of their lands and were paid a percentage of the income of their States. Their palaces and their treasuries, however, were taken over by the Central Government, and their private troops were incorporated into the Indian Army.

We spent our first day at Cooch-Behar exploring the palace and the palace grounds. We had tea in the garden and watched the Maharaja, an excellent athlete and shot, and some of the other guests, play tennis. The following morning we watched the ceremony of the changing of the guard smartly executed by soldiers of the Maharaja's private army. The drill used in this ceremony was the same as that used by the Guards at Buck-ingham Palace. The Maharaja complained to me that times were not what they used to be. He had only about forty elephants and less than two hundred servants with which to run the palace.

The following day we were to proceed to a place about forty miles west of Cooch-Behar, where a herd of cattle had been attacked, and a tiger kill reported. The elephants had already been sent there and we were to leave early the following morning for the camp that had already been set up. The next morning we had breakfast at six o'clock and the party started out by jeep.

To reach the tiger country where the camp was located, we motored over narrow roads, some of which would make a washboard seem relatively smooth, and we were ferried across rivers on large rafts constructed of bamboo. We arrived at the camp and found that large tents had already been erected and pad elephants were standing ready to take us to the place allotted for the hunt. The pad elephant, as its name implies, has a large pad lashed to its back. A rope runs along either side of the pad and the rider holds on to this while the elephant is in motion. One after the other, the elephants were instructed by the mahout to kneel. Our mahout sat on the elephant's head behind the ears and carried a short pronged steel hook, with which he occasionally bonked the elephant on the head, either in anger or affection. The Maharaja of Dewas, a most interesting man, a delightful companion, and a keen hunter, came along with my wife and me on the elephant assigned to us. With his great hunting experience, he could tell me what to do, and what not to do, on an elephant. The line of thirty pad elephants moved across four miles of open country covered with jungle grass from four to six feet in height and we reached the place where the howdah elephants were in position. These are the elephants which had been especially trained to stand in position, rigid and motionless, when the tiger is driven towards them. The howdah on their backs is a wicker cage about three feet wide in front and three-and-a-half feet high, tapering back to a slightly lesser width. It contains two seats. The hunter sits in the front seat and there is a gun rack and ammunition pouches on the inside front of the howdah, and thermos bottles with water or other refreshment underneath the seat.

There were five guns for the shoot that morning, each mounted on one of the five howdah elephants that were in position in line forty yards apart. In front of this line the jungle grass had been cut down, making a clearing twenty-five yards wide which ran the full length of the howdah elephant line. This was the clearing of the ring and the tiger would have to cross it if the beat were to be successful.

The pad elephants, with the Maharaja on the leading elephant, started into the jungle grass a quarter of a mile to our right, and moved straight out for a distance of half a mile. They then swung at right angles to the left and moved through the grass until they were directly in front of us about half a mile away, twenty-five yards apart and facing us. This line of elephants then started to move towards us and the beat had commenced. It had not proceeded very far when a boar ran out across the ring and the elephant on which I was standing started to sway ever so slightly. The Maharaja who was with us on the howdah told me that elephants do not like boar, as the boar sometimes panic and occasionally charge the elephant's feet and try to rip them with their tusks. He told me that I could expect a well-trained howdah elephant to be almost motionless on the appearance of a tiger, as the elephant was not afraid of tiger.

The line of elephants came closer and closer. Suddenly an elephant in the middle of the line trumpeted. The Maharaja immediately whispered to me, "Tiger"; the word was hardly out of his mouth when we heard a terrific double roar. The line of elephants continued to approach. Nothing further happened until suddenly we noticed a ripple in the grass twenty or thirty yards on the other side of the clearing, which moved towards us and then turned abruptly to the left and moved out of sight, passing in the grass in front of the two howdah elephants on my left. The tiger had "broken out" instead of crossing the open space.

As the pad elephants closed in we proceeded back to the camp. The ride on the elephant, either pad or howdah, was not at all tiring, the walk of the elephant having the effect of a long, gentle, rocking motion from side to side. When we reached the camp we found luncheon spread under the trees on the river bank. The inhabitants of a neighbouring village were gathered there to watch us eat, knowing that when we were finished they also would share in the picnic. The elephants were walked into the river beside the camp, and watered. After lunch we engaged in several other beats, all of which produced boar and deer but no tiger. We passed through some country where the elephant grass was ten feet high and I remarked to the Maharaja of Dewas that I had never seen grass this high before. He told me that this was only small grass, and that later in the afternoon we would pass through an area where the grass was twenty-five feet high. Sure enough, we later did pass, with elephants in line, into an area where the elephants to the right and left of me were lost to my view in the grass. While I was standing upright in my howdah taking moving pictures, the grass still reached six or eight feet over my head.

The last beat was what was called a "scrub beat". Here the line of elephants moved slowly through an open area with low grass two to six feet high, and game put up in front of this line was shot at to provide for the game dinner we were to have the following night. I kept on taking movies, as I was not quick enough to pick up the game moving rapidly through the grass in sufficient time to be reasonably sure of a dropping shot.

On our return to the palace, after a bath and change which we found acceptable, we sat down to dinner. The main course consisted of "deer strogonov", the preparation of which was supervised by a White Russian guest by the name of Boris.

The following evening the game dinner was served on one of the upper balconies of the palace which the ladies had arranged to resemble the floor of a typical New York night club. The walls were adorned for the occasion with very clever sketches, decorations and murals previously drawn by some of the guests. In this setting music and entertainment contributed to a most enjoyable evening.

The next morning we bade good-bye to our host and returned to Calcutta.

I HAD OTHER hunting experiences in India, both before and after the tiger hunt at Cooch-Behar.

On one occasion I was the guest of a Sikh whom I had met while he was visiting Canada. He had then insisted that should I ever come to India I should be his guest on a hunt to be arranged by him. He lived in Nagpur and my wife and I flew there from Bombay. For a number of years I had suffered from a sinus infection. In Bombay I had a recurrence of this infection and I arrived in Nagpur with a temperature of 102°. However, I insisted on going on to Chanda as all arrangements had already been made. If necessary, I could be put to bed when we arrived at the camp.

We motored south 120 miles from Nagpur to Chanda. The road, a very fine one, had a pavement, flanked on either side with a dirt road of equal width. We passed an endless procession of cattle and bullock carts moving along the side of the road, and were at times enveloped in clouds of penetrating fine dust. Only those who have travelled in India on its dirt or jungle roads will realize the extreme fineness of this dust, which seems to have the capacity of penetrating the interior of closed cars and covering equipment and guns, no matter how well they seem to have been stored. This was not my first experience of Indian dust. I had sealed the muzzles and breech ends of my rifles, as well as all moving parts of my telescopic sights, with scotch tape. We tied handkerchiefs around our faces, below the eyes, to act as filters, in imitation of the native who, in similar awkward circumstances, winds his cotton scarf around his face.

We arrived in Chanda in time for bed and spent a very comfortable night in the rest house. These dak bungalows are constructed by the Government, and are in suitable locations throughout the jungle areas to provide accommodation for government officials on their inspection tours of the forests. When not in use for such purposes they can be rented from the authorities of the district for hunting parties. The buildings are well constructed. In general, they consist of a combined living and dining-room flanked on either side by a bedroom and dressing-room. The rest house at Chanda, however, was considerably larger, having four bedrooms, four dressing-rooms and four bathrooms which, of course, were of the most primitive. There is also a smaller building from which the servants provide the food and services required by the occupants of the rest house.

The following morning we travelled twenty miles east of Chanda to Kolsa, which lies on the magnificent plain of Nagpur, a beautifully wooded area, generally flat, and crisscrossed with narrow dirt jungle roads. Here our camp headquarters was again a rest house. Our shikari, or hunter, with the bearers and attendants, awaited us here.

The general plan was to spend the week in this jungle area. Should a kill be reported by the natives in any of the neighbouring villages we would be advised and would try to deal with the marauder. The area abounded in deer but there were only a few tiger and panther.

An old elephant called Bolapyari, meaning "Beautiful Flower", had been provided for the hunt and we spent the next couple of days going into the jungle on the elephant, watching and photographing deer, and picking off two for supplies for the camp. It was a new and interesting experience for my wife and me, aboard Beautiful Flower. She was gentle, intelligent and obedient.

When we came to a stream with a bridge over it she would test its strength with her foreleg. If she considered it strong enough to bear her weight she would cross the bridge, if not, she would turn and wade through the stream. If we encountered heavily treed jungle and she could not pass between the trees, she would lower her head against one of the obstructing trees and slowly push until the obstruction was removed. Occasionally we would be blocked by heavy branches of vines dropping down from above, or overhead roots. It was fascinating to watch her assess the obstruction and then either grasp one very thick vine and tear it down, or wind her trunk around a group of smaller ones and jerk it out of the way. At the camp she would gently take balls of rice out of our hands. In every way Bolapyari was a real lady.

On the third day one of the natives reported that a tiger had been heard roaring about four miles west of our location. The shikari, a tracker, and myself went aboard Bolapyari and started

across country through lightly wooded jungle with bamboo undergrowth, to see if we could locate the tiger. After we had
proceeded about four miles, raising many herds of chital deer,
we arrived in open territory. It was slightly rolling terrain covered with jungle grass three to four feet high. To our left, some
500 yards away, a stream with trees along both its banks mean-
dered through the plain. We became aware of the chattering
of monkeys calling to each other. The tracker and shikari
thought that we should turn towards the stream, which we did.
They seemed to think that this disturbance might indicate the
presence of the tiger.

We circled around in this area for three-quarters of an hour,
during which we saw nothing but deer. Finally we decided that
we had better start back to the camp. Before doing so we shot a
chital to take back with us for food. When we went over to pick
up the chital, old Bolapyari was ordered by the mahout to sit.
She did, but she had no sooner done so than she started to raise
herself on her forelegs again; and on being ordered again to sit,
she kept sitting down and raising herself. We were able, at
last, to clamber off the restive elephant, and with some difficulty
lashed the chital on her back. We returned to the camp without
further incident.

About one o'clock in the morning we were awakened by the
village dogs barking furiously, and became conscious of a tremendous commotion as if everything had suddenly become alive
in the stillness of the night. We heard an increasing crescendo
of the cries of peacocks and jungle fowl, the chatter of monkeys,
and it seemed as though a wave of terror was passing from our
right, towards us, then by us; finally we could hear the tumult
subsiding in the distance beyond us. My wife and I had never
heard such an unearthly pandemonium before.

By morning we had the solution both to the restiveness of
Bolapyari and the wave of terror in the night.

Apparently when we stopped to pick up the chital the tiger
was somewhere very close to us in the jungle grass. His presence
had been sensed by the elephant but not by us, and this was the
reason for the elephant's restiveness while we were attempting
to load the chital. Later the tracker took me beyond the camp

and showed me where every large footprint of Bolapyari was followed by a pug mark of a medium-sized tiger. The tiger that night had followed in the same route that we had taken when returning to the camp on the elephant, then had pursued a course swinging near the small native village, only 400 yards away from us, then behind our camp and back into the jungle.

On the following morning bearers arrived from a village about seven miles away. They told us that a panther had attacked their herd, killing one of the cattle. If we arrived at the village by noon, they would have all the villagers off the fields and would be ready to organize a beat to drive the panther out. We arrived at the village at that hour and found a hundred and fifty Indians gathered together.

We drove in a small bullock cart about half a mile outside the village where the kill had taken place. It was believed that the panther would be sleeping somewhere in the jungle, its position being indicated by the direction in which it had dragged its kill before it fed. The difference between a panther and a tiger kill is unmistakable. The panther always kills by leaping at the throat and sinking its fangs into the throat of the animal, whereas a tiger always leaps upon the back of the kill, and with its powerful forearm twists the head and breaks the animal's neck.

The shikari lined up the beaters along the road behind the machan and gave them their instructions for the beat. At this point I should explain the method of organizing a beat. A machan, or small platform, well camouflaged with leaves, is built twelve to fifteen feet up a tree and jungle brush is cleared in front of it for a radius of thirty or forty yards, to allow the best possible field of fire. The machan is located on a route that the animal is likely to take when being moved forward by the beaters, usually in a draw or nullah, or very often alongside a small dry river bed. The animal is more likely to follow a course of this kind which offers some cover and also provides the easiest route, rather than move over high ground.

The natives are divided into stops and beaters. The right line of stops is placed in position starting at the machan, moving out at an angle of about forty-five degrees from the machan, the men taking up a position in trees some thirty yards apart from each other. The left line of stops similarly begins at the machan and runs at an angle of forty-five degrees to the left.

There are, then, two lines of stops, one on each side of the machan, flaring out from it at an angle and in effect providing two lines of men up trees, with the narrow end of the funnel at the machan end. In this particular case we had thirty stops on each side, or a line of stops running 900 yards on either side of the machan.

The beaters are led through the jungle at the outside of the stops and then moved to form a semicircle across the wide end of the funnel. They carry pans, cymbals and other noise making instruments. Some carry axes as well, and here and there among them an occasional muzzle loader.

The function of the stops is to maintain a tapping on the trees as they see the animal approach. This turns the panther from one side to the other as he moves ahead of the beaters. The idea is to move him down this ever-narrowing funnel of stops to enable the hunter to get his shot. Without stops it would be practically hopeless to get a shot in a beat, as the animal might go anywhere. Sometimes, even with the stops, the animal breaks out between them.

The beat started at three o'clock. We soon became conscious of the faint shouts of the beaters in the far distance and these became louder and more audible as the beat progressed, finally swelling into a great crescendo. Startled deer ran in front of us and by us. Occasionally a wild boar came crashing through the jungle, but there was no sign of the panther. It is difficult to describe the air of tension and excitement on the machan, though I have experienced it many times since. The beaters were now within fifty or sixty yards in front of us and from time to time I saw a flash of white in the jungle as the beaters moved towards me.

Suddenly a large panther, walking very slowly and deliberately, moved into the clearing on my right, seemingly unperturbed by all the din pressing him forward. The line of beaters was not more than twenty yards behind him. My wife, sitting beside me with the moving picture camera, was so engrossed by her first sight of a panther that she quite forgot to use the camera. I watched and waited until the panther had moved to the right of the machan, as a bad shot would have put him back on top of the beaters.

As he was starting to move by the machan, as slowly and unconcernedly as before, I found his shoulder with the double-barrelled .375 and fired the right barrel. He went down in the jungle grass. The crack of the rifle was followed almost simultaneously by the beaters shinning up trees. About fifteen seconds later, although mortally wounded, he tried to drag himself away; a second shot despatched him. We shouted to the beaters that it was safe to come down from the trees. As they descended they formed a large circle around the body of the panther, throwing sticks to ascertain if there was any movement to signify life. During this process he was still covered by my rifle. The panther measured seven feet. He was placed on a leaf-covered litter built by the natives and carried back into the village in triumph.

I was still running a temperature from my sinus infection and had strapped a hot water bottle over my chest under two sweaters during the hunt. It would not surprise me if this were the first time that a hot water bottle was part of the equipment required for a beat.

No MATTER HOW OFTEN I experienced it, I never ceased to thrill to a night watch on a machan. We would mount to our perches before sundown at a time when the air was filled with the chatter of monkeys and the twittering calls of birds. Gradually, as the light faded, the noises and calls of the jungle subsided into an uneasy silence. This is the hour when the tiger and the panther are abroad stalking their kill. The temperature drops sharply with the going down of the sun and we would begin to appreciate, as we had not earlier, heavy woollen underwear, down-filled jacket, balaclava cap, and woollen muffler. In the dead silence we would become aware of the calls of the shepherds. Each shepherd has his own peculiar cry or snatch of song which he repeats throughout the night at short intervals. It is the immemorial method which the shepherd uses to guard his flocks against the night marauders.

Below us in the clearing lay the live buffalo or the tiger kill staked out as bait. In the darkness I would watch this through my glasses, and watch, too, the deer and other animals that occasionally drifted across the clearing. If I were lucky, I would hear somewhere on the edge of the clearing the faint rustling in the jungle grass which always set me breathing hard and my heart pounding. I did not need the touch of the shikari's hand on my arm nor his voice in my ear whispering, "Tiger", to know that I was faced with a possible shot and that the slightest movement or rustle from the machan might lose me my chance to shoot.

We were not always lucky. On one occasion I was hunting in Sillipur in the company of a young Rajah who was endeavouring to organize shikars in his district. I was his first client and his staff work was not always efficient. During our stay in one camp, we received a report that a tiger had attacked a herd and had killed a large buffalo on the edge of a village five miles away. We immediately went over to the village and found that the attack had taken place less than a hundred yards from its huts. A narrow nullah about fifteen feet deep, filled with scrub, passed the edge of this village. One of the buffalo of the village herd had wandered into the nullah and had promptly been killed by the tiger. I went back to the camp, where I was to be picked up after a machan had been erected in a large, spreading tree overlooking the scene of the kill. The dead buffalo, however, had to be moved up the side of the nullah towards the tree and placed in such a position that a clear shot could be obtained, if the tiger came back to feed.

The arrangements and timing were again faulty, as had been the case throughout my entire stay. I was not picked up until sundown and climbed up into the machan after dark. By this time we were all very tired and found it difficult to resist the overwhelming desire to sleep. I had not been in the machan very long before I succumbed to this desire. I was wakened by the Rajah, and most of the early part of the night was spent in our alternately waking one another. Finally, the Rajah awakened himself with a loud snore, turned to me and admonished me for making too much noise. By this time I had lost all interest in the proceedings and could not have cared less if the tiger had joined us on the machan, provided he curled up and went to sleep. We both slept soundly throughout the night and were wakened by our bearers at daybreak.

Pug marks showed that the tiger had come back through the nullah and sat down behind a clump of grass a few yards away from his kill. He must have decided that it would not be dignified for him to feed within earshot of the pandemonium created by our snores.

Hunting, in India, is not always conducted from a machan, or from the back of an elephant, though to hunt on the ground involves a certain amount of risk. The tiger can move and leap like a flash. I have seen one make a leap of about ten yards; and the place where another had jumped fifteen feet straight up in the air, reached his forepaws over the sheer edge of a nullah, dragged himself to the top and then made his kill. I have also seen tigers tearing through the jungle, moving at great speed in long easy bounds. The vitality of these beasts is so extraordinary that even though mortally wounded, they are capable of pressing home an attack. For this reason, the hunter on foot at close quarters is advised never to take a frontal shot except as a last resort. In India the general opinion is that if a man hunts long enough on foot, sooner or later he is going to be killed.

I had several experiences of hunting on foot, both by day and at night. During my sojourn at Sillipur, the Rajah had intended that I should hunt from what he called an underground machan, but the arrangements were confused and when I got into this structure followed by one of the Indians, I found that the space was too small and cramped for us. When I pushed the barrels of my gun through the aperture in front, I discovered that I could only fire at an angle of thirty degrees or more from the ground.

I wriggled out of the machan again with difficulty. The sun was about to set and it was too late now to build a machan in the big tree at the other end of the pond. The Rajah asked me how I would like to sit out on the ground with my back to the tree.

ON THE MATAPEDIA

My daughter, Marian Adams, with our guides. The salmon weighing 42 pounds was a record for the year. I have been fortunate enough to spend the later summers of my life where the river flows between the wooded hills which form the beautiful lower valley of the Matapedia.

HUNTING IN INDIA

Top The panther measured 7 feet. He was placed on a leaf-covered litter, built by the villagers, and carried back to their village in triumph.

Bottom We were not always lucky. One hunt in which we were lucky was a meticulously organized shikar near Ranchi. The tiger was killed by another member of our party. My wife is second from the left of the standing group.

I swallowed once, and said I would if he would: he swallowed twice and said it was a deal.

We pulled up the peg with which the bullock was tethered and staked him into position at the edge of the water twenty yards in front of the tree. Then we cut some branches and thorn bushes and built the equivalent of a duck blind on the ground at the base of the tree. With our backs to the tree, we sat down to wait and sent the natives away. It was soon dark. The moon came up and we watched our bullock through the leaves and camouflage in the stillness and beauty of a bright moonlight night.

Two hours passed slowly. Suddenly to our right and behind us we heard that almost inaudible rustle which indicates the movement of a tiger. I tried desperately to freeze. The Rajah was so quiet that I could not be sure he was at my side. The rustle and stopping continued until it was directly behind the tree; then it proceeded for some distance beyond us. The tiger turned around. He followed the same course in reverse, passing behind the tree a second time. We sat frozen to the spot, hoping that he would come out of the grass and move in front of us towards the pond. He moved behind the tree for the third time. We heard him stop in the distance. Again we heard the approach behind us. Finally he stopped in the grass twenty yards behind the tree. Then the stillness was rent by his double roar. It could only have meant, "You stupid pair of so and so's, I want to come out, but I know that you are there. *Goodnight!*" Then the rustle receded into the distance and we heard him no more.

I enjoyed wandering about the country deep in the jungle, though it was rough going over the hills and along narrow buffalo tracks which were difficult to negotiate even in a jeep. Occasionally our route would take us through an Indian village. The villages were often surrounded by walls made of thorns or plaited bamboo which served as a protection against marauding tiger for both the villagers and their cattle. The inhabitants lived in mud or thatched huts. In many cases the children fled at the approach of our jeep.

One of the most interesting methods of hunting tiger at night is to drive through the jungle on bullock trails and jungle roads, with the windshield of the jeep laid down on the hood. It is, in effect, hunting on foot, with this exception that, moving along at six or seven miles an hour, it is possible to cover a much greater area each night. During one of my visits to India I spent several days in Somanpali hunting in this manner.

The forest here abounded with boar, cheetal, sambar, and it was believed that a herd of gaur, or Indian bison, was in the area. We spent the first few days exploring in order to determine which roads would provide the most interesting night hunting. We saw a number of deer, but found it difficult to get from the natives any information that might be useful in locating tiger. They claimed that there were several known to be in the area, and that their kills had been spasmodic and at widely separated locations, as they often are in the winter months. When water is plentiful during and after the monsoon time, before the dry season, the animals do not have to congregate at water holes.

One afternoon, as we were driving along the road, we spotted our first gaur. It was a large, brownish-black animal, with a bulky body and huge shoulders; it had an enormous pair of horns that swept out from the head and then curved inward. It was a solitary bull, standing alone, broadside on, a hundred yards off the road in the jungle. One shot in the shoulder from a 7.9 mm. Mauser brought it down. We drove back to the village, after having marked the spot on the road, and made arrangements for the natives to bring in the bison. Later that day we saw that the animal had been skinned, the hide being used by the villagers to make water bottles. We attended the village barbecue that night, where a feast was in progress. The natives were grouped around a large fire, and the roasted carcass was consumed with great gusto, washed down with some sort of local native brew.

On the following day I had my first real adventure in that area. We started after sunset and drove slowly along a narrow bullock trail leading through a dark forest jungle. At places we had difficulty in passing trees or their roots, and virtually had to wriggle the jeep along this dark, forbidding path. The shikari and another Indian in the back seat were throwing their beams into the jungle on either side of the road as we moved slowly on, picking up and passing a number of deer.

Suddenly, on our left, we saw a pair of large orangey-red eyes staring at us. The jeep stopped and the shikari whispered, "Tiger." I had my 7.9 Mauser with telescope in my hand, and the shikari was holding my double-barrelled .465. The eyes quickly disappeared as I raised my rifle. The shikari whispered that the tiger would not move very far. In a few minutes the beams again picked up the tiger, who had moved some yards parallel with the road, but in a direction opposite to that which the jeep was facing. The eyes again quickly disappeared. I told the shikari I was going to leave the jeep, as the tiger was moving behind us and I was certain that if I took a position a few yards behind the jeep I would get a clear shot. I asked him and the other Indian to join me and to carry the powerful hand flashlights, which we also had in the car, in addition to the flexible beams.

The shikari strongly advised against this, saying that if I did not drop the tiger, a possible charge in the dark involved too great a risk. It had been strongly impressed upon me, on my first visit to India, that no shot should be taken at any time unless I felt reasonably certain it was going to be a dropping shot. That advice is only too sound, as a hunter is honour bound to follow a wounded animal, and in this way risk not only his own life but the lives of the shikaris and trackers that accompany him.

From experiences that I have had, I know of no phase of hunting that can be more dangerous than tracking a wounded tiger or panther. More lives have been lost while tracking a wounded animal than in any other way. I do not include in this the depredations of man eaters, who fall into an entirely different category.

Being of a somewhat phlegmatic nature, and not very readily excitable, I still do not know why I exercised such poor judgment that night. I said I was going out to take the shot if the shikari would come with me and hand me my double-barrelled rifle the minute I fired. The three of us got out of the jeep, the shikari and his companion carrying hand flashlights. When we were some fifteen yards behind the jeep, I asked them to put the lights over my shoulder and flash them into the jungle. The lights went on; again I saw two glaring eyes and this time the dim outline of the head of a tiger standing looking directly at me, sixty or seventy yards away. I moved slowly to a tree, rested the

light Mauser against it, picked a point between the eyes of the
tiger, and squeezed the hair trigger. Immediately following the
shot, the flashlights went out and I hurriedly reached back for
my second gun.

To my dismay there was nothing there, and I heard the clatter
of the Indians as they jumped into the jeep. I doubt if there
is any known device capable of recording the minute interval
that elapsed between my hearing this clatter, and my joining the
others in the jeep. The car was put in gear and driven some
distance ahead through the trees. We here decided that we
would go back at daybreak and attempt to locate the tiger, which
the driver believed had dropped, as he had not heard any movement in the jungle immediately following the shot.

I was wakened at daybreak, and after a pot of tea, we drove
back along the road. We found no difficulty in locating the spot
from which the shot had been fired the night before, as the ejected
cartridge lay on the road in the midst of our footprints.

We could see by daylight that the undergrowth in the woods
consisted of clumps of grass which in some places were six feet
high. As the fate of the tiger was not known, our shikari thought
that we should take all the precautions usually followed in tracking a wounded animal. There were six of us. We lined up at
the edge of the road with a tracker on my left, two men on my
right, then the shikari carrying my second rifle, with another man
on his right. We were spread out about five yards apart. The
Indians took off their sandals and climbed the trees at the edge
of the road. They reported that all was clear ahead, with the
exception of several clumps of grass within sixty yards. They
came down from the trees and we moved in line, still the same
distance between us, into the wood, with our safeties off and
rifles at the ready to avoid being jumped. The Indians threw
sticks into the large clumps of grass as we approached them.
After we had covered somethings less than the distance that the
men had reported clear on their first view from the trees, we
stopped, and they again climbed trees to see if any trace of the
animal could be seen. We continued this procedure half a dozen
times, working our way into the forest to a distance of between

three and four hundred yards. By this time it was easy to see how, and why, fatal accidents occur while tracking.

At the beginning everyone is exceedingly careful and the distance between the men advancing in line is fairly well adhered to. By this means, if there is a charge, the trackers at least have the protection of the guns that are covering them. I found, however, that by the time we had gone in a quarter of a mile, the trackers became more careless and before I knew what was happening, one would dart off alone twenty-five or thirty yards away to heave something into a clump of grass or bush. If, by any chance, it had sheltered a wounded tiger there would have been one leap and that would have meant the end of the tracker.

By this time, we had thoroughly covered the ground for a considerable distance in front of the tree from which I had fired at the tiger. We did not find a trace of blood, or indeed anything to indicate the wounded animal. Finally, the shikari came over to me, scratching his head, and said, "Sahib, I am afraid the tiger did not receive your bullet." How could a miss be described with greater delicacy?

This more than puzzled me, as I had sighted with the telescope and the range could not have been more than eighty yards. I had my heavy double-barrelled rifle with me in the morning and when we returned to the camp for breakfast, I found the reason for what was probably, for us, a very lucky miss.

I had found jolting around in a jeep, with its metal floor, over the rough roads and terrain, extremely hard on the butts of my rifles even with rubber butt plates. To overcome this, after my first trip to India I had the entire stock fitted with a canvas covering which protected it against chafing. I had not, however, taken sufficient precautions to keep the settings of my telescopes locked. When we returned to camp that morning and I examined the rifle which I had fired the night before, I found that the elevation set-screw of my Hensolt telescope had been shaken loose, had dropped out of the telescope and had been lost. I fired the rifle as it was, and it was shooting eight inches high at one hundred yards. Fortunately, I had a spare Hensolt 'scope with me, which I mounted on this rifle, which I then zeroed. I covered the locking screws with several strips of scotch tape. Since then I have had no further trouble of this kind.

In the Somanpali district I had an encounter with the largest tiger I have ever seen anywhere. On our last night in the district we had decided to patrol a road on which a tiger had escaped us the night before. We started after dark, as always full of hope, and moved up and down the road for some miles, the trees on either side of the road brushing the sides of the jeep.

About one o'clock in the morning, we passed the spot where the tiger had killed the night before. Suddenly there appeared in the headlights of our jeep the dim outline of a huge tiger. The driver jammed on his brokes, enveloping us in a cloud of dust. I told him to get into low gear and run the jeep right up behind the tiger. Turning to the shikari, I told him to be ready to throw his flash on my sights, as I hoped to get a chest shot as the tiger turned off the road. It is unlikely that a shot from behind would have killed him. Most likely it would have resulted in a wounded, dangerous animal that we would have had to track.

We were all tense as we slowly overtook the tiger. When we were less than twenty yards behind him, we realized that we were following a tremendous beast, its shoulders looming above the hood of our jeep. The head, carried low as he moved, could not be seen. In spite of the noise of the jeep and the glare of its headlights, the tiger never varied his ponderous pace or turned to look at us, as we followed in this fashion for several minutes. The thought went through my mind that I had never been in a circus procession before, headed by a wild tiger.

Suddenly, without any warning, he turned into the jungle. In that split second, I threw up my gun and fired, in spite of the fact that the shikari was not quick enough with the light. The blast of the rifle enveloped us in a cloud of dust. We heard nothing and I quickly reloaded the right barrel. As the dust cleared, the tiger was not to be seen. We threw the beam into the wood to our right, but could see no sign of movement. Then, to our surprise, the tiger walked out of the woods on to the road a hundred yards behind the jeep and proceeded down the road as slowly and deliberately as he had walked before, and then turned into the forest on our right. We marked the spot. When we returned the next morning I found that my bullet had splintered a small tree which stood directly in the line of fire as the animal turned into the forest. This had saved his life—and possibly some of ours as well.

It was a night that I will long remember.

How large that tiger was I shall never know. I returned from that trip to India by way of England where I was a guest at a week-end shooting party with the Sopwiths in Hampshire. Among my fellow-guests was Colonel Rex Benson, D.S.O., M.V.O., M.C., aide-de-camp to one of the Viceroys of India. When I told him of my encounter with my large tiger he, in turn, told me a story about another large tiger. He had been on a tiger hunt with the Viceroy which had been arranged by a Maharaja who was very proud of the size of the tiger that roamed his State. Both the Viceroy and his aide, who must have had considerable confidence in their marksmanship, took their positions on the ground. As the beat progressed, two tigers appeared, one of which was shot by the Viceroy and the other by his aide. The tiger which the former had dispatched was measured, and the Maharaja congratulated his guest upon his feat of bagging the largest tiger known to have been killed in India. It measured something well over twelve feet. He announced that a monument would be erected to commemorate this achievement. They started measuring the tiger killed by the aide who, unobserved, picked up the end of the tape and noticed that it started at two feet! Some time later, again in India, I saw the actual monument which the Maharaja, true to his promise, had erected at the side of the road. Fishermen kindly take note!

PART SEVEN

CANADA AGAIN

CHAPTER XVI

THE LAND THAT FREEDOM CHOSE

IN AN EARLIER CHAPTER I told how, in 1910, as a boy of seventeen, I competed in the Oratorical Contest of the Berlin Collegiate and Technical Institute and with an oration on "Canada" won the contest, and the Mackenzie King Medal. I have the final draft of this address before me as I write. One of my sons, looking at it recently, remarked facetiously that my handwriting seems to have deteriorated over the years.

It is a strange, yet not unpleasant experience to look at the pencilled markings on these yellowing sheets of foolscap, to read what I had to say then, and to meditate on the changes that forty-five years have brought to Canada and to the boy who chose his country as the subject for an oration. There is little that is original in what I had to say. I spoke of Canada's favourable geographic location; of its population drawn from the peoples of many lands and the problems connected with their fusion and assimilation; of our method of government under British rule. I waxed eloquent on the generosity of Nature in so liberally endowing Canada with a wealth of products of the field, the forest, the mines and the seas. I donned the mantle of the prophet, gazed into the future and saw three possibilities for Canada: annexation to the United States, complete independence, or Imperial federation. With youthful seriousness I urged on my hearers the need for maintaining the powerful ties that bound our country to the British Empire.

In a word, I demonstrated in all this how ill the role of prophet became me. Of the three destinies that I outlined for Canada, none has come to pass. Even in 1910, though I seem to have had no knowledge of it, the statesmen of Canada were giving the lead in the evolution of the modern political miracle, the Commonwealth of Nations. There was, in my speech, no foreshadowing of the fact that Canada's emergence into full nationhood would be hastened by her participation in two World Wars or that five of my own youthful years would be spent as a member of the Canadian Army in the first of these. I was apparently content, in 1910, that Canada should remain a producer of primary products; yet in my own time she was to become a great industrial and manufacturing nation, and I was to play a part in bringing about the change.

In that boyhood address I spoke, as even today's orators on the theme of Canada speak, of the two cultures which exist side by side in our land, and I pointed to the need for their fusion. In my own time I have seen our society of two cultures reach a maturity which has worked a far-reaching change in our stature as a nation.

A nation reaches full independence when it assumes direction of its own foreign affairs. When, after the first World War, Canada took over this right, foreign affairs were considered so important and so specialized that they came to be regarded as the special province of the Prime Minister; and that, in our country, meant Mackenzie King. It is not uncharitable, I think, to say that Mr. King's conduct of foreign affairs was characterized by a certain imprecision. I myself, as I have noted elsewhere, saw something of this trait in the negotiations leading to the Bren gun contracts, when Mr. King refused to have the matter of the decentralization of munition plants placed on the Canadian agenda of the Commonwealth Conference in 1937, on the grounds that it might be construed as a prior commitment in the event of war. Yet there was a certain logic in what seemed to many Canadians, and others, a singularly undistinguished and inconspicuous attitude towards the great questions of the day; for the first and guiding principle in the formulation of Canada's foreign policy under Mackenzie King was this, that no action in any area should be taken that might endanger the unity of Canada as a nation. Well, whether through wise policies of our statesmen or whether it has been brought about and speeded up by the nature of the times in which we live, our polyglot peoples are

now on the way to being assimilated, our two cultures fused, and
our ten provinces welded into one nation, which they must be
if our country is to survive. Today our foreign policy is less likely
to be inhibited by the fear of offending one part of our country, or
another, and must be formulated as a result of a dispassionate
analysis of the foreign situation and our responsibilities.

And so I have seen a brigade of Canadian soldiers dispatched
to take part in an international police action in Korea at a time
when Canada was at peace, and with few dissenting voices raised
against the sending of the force. In our own factories I helped
build the marine turbines and the pumps to equip the Canadian
destroyers which served in Korean waters. I have seen other
great changes in this area. I served in the Reserve Army in
Canada when it was difficult to find enough volunteers to undertake spare-time training in summer camps; today we have a
standing army of more than a division, with one brigade in
Korea and a second in Europe in fulfilment of our commitments
to the European Defence Community. I crossed the Atlantic
during the first World War in a troopship under convoy of the
Royal Navy; in the second World War the Royal Canadian Navy,
with nearly 900 ships and 100,000 men, patrolled the Atlantic,
keeping Britain's lifeline on this continent secure; later in the
war it supported the army in its landings in France. My son-in-
law, Bruce Adams, still wears a caliper as a result of injuries he
received while flying a Spitfire during the Battle of Britain.
He is one of the many Canadians who flew with the R.A.F.
during those fateful days. Before the war was over, forty-eight
R.C.A.F. squadrons were distributed over the various commands
and participated in actions from North Africa to the Far East.
Today we have squadrons of Canadian flyers manning Canadian-
made planes based in Europe, as evidence of our will to back up
our allies in the North Atlantic Treaty Organization.

None of this is adduced in a spirit of militarism. Canada is
not a military nation, either by inclination or design, though in
two world wars she has organized and administered armies that
fought with a gallantry and efficiency that brought new glory to
the name of Canadian. But it is presented as evidence of the
stature that Canada has acquired in the family of nations in the

forty-five years that have passed since my days in Berlin Collegiate, and of the changes that have come about in our country. Few of these could have been foreseen in 1910.

Other evidence of a similar nature can be adduced: the election of the Hon. L. B. Pearson, our Secretary of State for External Affairs, as President of the General Assembly of the United Nations; the participation of Canada, of which I have written elsewhere, in a Four Power Conference on the standardization of weapons; the appointment of General E. M. Burns, D.S.O., O.B.E., M.C., to the Israeli-Arab Truce Commission of the United Nations and the recent choice of Canada as one of the three nations charged with carrying out the terms of the Geneva Conference for the pacification of Indo-China.

In my various journeyings about the world I have found everywhere a feeling of good will towards Canada and Canadians. Many things have contributed to the creation of this good will: respect for the form and accomplishments of our government; the distinguished record of Canadians during two wars; the ability of Canadian industry and the quality of its products; and the fact that in conducting commercial relations with other countries we have no axes, political or diplomatic, to grind. Above all, this good will is a tribute to the men who represent Canada in other countries as ambassadors, high commissioners and trade commissioners. I have already written of John Kearney in India and J. M. Boyer in Egypt, and of the fine work they were doing for Canada in these countries. It seems to me that Canada is well served by the men of our foreign service, and always has been. I have known many of them personally. The Right Honourable Vincent Massey, the first Canadian Governor-General of Canada, was formerly ambassador to the United States and later High Commissioner to the United Kingdom before and during the strenuous days in London during the second World War. Mr. Leighton McCarthy, our first ambassador to the United States, was a partner in the firm of McCarthy and McCarthy where I made my inglorious debut as a lawyer. I served as Brigade Major on the staff of General Victor Odlum who was our first ambassador to China, and during the Bren gun negotiations I worked with General LaFlèche, who later became our ambassador to Greece. I have dealt with Fraser Elliott whom I met in Australia when he was Canadian High Commissioner there. I can testify, from my own experience, to the skill and efficiency with which they go about their duties and win friends for Canada. Our country is indeed fortunate in the calibre of the men who represent her abroad.

In 1910 the population of Canada was just over five millions. Of these, about a million and a quarter were employed, nearly half as farmers. It is not strange, then, when I reached that section of my oration in which I extolled our great natural resources, that agriculture, like Abou Ben Adhem, should lead all the rest. In my early youth, and indeed for many years thereafter, Canada was considered, primarily, an agricultural country.

I can remember well my early trips across Canada. The Prairie Provinces I recall as great fields of golden grain swaying in the breeze. Yet even in those days the people in the West were conscious of the dangers inherent in a one-crop economy and much of the discussion at that time among the Prairie dwellers centred on the possibility of finding a "second crop". A few years ago George Stewart, the President of Imperial Oil, arranged for me to visit his company's oil fields at Leduc, Alberta, and as I toured the installations and speculated on the changes that these would make in the life of the people of Alberta, it occurred to me that that province, at least, had found its "second crop". It is, indeed, the tremendous development of those natural resources, of which I spoke so eloquently forty-five years ago, that has changed the face of Canada during my lifetime and made the agricultural nation of 1910 the important industrial, commercial and trading nation of 1954.

What these great natural resources are I shall not here enumerate. They are familiar to everyone who reads a newspaper or listens to an after-dinner speaker. But the first and greatest of them is a plentiful and cheap supply of power without which no country can develop its resources. Canada is second only to the United States in her production of hydro-electrical power, and vast new developments at Kitimat in British Columbia, Grand Falls in Labrador, and on the St. Lawrence River ensure that she will maintain or improve that position. Moreover, the uranium discoveries in this country presage that important sources for the development of atomic power for industrial purposes will be available to supplement the supply of hydro-electrical power. It was the application of power to the development of our natural resources that led to Canada's pre-eminence as a producer or processer of newsprint, nickel, asbestos, platinum, pulp, uranium, gold, zinc, silver and sawn timber, and brought our country to the point where the products of our mines and forests far exceed in importance the products of agriculture.

I am one of those people who, if they see a light burning in an empty room, turn it off. To me, waste of any kind has always seemed a special form of wickedness. From the moment that, in my travels about this country, I first became aware of the real nature of the natural resources of which I spoke so glibly in my oration, I have felt the need for a Federal plan of conservation of these resources intimately integrated with a plan for each of the provinces and the industries concerned. The presence of natural resources in this land does not entitle us to enjoy in perpetuity as a blessing something which we received as an inheritance. Inheritances can soon be dissipated unless the heirs have the will and the ability to use and conserve them with intelligence. A long-range, well-integrated plan to ensure a continuity of execution, allied to the best in scientific research and technological development, is vital to the preservation of our national fortune.

IT WAS THE DEVELOPMENT of our natural resources that led, in turn, to the industrialization of Canada.

When my father first came to Canada from the United States, as I have already narrated, he associated himself with the Hahn Brass Company in New Hamburg. He was, in his way, a pioneer in Canadian industry. Industry has been the main preoccupation of my adult life, and now that I have retired from it, my sons have followed in my steps. The history of my family as manufacturers has almost exactly paralleled the period of the great development of Canadian industry.

Statistics are supposed to have no place in a book of this nature; by many they are believed to be dull. I apologize for introducing a few here, and plead that I do so only to make more vivid the tremendous extent of the change that has been wrought in our national life in the forty-five years of which I have been speaking. In 1910, as I have already said, our population was a scant five million. Of these, about one and three-quarter million people were employed, half of them as farmers. The value of our manufactures in that year was $215 million, and of our exports $195 million. By the end of the first World War the population had increased to over eight million, of whom three million were employed. The trend from farming to industry was already apparent, for only one third of those employed at that time worked on farms. The value of our manufacturing had reached a billion and a half dollars and of our exports nearly a billion.

In this year of grace in which I write our population has passed the fifteen million mark. Of these, five million are employed, but less than nine hundred thousand of them work on farms. The value of our manufactures is well over seven billion dollars and of our exports over four billions.

It would be idle to pretend that the evolution so vividly depicted by these figures was a natural one. It was aided and accelerated by two World Wars which imposed upon Canada the duty to tool up for the production and manufacture of all the multifarious objects required by modern armies in times of war. The acceleration was particularly rapid during World War II and much of the credit for it goes to the Right Honourable C. D. Howe, P.C., then the able, driving Minister of Munitions and Supplies, now Minister of Trade and Commerce, whose vision, capacity for organization and sound and quick decisions, and great confidence in the ability of Canadian industry, did so much to further Canada's tremendous contribution during the war and the unprecedented expansion of industry which followed it.

But whatever the cause, the evolution did occur; it still continues. With additional discoveries of oil and natural gas being made in the Western Provinces, it is not unlikely that important industrial establishments will be made in these provinces.

In my library I have "A Catalogue of a New and Compleat Atlas, or Set of Twenty-six [TWO-SHEET MAPS], all Compos'd and Done, According to the Newest and Most Exact Observations, by [HERBERT MOLL], Geographer". This set of magnificent maps is dated about 1708 and each is dedicated to some person of quality. The map of North America is dedicated to "The Right Honourable John, Lord Sommers, President of Her Majesty's Most Honourable Privy Council &c." and bears a fine engraving of this gentleman's family crest. It is interesting to compare a modern map of Canada with the Canada represented in the engraving of Herbert Moll, Geographer. In the latter, the sea adjacent to our Maritime Provinces, then called New Scotland, is labelled "Sea of the British Empire"; while the sea between North America and Europe is designated "Western Ocean". On the West Coast California is shown as an island, and all the territory extending westward from Lake Superior, "Upper Lake" in the map, is named, in large capitals, "Parts Unknown".

There is a vast difference between the Canada depicted in the masterpiece of Herbert Moll, nearly two hundred and fifty years ago, and the Canada that the modern map reveals. Yet the changes that are recorded there are no greater in their way than the changes that have taken place in the economic, social and political pattern of the lives of Canadians in the forty-five years that have passed since the day in 1910 when I advanced to the edge of the platform in the auditorium of the Berlin Collegiate and began my oration on "Canada".

These years have witnessed a shift in our population to the point where today eighty per cent of Canadians are urban dwellers. We have, to add to the comfort of our way of life, twice the services and facilities that were available forty-five years ago. In that period the weekly working hours have been cut by a third and we have at our disposal both the leisure and the equipment to devote to the pursuit of our interests. In addition, a social evolution has taken place in Canada, as elsewhere in the world, which has produced a form of taxation intended to redistribute the wealth of the nation by raising the funds necessary for such welfare and social services as family allowances and old age pensions. Canada, in 1954, has, from one point of view, the best standard of living in the world, and this brings me, at last, to the point I have been aiming at since the beginning of this chapter.

MY OLD FRIEND, the late Lee Ainsworth, used to be very fond of saying, "There are always three opinions: your opinion, my opinion and the right one." Let me make it clear immediately that what follows is my opinion only.

I should be rash indeed if I attempted to forecast what lies in store for Canada in the next forty-five years. At this writing it is not clear what impact the St. Lawrence Seaway, whose construction as a joint undertaking with the United States has been announced since I began this chapter, will have upon our national life; but statisticians claim to believe that by 1970 Canada will have a population of twenty millions of whom two millions will live in the city of Toronto. If this is so, then it is obvious that the trend to urbanization and industrialization is to continue.

The greater population will provide a larger domestic market for the products of Canadian industry. Yet if Canada is to continue to prosper she must expand her business abroad; and it is precisely in this area that the danger to our national life lies.

I have told already of my travels in Europe and Asia and of the great good will for Canada and Canadians that I encountered everywhere in my journeys. I found, too, a willingness to do business with us, and I have narrated elsewhere my own endeavours along those lines. But, in spite of this good will and a real desire on the part of other nations to trade with Canada, during the past five years I have witnessed our international trade becoming more and more restricted. This is only in part due to currency restrictions. In the industry with which I am most familiar, within a period of less than four years after the war, we were underbid in overseas markets by foreign competitors by as much as forty per cent. The difference was caused by the variations in the costs of raw materials used here and in the home lands of our competitors and in the cost of man hours. In one of our most important Canadian industries the average wage rate is almost three times that in the factories of our most important foreign competitors. It is obvious that the principal preoccupation in these countries is not with plans for the reduction of working hours and the increase of wages.

The present high standard of living enjoyed by Canadians has been won, and rightly won, by organization, negotiation, and direct action. The early days of industry in Canada, as elsewhere, were marked by unfairness and abuses in the relationship between management and its co-workers, caused, as most of the woes of the world are caused, by the imperfections of mankind. In an earlier chapter I told of an evening I spent with General Bill Knudsen listening to his reminiscences of his days as an immigrant from Denmark at the turn of the century. Bill's first job was in an iron foundry in Buffalo. The pickling of castings in this foundry was done by a worker called Joe whose job it was to immerse the castings in a huge vat of muriatic acid. Joe had one small weakness. He was addicted to the bottle, and from time to time he would be off the job for a day or two, returning with a violent fit of hiccoughs and the explanation that he had had a cold. These lapses annoyed the manager of the plant and one day when he went to the pickling vat and found Joe missing he instructed Bill Knudsen to fire the absentee on his return. Bill remonstrated with the manager, pointing out that Joe had a particularly dirty job and an unhealthy one, exposed as he was, all day long, to the fumes of muriatic acid. He asked the boss to overlook Joe's absence just once more. The manager's answer was that he didn't care so much about Joe's being away a couple of days but, he said, "One of these days Joe will come in here drunk and fall into the tank, and then we'll have to clean out the vat and buy a lot of new acid."

We've come a long way from those bad old days and no one would wish to return to them. It is fundamental and just that Canadians, whatever their occupations, should enjoy the highest standard of living that we are able to create and maintain. But I am convinced that our standard of living must rest on solid pillars of performance and must not be so forced out of a relation with that existing in other parts of the world that it will make necessary a severe readjustment in our economic structure.

The forty-five years of which I have been speaking and in which my father and I have been so closely identified with Canadian industry have seen an evolution and a tremendous improvement in the working conditions and benefits which have accrued to the co-workers of management. Many of these were won, over the years, by a series of strikes, but neither my father nor I ever had a strike in our factories, although at its peak my "family" consisted of seventeen thousand people.

The happiest periods of my life have been those that I spent with my fellow-workers, the craftsmen and artisans of Canada, labouring at the task of developing our natural resources and expanding Canadian industry. We have worked together in harmony, understanding, mutual trust and respect, having as our common goal the creation of those goods which would be of the greatest benefit to the people of our country. Elsewhere in these pages I have recorded my admiration for, and paid tribute to, the high purpose, skill and stability of the co-workers with management in the industry of Canada, who have proved that they are capable of manufacturing a quality of products which cannot be excelled anywhere in the world. I feel that my experience as a manufacturer and this background of labour-management relations entitles me to say what I must now say.

Collective bargaining was introduced after my father's day. I remember when a group of men came to see me to suggest that they form a union in my plant. I recall that they were taken aback when I told them to go ahead and organize anything at all that would be in our mutual interests. My own feeling, I said, was that we must deal with all our problems on the basis of the long-range requirements of our country and if, with that in mind, our negotiations were conducted towards settlements that would be fair both to management and its co-workers, we should have no difficulty in getting along. And that is exactly the way it worked.

In my book, management and its co-workers together form a team. An efficient plant is one manned by personnel who realize that they are part of a team competing in a league with similar teams and that if their team is to emerge and to remain at the top of the league they must work and plan accordingly. When, as has been the case recently, teams from other parts of the world can place their manufactured products in our markets, and substantially undersell us at home, then the time has come to reflect on what is the matter with our team and to review its methods of training and playing.

Unions in Canada tend to be dominated and their policies influenced by union activities in the United States. These leaders are not familiar with, nor do they seem to be interested in, Canada or the differences between our economy and that of the United States. Their constant preoccupation is with higher wages and lower hours. I apologize once more for introducing statistics and assure the reader that this will be the last time that I shall sin in this manner. The population of the United States is better than a hundred and fifty millions; ours is about a tenth of that. The United States depends for the welfare of its economy upon an export of only five per cent of its production. We, with our smaller population, require an export market for twenty-three per cent of our production. It requires no great mathematical knowledge to see from this that the United States is less dependent on its export trade than we are. Yet our U.S.-dominated unions persist in increasing the cost of our man hours, at the same time lowering our production. In this way Canadian goods are pricing themselves out of the many desirable export markets that exist in the world today.

The cost of labour varies in each country with the standard of living. A country with a low standard of living, if it has the administration to organize and the skills to produce, can deliver substantially the same type of goods to other countries where the cost of the man hour and the standard of living are higher. The way of life in many countries which I have visited is shockingly substandard; I have found people barely existing under conditions which obviously require a complete upward revision of the entire living standards. If, then, we are to maintain the standard of living that we have created on this continent, we must see that it results in higher efficiency and more economical production.

Until the standard of living we enjoy can create a productivity that enables us to meet foreign competition on a much better basis than we can do today, I believe that, ostrich-like, we have our heads buried in the sand. We cannot dismiss, with the cry of "dumping", goods sold in our country, manufactured by people who are willing to work both harder and longer, or who can produce more in the same period of time. We must have a realistic assessment of the position which we have established and which some people pretend to believe we are entitled to maintain regardless of what goes on in any other part of the world. The team of management and labour must at all times recognize their responsibility as a part of the economic structure of Canada and never lose their awareness of the competitive position of our country in relation to the other producing countries of the world.

The periodic advance of wages, followed by the inevitable rise in costs, reminds me of a football match where people suddenly become so excited that the front row stands up; this causes the second row to stand up, and then the third and the fourth ones, until all the rows are standing including the top one. No one sees any better than he did before, and the team does no better because everyone stood up. Wages are considerably higher than they were years ago, but it is equally true that the cost of many things we purchase on this continent today are correspondingly higher; and similar goods can be bought more cheaply in almost every other country in the world.

When either management or labour is discussing or outlining objectives, it is fundamental that these must be in the long-range interest of Canada. Until the objectives of both management and labour parallel each other and are based upon what is in the best interests of Canada, success for their projects cannot be attained. Neither management nor labour has the monopoly of all the virtues or all the vices.

Before my retirement, I was active for some years as a member of an organization whose only purpose was to develop researches and studies into long-range requirements which would beneficially affect the future of Canada. The studies of this group had the benefit of the assessments made by its members who had travelled in the many countries of the world. We were, therefore, able to discuss reasonably intelligently the factors that affected Canada's position in its relation to the economy of the other countries of the world. The purpose of this group was in one sense selfless, and in another interested—selfless, because any suggestion to the benefit of the particular interest or short-range view of any one of its members would have been regarded with great disfavour; interested, because it was agreed that anything that could be done to contribute to what was in the best interest of Canada would ultimately be in our own interests. I know of no better suggestion that I can offer to the leaders who are today heading the labour wing of the labour-management team than that they should include a similar long-range constructive view for Canada's future as a basis for all their planning.

As to the foreseeable future of Canadian industry, the shape of things to come is rapidly becoming clear. When I organized my first business in 1922, as I have already related, I secured a licence to manufacture under a group of United States patents and began to import parts and assemble radios. As the business expanded, we manufactured some of our own parts, until soon we were making all the major components. Research and design were left to the United States licensor; our interest was confined to manufacturing and distribution; and this was the pattern followed at that time by many manufacturers. It soon became plain, however, that we must undertake our own research and design in this country. If we had not learned this lesson for ourselves, it would have been forcibly and painfully administered to us during the depression years when the crash of many American companies cut off Canadian industries from sources of research and design upon which they had relied. Canadian research and design made a great step forward during the second World War, as, of course, did Canadian industry, and now, as never before, we have the funds, the facilities, and the trained personnel to pursue more and more our endeavours in these fields.

As more original research is undertaken here, by industry, Canada should reach the position in relation to other nations of the world that other countries occupied thirty years ago in relation to Canada. She will become a licensor instead of a licensee, allowing the industry of other countries to manufacture under Canadian patents and designs and in this way be in a position to provide the same impetus to industry in other lands that Canada once received from the United Kingdom and the United States.

I ended my oration forty-five years ago with some lines from Tennyson's "You Ask Me Why", which summed up, I felt, everything I wanted to say about my country.

> It is the land that freemen till,
>   That sober-suited Freedom chose,
>   The land, where girt with friends or foes
> A man may speak the thing he will;
>
> A land of settled government,
>   A land of just and old renown
>   Where Freedom broadens slowly down
> From precedent to precedent.

The quotation is as apt for Canada today as it was when I first quoted it.

And now I have come to the end of this story of my life, this summing-up of some of the things that have interested me and experiences that I have thought significant. It has not, I hope, been too dull.

Some years ago, an artist friend designed a book plate for me. The central motif was a barque to signify my love of sailing, and the motto about it read, "Up anchor and let us go adventuring". My voyage through life has been an adventurous one, and when the good Lord chooses to guide my barque into port at the end of its charted course, I shall have encountered during the voyage much happiness, met with the sea in all its moods, and enjoyed a passage filled with His many and undeserved blessings.

INDEX